Beginning CakePHP

From Novice to Professional

WITHDRAWN

David Golding

Apress®

Beginning CakePHP: From Novice to Professional

Copyright © 2008 by David Golding

ISBN-13 (pbk): 978-1-4302-0977-5

ISBN-13 (electronic): 978-1-4302-0978-2

Printed and bound in the United States of America 9 8 7 6 5 4 3 2 1

Lead Editors: Steve Anglin, Tom Welsh
Technical Reviewer: Richard K. Miller
Editorial Board: Clay Andres, Steve Anglin, Ewan Buckingham, Tony Campbell, Gary Cornell,
    Jonathan Gennick, Matthew Moodie, Joseph Ottinger, Jeffrey Pepper, Frank Pohlmann,
    Ben Renow-Clarke, Dominic Shakeshaft, Matt Wade, Tom Welsh
Project Manager: Sofia Marchant
Copy Editor: Kim Wimpsett
Associate Production Director: Kari Brooks-Copony
Production Editor: Laura Cheu
Compositor: Linda Weidemann, Wolf Creek Press
Proofreader: Nancy Sixsmith, ConText Editorial Services, Inc.
Indexer: Becky Hornyak
Artist: Kinetic Publishing Services, LLC
Cover Designer: Kurt Krames
Manufacturing Director: Tom Debolski

Distributed to the book trade worldwide by Springer-Verlag New York, Inc., 233 Spring Street, 6th Floor, New York, NY 10013. Phone 1-800-SPRINGER, fax 201-348-4505, e-mail orders-ny@springer-sbm.com, or visit http://www.springeronline.com.

For information on translations, please contact Apress directly at 2855 Telegraph Avenue, Suite 600, Berkeley, CA 94705. Phone 510-549-5930, fax 510-549-5939, e-mail info@apress.com, or visit http://www.apress.com.

Apress and friends of ED books may be purchased in bulk for academic, corporate, or promotional use. eBook versions and licenses are also available for most titles. For more information, reference our Special Bulk Sales–eBook Licensing web page at http://www.apress.com/info/bulksales.

The source code for this book is available to readers at http://www.apress.com. You will need to answer questions pertaining to this book in order to successfully download the code.

To Camille and Kenny—
your sacrifices, above all,
make this all possible.

Contents at a Glance

PART 4 ■■■ Appendixes

Contents

PART 3 ■ ■ ■ Advanced CakePHP

PART 4 ■■■ **Appendixes**

About the Author

DAVID GOLDING began developing web sites in 1999 and first started using CakePHP on a bet he couldn't complete a web application in five minutes. Golding has a degree in European Studies from Brigham Young University and currently works in technology consulting and freelance web development. He lives with his wife, Camille, and his son, Kenny, in southern California and spends his free time playing golf and studying history. His musings can be found at www.davidgolding.net.

About the Technical Reviewer

 **RICHARD K. MILLER** is the executive vice president of a nonprofit foundation in Utah. He graduated from Brigham Young University with a bachelor's degree in business management but has been interested in technology since he began computer programming at age 10. His experience includes web programming, Internet marketing, and new media strategies such as blogging, podcasting, social networking, and online video. He is the developer of several MediaWiki extensions and WordPress plugins, including the widely used What Would Seth Godin Do plugin.

Acknowledgments

I owe much to those who have contributed to this book, especially since CakePHP is an improving framework and its online community is growing. Chris Nielsen and Benjamin Swanson directed me in which web frameworks to consider and how to build more robust web sites, for which I'm grateful. Steven Burton, Julie Cloward, and Richard Culatta at Brigham Young University provided the opportunities and support to explore web development and to teach others; your influence also contributed to my personal skill set, for which I'll always be thankful. Spencer Fluhman, in so many ways, has been a brilliant mentor and advisor; thank you for your professional counsel and support. Richard Miller's technical expertise and reviews made this book so much more solid, not to mention the professional skills that helped tighten up the loose ends. I wish to thank the Cake Software Foundation and other dedicated Cake developers for providing not only an exceptional framework but for taking the time to judiciously design an effective paradigm for web development. Felix Geisendörfer, Daniel Hofstetter, Tom O'Reilly, and Garrett J. Woodworth have all been especially helpful in providing examples and documentation that facilitated the writing of this book. And, most especially, the staff members at Apress have been remarkable; thank you for taking this book to the next level.

CHAPTER 1

■ ■ ■

Introduction

Programmers have used frameworks for years, though for web development the use of frameworks has been more recent. Probably the main advantage of using a framework in any project, be it web-related or not, is explained by the concept of "inversion of control." Many programs operate in such a way that the code is in control. In other words, the code decides when one operation should appear, how it should handle the user's response, and so forth. Imagine if this order of control were inverted. Rather than have a script or library that contains a series of operations, the program has a series of objects that can do nothing until you extend them (even though they may contain tons of tools you could put to use). In this way, the framework calls on you, not the other way around.

For example, let's say you are looking for a way to install a voting program into your web site. You browse the Internet and find a handful of useful PHP scripts that all promise to do that for you. After plugging in some unique settings, you place one of these scripts onto your server and launch the program. The program runs just fine, but if you wanted to change anything, you would have to go into the script, locate where the operation occurs that you want to change, and work the adjustment by hand. The script manages the flow of control in the sense that all of its operations are executed when the program runs, and if you want to control the program, you have to alter the script.

A framework, on the other hand, has an inverted flow of control. To produce a voting application in a framework, you would have to add to the framework those objects that would handle the voting. The framework would automatically pull together several resources to make the voting process happen, and you would have to intercept those resources or extend them to add your own functionality. A library will behave on its own, like the script example, and any changes must be made directly in the code. A framework is different in that it will wait for you to extend or add to it before it can really do anything for you. You will not need to go directly to the framework's code to make changes; instead, the framework will take your extensions and use those instead of its own libraries.

CakePHP (or, for short, Cake) is a framework, not a set of libraries, even though it contains dozens of functions and methods that simplify web development much like libraries do. As such, Cake waits on you to extend its objects and add your own customized resources. With Cake, gone are the days of individually scripting each and every function. Instead, developers are using a bundled package of scripts, libraries, and conventions that are designed specifically for web development.

From Novice to Professional

This guide is for beginners to CakePHP. Whether or not you have much experience with the PHP scripting language, working in Cake will require some new methods you may or may not have tried before. If you don't know what a "has-and-belongs-to-many" relationship is, don't know how to build your own class object, or don't know how to parse an array, then this book is a perfect place to start when getting into Cake.

Most of the available online resources require some sort of prior knowledge of web development to get a grasp on how to install and work in Cake. If you're like me when I started using Cake, you probably just want a handful of tutorials with code samples from square one that can get you up and running quickly and lead you in the right direction for more advanced techniques. In fact, when asking a question on forums or chat rooms, many beginners get little help or confusing leads from the experts. Simple questions can get a response like "Well, just read the online manual and API." Sometimes novices need a very simple approach to the software, and this guide is just that. As you begin to master Cake, this guide will also provide tips and a reference for helping you quickly add more features to your projects and catch errors.

This book will start by showing how to install Cake on a server and your own computer and will provide some detailed code samples and visual snapshots to walk you through the process. In Chapter 2, I'll show how to build a simple Cake application. You'll get used to the Model-View-Controller (MVC) structure and how to organize your Cake applications effectively. In Part 2, you'll build more extensive web applications in Cake, and you'll explore Cake's built-in helpers, including the Ajax helper, and work with more advanced features. By the end of the book, you will be able to create your own helpers, plugins, and other useful features that will reduce the overall amount of code to run your applications, and you'll also have a solid enough foundation to try other advanced features on your own.

Why Cake?

Ever since Ruby on Rails became a popular web-based framework, teams of developers have been creating clones of Rails or Rails-like frameworks for various languages: TurboGears for Python; Zend, Symfony, and many others for PHP; Catalyst for Perl; and on and on. With so many options out there, why choose CakePHP for your web project?

It's PHP!

Many web developers complain about switching to Ruby on Rails simply because the framework is built on the Ruby language. PHP, they say, is one of the more widely supported web programming languages and is standard with most web services providers, so why give that up for Ruby? For those who learned web development on PHP or those who have made PHP their primary development tool, the idea of ditching PHP for something else may seem daunting or time-consuming. For companies, switching to another language can require reallocating resources, changing web service providers, or reworking an expensive server configuration. Whatever the case, leaving PHP for another development framework can be costly and time-consuming. With Cake, you can enjoy the benefits of framework-based development without learning another language.

One of the difficulties in using some PHP frameworks has been their compatibility with PHP 4 and 5. Symfony, for example, requires PHP 5 and is not backward compatible with PHP 4. Cake, on the other hand, is compatible with both versions of PHP, a necessary feature for many developers with long-term projects that go back a couple of years.

Many PHP developers overlook the benefits of a framework and simply look for premade functions or classes to be used as includes in their scripts or, as with Perl, pullin modules that chew up lots of time on the server and provide little customization. Cake, however, is thoroughly object-oriented in its scope. It supplies objects that can be implemented and modified to your liking and is not just some module or set of includes that give you little control.

Rapid Development

Getting a web project off the ground can be cumbersome and technically demanding, especially when using older methods of development. Cake, however, makes the initial steps of building a web application easy. Rather than run installation scripts from the command line, Cake comes prepackaged as a folder you simply drop onto a server and is ready to run.

The command line does come in handy once you begin building onto the framework. Later, I'll discuss Cake's scaffolding features that cut down on routine development tasks. With Cake, creating user flows in the application early on is simple and can improve communication with clients. In some cases, a run-through of the application can be developed in minutes, allowing the client to get an idea of the project's architecture.

Once a project is fleshed out and launched, site maintenance is also improved thanks to Cake. Because of its hierarchy and organization, as well as its effectiveness at limiting redundancy, Cake helps developers adjust a web application on the fly. Cake also supports test databases and URL routes for testing new features or versions of web applications on the live setup.

Model-View-Controller

Cake enforces an MVC structure for your web applications. Basically, it effectively separates typical operations into specific areas: models for all your database interaction, views for all your output and displays, and controllers for all your commands/scripts for input and program flow. The typical PHP application mixes each of these three functions in the same code, making it difficult to maintain and debug.

This is the typical flow for PHP scripting (see Figure 1-1):

1. The client sends a request to a PHP script by typing a URL or clicking a link of some kind.

2. The script processes the data and then sends the database requests directly to the database.

3. The script receives any database output and processes the data.

4. The script generates output and forwards it to the client's browser.

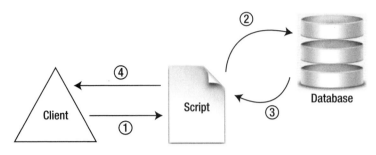

Figure 1-1. *The typical flow for PHP scripting*

In short, everything is contained in one PHP script. By using the include() function, developers strip out common functions into other external files, which makes it possible to reduce redundancy. The most complex PHP applications use objects that can be called anywhere in the application and modified depending on the variables and settings passed to them. Developers, when using objects and classes, can structure the application in numerous ways.

MVC improves upon the typical PHP flow and is an effective technique for making class objects available over the whole application. The main goal behind MVC is to make sure that each function of the application is written once and only once, thus streamlining code by reducing redundancy. Cake accomplishes this goal by not only providing the resources to make MVC possible but also by using a consistent method for where to store operations in the application. Simply naming your own files a certain way allows Cake to piece together the various resources without using any code specifications.

MVC can vary depending on the framework with which you're working, but generally it works as follows (see Figure 1-2):

1. The client sends a page request to the application, either by typing a URL or by clicking a link of some kind. By convention, a typical URL is usually structured like this:

   ```
   http://{Domain}.com/{Application}/{Controller}/{Action}/{Parameter 1, etc.}
   ```

2. The dispatcher script parses the URL structure and determines which controller to execute. It also passes along any actions and parameters to the controller.

3. The function in the controller may need to handle more data than just the parameters forwarded by the dispatcher. It will send database requests to the model script.

4. The model script determines how to interact with the database using the requests submitted by the controller. It may run queries with the database and do all sorts of handy data-sorting instructions.

5. Once the model has pulled any data from or sent data to the database, it returns its output to the controller.

6. The controller processes the data and outputs to the view file.

7. The view adds any design or display data to the controller output and sends its output to the client's browser.

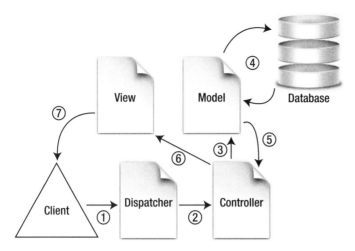

Figure 1-2. *How Cake makes use of the MVC structure*

The benefit of using MVC to develop web sites is that repeated functions or tasks can be separated, thus allowing for quicker edits. It can even help in debugging. Say an error keeps occurring during the interaction with the database. Usually the problem will be somewhere in a model. Knowing that all database interactions occur in just one place makes it easier to solve problems.

CRUD Operations and the Bake Script

Almost all web sites use CRUD operations: create, read, update, and delete. A blog, for example, will need to create posts; users will need to be able to read each post; the author will likely want the ability to edit the post in the future or update the post; and the author will also want access for deleting posts.

Cake makes these operations a breeze with its automated CRUD functions. Instead of writing each CRUD operation by hand, it has prebuilt classes that do it for you. Cake includes the Bake script, a handy command-line tool that generates editable CRUD code based on your database schema and customized parameters.

Scaffolding

Getting a web site off the ground is much easier with Cake's scaffolding abilities. With just one simple line of code, you can call out Cake's prebuilt scaffold to render views based on the database. In other words, it figures out how some standard interface views should work with your database and outputs the HTML forms, all without you having to write one bit of HTML. Although the scaffolding feature is not intended for full production views, it lets you begin testing logic and functions without wasting time building views or HTML output.

Helpers

Cake comes with standard HTML, Ajax, and JavaScript helpers that make creating views much easier. Your HTML output will be greatly facilitated by intuitive strings of helper code that render the markup for you. And getting Ajax to work, although a little tricky at first, is much easier and far more efficient than if you had to worry about DOM peculiarities. What's more, you can download other helpers written by fellow Cake developers to boost the strength of the framework or even write your own to cut down on repetitive or clumsy markup.

Customizable Elements

You can customize each of Cake's features to fit your application. For example, you can bring FCKeditor, the popular WYSIWYG editor for web browsers, into Cake as a plugin. Using customized helpers, you can bring all the functionality of FCKeditor into your Cake application and actually trim out extra lines of PHP code to get it working. Later, I'll discuss other Cake elements such as components, helpers, and plugins, all of which can be customized by you for your specific needs or brought into your application as third-party resources from other developers.

Large Community

Should you need help down the road, a massive online community exists to provide it. In reality, the PHP community is the largest open source programming group on the Web, so if you need a quick workaround for a problem in Cake, someone somewhere will have some help for you, usually within minutes. Cake specialists have also established online forums, chat rooms, and blogs to help others improve and learn the framework. Compared to other PHP frameworks, this community is one of the largest on the Web.

Code samples are a must for anyone getting involved in web development. PHP dominates this field, and Cake has a growing repository of code samples as well. If you are considering another framework, this fact just may tip the scales in favor of Cake if you are wanting to piggyback on someone else's work.

More Features

Cake aims to simplify the development process for building web applications by providing an overall method for organizing the database and other resource files that cuts down on code. Although this general approach to web programming is itself a major feature Cake offers, its repository of other powerful resources such as built-in validation, access control lists (ACLs), data sanitization, security and session handling components, and view caching make Cake worth any serious developer's time.

Summary

As a framework, Cake inverts the flow of control and provides you, the developer, with an effective method for extending your web application in less time. Cake is built in PHP and therefore allows you to take advantage of a web-based framework without having to learn or use another programming language. Other benefits to using Cake include its MVC structure, which separates resources and functions of the application; the Bake script, which automates CRUD scripting; the scaffolding features, which reduce basic view rendering into one line of code; the built-in helpers, which reduce HTML output operations into single-line call-outs; and the large and still growing Cake community.

PART 1

■■■

Getting Started

CHAPTER 2

■ ■ ■

Installing and Running CakePHP

One of Cake's selling points is its ease of installation. At this point I could add a long tutorial explaining how to install Cake for every possible server configuration, but I won't. Cake should be simple enough to install, and if you do experience trouble getting off the ground with it, chances are the problem lies in a more unduly complex server configuration. Appendix A addresses some of the choices beginners make in setting up a localhost environment in case you run into installation questions during this chapter. By and large, any troubles getting Cake to work are due to localhost issues, not enterprise server or web service provider setups.

Throughout this book, you will develop some Cake applications that I expect you to build on your PC and not on a web server. All my instructions, therefore, will be for a localhost environment, not a remote one, though the setup routines I discuss in this chapter apply to a remote installation as well.

A Simple Start: Running Cake on a Localhost Environment

Before you begin running Cake, you will need the following already working on your localhost (see Appendix A for more details about installing these components):

- Apache server with `mod_rewrite`

- PHP 4.3.2 or greater

- MySQL (Cake does support PostgreSQL, Microsoft SQL Server 2000, Firebird, IBM DB2, Oracle, SQLite, ODBC, and ADOdb, but I'll stick with MySQL in this book because it's the default database engine in Cake)

All three of these are easily installed with programs such as XAMPP by Apache Friends (`www.apachefriends.org`) or MAMP by Living-e (`www.mamp.info`). Or if you prefer, you can manage a custom HTTP server setup for each on Windows, Linux, and Mac operating systems manually. In your web browser, you should be able to access a root folder on your localhost by entering **http://localhost** in the address field.

Getting Cake

The first step is to download the latest stable release of Cake version 1.2 from www.cakephp.org. Once you've downloaded and extracted the Cake release file, you should end up with a folder named something like cake_1.2.x.xxxx with a handful of folders inside it (see Figure 2-1).

Figure 2-1. *Contents of the main Cake install folder*

The app folder is where almost everything happens in your application. It houses all the controllers, models, views, layouts, and all other JavaScript, CSS, Flash, image, and other files. Of course, if you take a peek inside the app folder, you'll notice that all these areas of the application are organized into several subfolders.

The cake folder contains all of Cake's libraries and scripts. You can replace this folder with newer releases of Cake, and it should still work with the application. Inside, you will find dozens of individual PHP files that contain all of the classes and scripts necessary for Cake to run.

The docs folder holds change log information and other readme files.

Any other non-Cake PHP scripts you intend to work into your application are stored in the last folder, vendors. Later in the book, you'll also use vendors to store some fancy PHP scripts that work independently of Cake.

Launching Cake

Running Cake is really this simple: rename the main Cake folder to how you want the application to be called in the browser and drop it into your localhost root. I have named mine first_app and have placed the folder in my localhost root. This root folder will depend on how your localhost is configured. It may be named webroot, www, or public_html (these are some of the most common folder names for the server root directory). Be sure to identify where your localhost root is and drop the renamed Cake folder into it. By typing **http://localhost/first_app** in my web browser, I get the Cake welcome screen (see Figure 2-2).

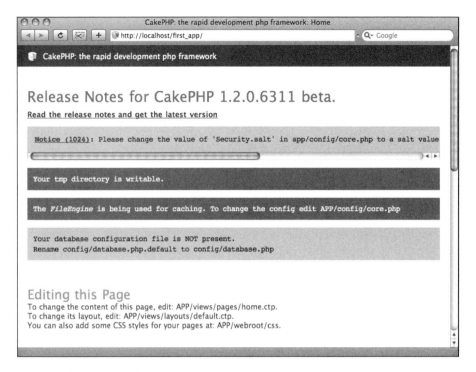

Figure 2-2. *The Cake welcome screen*

If you get a screen like this, congratulations—Cake is now running. If for some reason you get this screen but it appears without any graphics or colors or (worse yet) if the screen is just blank, you may be encountering one of the following errors.

■**Caution** A lot of what is discussed in this chapter will depend on how you configure your web server. If the localhost is accessed by typing **http://localhost:8888** or some other address, make sure you substitute my instructions with the appropriate settings. You should be versed in localhost setups before launching Cake, especially since so many variations of localhost setups exist that I won't discuss in detail here.

Permissions Error

There may not be the necessary file permissions in place. If this error occurs, you may see a blank screen or a 403 error. The 403 HTTP server error occurs when the server denies access to whatever is being requested by the user. Several settings, file permissions, or PHP configuration bugs could trigger the 403 error. To fix this, set the first_app folder permissions to 0755 with chmod in the command line, or use your operating system to give read, write, and execute permissions to the user and read and execute permissions to the group:

```
chmod -R 0755 /path/to/cakephp/folder
```

Refresh the first_app URL; if you see the screenshot shown in Figure 2-2, the problem is fixed.

USING THE COMMAND-LINE INTERFACE

Whether you are working in Windows, Mac OS, or Linux, the command line will be necessary later to take full advantage of Cake's features. Mac and Linux users should have no problem running the command line because it is built into these respective operating systems. Like the web server setup, running the command line can take on multiple configurations that would be too exhaustive to cover here. Be sure to get the command line working in such a way that you can run standard Unix commands. Mac users should run the Terminal application to run their commands. Linux users will undoubtedly be familiar with the Linux console to run shell commands. Windows users may need to install a command-line interface (CLI) to run all the necessary Unix commands. I recommend using Cygwin (www.cygwin.com) or MinGW (www.mingw.org) to launch the command line in a Windows environment.

Apache AllowOverride Error

This error occurs when you see the content, but it doesn't appear like Figure 2-2; no color, no styles, no layout, and no font changes appear—it's just black text on a white background. If you continue with the rest of the tutorials here, you'll be able to see Cake running, but some things will not work properly or you may notice inconsistencies when you begin to expand your Cake application, especially with the scaffolding and the styles. This is a little more complicated to fix than the permissions error, but it's not really difficult.

You'll need to find the httpd.conf file in your localhost setup. It's usually stored in a folder named conf, bin, lib, or var. You can edit the httpd.conf file with any plain-text editor.

Search for a chunk of code that looks something like this in the httpd.conf file:

```
1    <Directory />
2        Options Indexes FollowSymLinks
3        AllowOverride None
4    </Directory>
```

Don't let line 1 throw you off. The slash after Directory is referring to the root folder. If you need to apply these changes to the specific Cake application folder, then add the path to Cake rather than the root folder:

```
<Directory /path/to/cake>
```

Change line 3 from AllowOverride None to AllowOverride All, and restart Apache. If you see the regular Cake welcome screen (shown earlier in Figure 2-2) once you launch the first_app URL, the problem is fixed.

Running the Setup Routines

Every time you install a Cake application on your localhost, you'll follow these routine procedures:

1. Prepare the tmp folder.

2. Change the Security.salt value in app/config/core.php.

3. Enter MySQL database connection settings.

4. Design your database schema (unless you are using an existing schema).

Preparing the tmp Folder for Cake to Read and Write Temp Files

The tmp folder is located in the app folder. By default, its permissions are set to 0777, but it is possible for it to change to a server permissions default. The Cake welcome screen tells you whether the tmp folder is writable. If this bar lights up green, then the tmp folder doesn't need to be adjusted. If not, run the following at the command line to change the tmp permissions and its enclosures:

```
chmod -R 0777 tmp
```

Then refresh the startup screen. It should change to "Your tmp directory is writable" (see Figure 2-3).

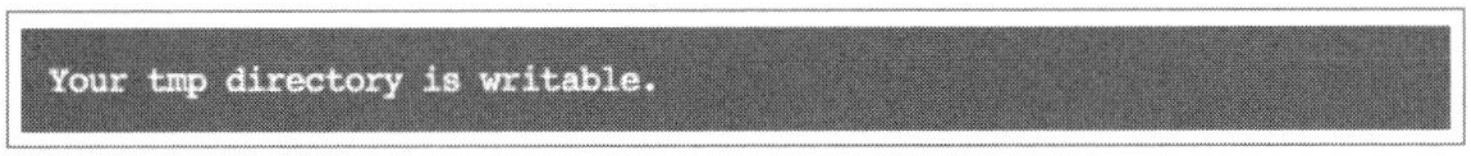

Your tmp directory is writable.

Figure 2-3. *Cake tells you whether your* tmp *folder is writable.*

Changing the Security.salt Value

When a session is initialized, the server groups a set of requests together using a session ID, a database, or a cookie. Whatever the method, the idea behind the session is that the server can maintain a pseudoconnection with the user, even though the communication could get interrupted along the way. You've run into this when you've logged into your web-based e-mail account or some similar web service. The site application knows that you're logged in and maintains that status until you log out or a certain length of inactivity transpires.

Luckily, Cake makes session handling easy. But you need to make sure that its session string is secure. You wouldn't want any users to toy with the session handling in an effort to break into your applications.

To add some security to the session variables, open the app/config/core.php file, and locate line 153, or thereabouts. You'll find a line that looks like this:

```
Configure::write('Security.salt', 'DYhG93bOqyJfIxfs2guVoUubWwvniR2GOFgaC9mi');
```

This line is how Cake writes definitions. Rather than use the PHP define() function, Cake's core configuration uses the Configure::write() function to better manage global variables. Here, the Cake core uses the Security.salt definition for creating hashes and other session variables.

Because that funky line of characters comes with Cake, everyone who uses Cake has the same session string. Let's change the second portion, the character string, to something unique. Go ahead and fill in any alphanumeric string, about 40 characters in length, and paste it here. I ended up with this:

```
Configure::write('Security.salt', 'mEayuDrXBhZkdiEJgFzPXvbcBrmKo9CdVGtKyPBr');
```

Now Cake has a salt value for when it needs to run any security configurations and hashing that aren't the default value.

Entering MySQL Connection Settings

Cake needs to know where your databases are located to save and retrieve data. You do this by editing the app/config/database.php.default file. You'll need to rename the file to database.php (remove the .default from the end) and edit it in the plain-text editor of your choice. However your localhost is set up, you will need to know the MySQL login and password for Cake to connect to the database. This is generally set to a default value unless you configure the administrator's account (for example, the login and password have default values of root and so forth). In the database configuration, there will be a place for you to enter the login and password values. Listing 2-1 shows the default DATABASE_CONFIG class in the database configuration file.

Listing 2-1. *The Database Configuration File*

```
1    class DATABASE_CONFIG {
2
3       var $default = array(
4           'driver' => 'mysql',
5           'persistent' => false,
6           'host' => 'localhost',
7           'port'=>'',
8           'login' => 'user',
9           'password' => 'password',
10          'database' => 'project_name',
11          'schema'=>'',
12          'prefix' => '',
13          'encoding'=>''
14      );
15
16      var $test = array(
17          'driver' => 'mysql',
18          'persistent' => false,
19          'host' => 'localhost',
20          'port'=>'',
```

```
21              'login' => 'user',
22              'password' => 'password',
23              'database' => 'project_name-test',
24              'schema'=>'',
25              'prefix' => ''
26              'encoding'=>''
27          );
28      }
```

In this class DATABASE_CONFIG, there are two databases it will connect with: default and test. If you have no intention of creating a separate test database, you can delete lines 13–21. Plop your database settings into the necessary lines, as shown in Listing 2-2.

Listing 2-2. *Adding the Localhost Settings to Your Database Configuration*

```
3   var $default = array(
4              'driver' => 'mysql',
5              'persistent' => false,
6              'host' => 'localhost',
7              'port'=>'',
8              'login' => 'root',
9              'password' => 'root',
10             'database' => 'cake',
11             'schema'=>'',
12             'prefix' => '',
13             'encoding'=>''
14         );
```

In this tutorial, you're creating a generic Cake application. Later in the book, you'll name the database based on the application you're building, but for now, you'll just create a database called cake. The settings shown in Listing 2-2 will tell Cake how to connect with this database, but you aren't done yet...you need to create the database!

Designing Your Database Schema

It's best to know how the database design will work from the outset. So, take some time to get at least a moderate idea of the program you're building first, and then build some tables and fields to fit that design. Chapter 4 will walk you through a detailed tutorial on how to design the schema to fit Cake applications. For now, just remember that building the structure of the database naturally occurs here when installing a new Cake application.

This application is very simple with nothing really in the database. You just want to connect Cake to the database. Fire up the MySQL application of your choice (I'm using CocoaMySQL), and connect to MySQL. Create a database called cake.

Now that a database actually exists for Cake to connect with, you can go to http://localhost/first_app in your browser, and it will display a new screen, as shown in Figure 2-4.

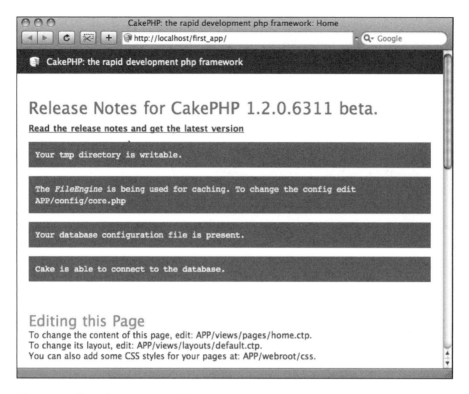

Figure 2-4. *The welcome screen when everything is ready to go*

Cake is now installed and working correctly. It's time to dive in and start building web apps!

Summary

Installing a new Cake application is simple and requires very little configuration to get up and running fast. Just remember to unpack the main Cake install file and rename the resulting folder to whatever you want your application to be titled. By checking the welcome screen, you can determine whether Cake is running correctly or whether a localhost error is present. Correcting errors is not too difficult. Just set the permissions correctly or adjust your Apache server configuration to handle Cake, and those errors should, in most cases, disappear. Your Cake application will require a few setup routines such as preparing the `tmp` folder, changing the `Security.salt` value in the core configuration, and connecting Cake to a working database. After these routines are complete, your application will be ready to be extended by creating models, views, and controllers. The next chapter explains how to add to your new application via a simple to-do list application using Cake's built-in scaffolding feature.

CHAPTER 3

■■■

Creating a To-Do List Application

Now that you've set up Cake on your own computer, it's time to begin building applications. In this chapter, you'll create a to-do list application in Cake using the built-in scaffold feature. This is the simplest approach to application building in Cake. It will only require creating a couple of plain-text files as well as a database with a couple of tables. You won't deal too much with the design but rather let Cake generate all of your HTML output.

Exploring the MVC Structure

Cake is designed using the common MVC structure. What this means is that the framework splits apart different processes into separate areas (see "Model-View-Controller" in Chapter 1). In the app folder, you will notice a folder for the program's models, a folder for controllers, and a folder for views. Right now the application is bare, so you won't find any files inside these folders. As you build the application, you'll create the necessary models, views, and controllers that correspond to the functions of the application.

In a way, these pieces of the framework talk to each other. Say, for example, that the application needs to run a user login process. It takes the user to a screen that displays two fields: a username field and a password field. This display, the actual HTML, would be contained inside a view file stored somewhere in the app/views folder. When the user fills out the login information and clicks Submit, the form gets processed in one of the controllers. At this point, the controller needs to find out whether the given username and password match in the database. So, the controller will talk to its corresponding model asking whether the supplied values match a record in the database. The model replies with a true or false response, and from there the controller decides either to return to the login screen and display an error message or to allow the user access to another area of the site.

The following is the login process in the MVC structure (see Figure 3-1):

1. The client enters a username and password and then submits the form.

2. The view that contains the form passes the form data to the controller for processing.

3. The controller sends a find request to the model asking whether the submitted information matches anything in the database.

4. The model generates the query and runs it through the database.

5. Based on the response in step 4, the model returns either a true result or a false result to the controller.

6. The controller processes the result and fetches the appropriate view to be sent to the client (either a success screen or an error message).

7. The final output view is displayed to the client.

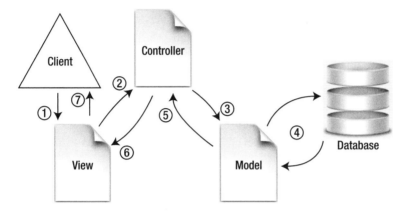

Figure 3-1. *A flowchart of a login process in the MVC structure*

MVC structures are useful because they allow you to separate the different processes of the web site. When needing to change or add new form fields, for instance, you need only to locate the appropriate view file and make the change. Instead of sifting through PHP output functions or scripts, you know that all the views are contained in the views folder. The same is true of controllers and models. Certain functions are available across the whole application without requiring any includes. Managing all the paths for include files or libraries in a non-MVC application can become difficult as the program grows; in this regard, the MVC architecture helps keep the application more agile. Table 3-1 explains what the models, views, and controllers handle; where these files are stored in Cake; and how the files are named.

Table 3-1. *MVC Structure Areas*

Area	Type of Process	File Name and Location in Application
Model	Handles all database functions	app/models/{Model name}.php
View	Handles the presentation layer and displays, including Ajax output	app/views/{Controller name}/{View name}.ctp
Controller	Handles all logic and requests	app/controllers/{Controller name}_controller.php

The To-Do List's MVC Layout

The first order of business is to understand how the MVC structure will work with the specific needs of the application. For the general to-do list application that you'll build, you will need to arrange certain processes throughout the MVC structure.

The to-do list application will have items that the client will want to complete. For each item there will be a description or title, a due date, a priority level, and a true/false field for whether the item is completed. So, in the MVC structure, you will split the processes into their respective elements. First, you'll create a controller for the items the client will want to save. Second, you'll create a model that will fetch items from the database and manage any other data-handling processes. Next, you will have Cake generate the views that will allow the client to list, edit, delete, and create new items. That's all there is to it.

Before you can begin saving items in the database, you must first create the database tables and fields. In general, when designing an application, the order of creation goes something like this:

1. Design and create the database.

2. Create models.

3. Create controllers.

4. Create and adjust views.

You already have a folder in your localhost root named `first_app` that has Cake 1.2 running. Let's rename this folder to `todo` and build the database. You should be able to launch the to-do list application by typing **http://localhost/todo**.

Designing and Creating the Database

In thinking about how the database should be designed, first you need to know something about the application you're building. Most programmers like to sketch use cases or flow-charts that explain step-by-step how the user will interact with the program and how the application will react to their inputs. I have already discussed how the application will work under an MVC structure; translating this into the schema so that the database works correctly with Cake is the next step.

■**Note** If you haven't already done so, make sure you have created a database to be used with this application and put the configuration parameters into the `app/config/database.php` file.

Create a table in the database and name it `items` (be sure to use lowercase). Then give the table the fields shown in Table 3-2.

Table 3-2. *The To-Do List Application Table Structure*

Field Name	Field Type	Length	Other Parameters
id	int	11	Set to unsigned; give it the primary key, and set it to auto_increment.
name	varchar	255	
date	datetime		
priority	int	2	
completed	tinyint	1	

Giving each record a unique id value is essential for Cake to function without trouble. This application is simple, so you may be able to get by without creating an id field set to auto_increment. However, it's good practice to make sure that all your records in the database can be identified by a unique value and that it's named id, because then Cake can generate scaffolding around your table without any code on your part. Once you begin creating associated tables, then it will be mandatory to include an id field.

■**Note** When specifying how to design the database schema, I will provide you with MySQL dump table creation code rather than walk through each field and its types and values (for example, `id` int(11) unsigned NOT_NULL auto_increment).

Creating Models

Now that you have a table in the database, Cake will need a model file to talk to that table and fetch results for the application. In the app/models directory, create a new file named item.php. This file name conforms with Cake's naming conventions, and you will need to make sure when creating models that you name the files correctly. Should you give this file a different name, you would then have to specify the nonstandard file name in the controller and (depending on what accesses the model) elsewhere too. Remember the inversion of control structure of the framework—Cake will automatically look for a file named item.php in the app/models folder, which saves you from writing unnecessary code.

In the item.php file, paste the code shown in Listing 3-1.

Listing 3-1. *Contents of the* app/models/item.php *File*

```
1    <?
2    class Item extends AppModel {
3        var $name = 'Item';
4    }
5    ?>
```

■**Caution** Depending on your localhost or remote hosting setup, you may need to change line 1. In all the examples in this book, I'm using a type of PHP shorthand. In some setups, though, PHP shorthand is not available. If this is the case, just use `<?php` on line 1 instead. Semantically, shorthand makes your code cleaner and easier to read, so to improve the readability of this book, I'm going to stick with it. You will want to double-check the examples if you have set up your localhost differently or if you're sure that PHP shorthand is not available on your setup.

What's Happening in This Model

All models will always contain some of the same header code. First you will notice on line 2 that you have created a PHP class named Item and that this class extends another class named AppModel. Cake has already created the necessary PHP objects to connect to the database, so in a way all you're doing is adding to that preconfigured object. For good measure, line 3 gives an object variable named name the value of Item, which allows for backward compatibility with PHP 4. Lines 4 and 5 close out the file.

Model Possibilities

Inside this class you can place model functions or specify table associations that directly interact with the items table in the database and return results. Possible functions include field validation, complex find queries and operations, and elaborate table design cleanup.

For now, the Item model is ready to go. Let's make the controller.

Creating Controllers

In the app/controllers folder, create a new file for the items table in the database. Controllers, by default, link up to the table after which they are named. In this case, you have created an items table, so the convention in Cake is to name the controller file after this table, using an underscore and the extension controller.php. So, name this new file items_controller.php, and place it in the app/controllers folder. Paste the code shown in Listing 3-2 into this file.

Listing 3-2. *Contents of* app/controllers/items_controller.php

```
1    <?
2    class ItemsController extends AppController {
3        var $name = 'Items';
4        var $scaffold;
5    }
6    ?>
```

What's Happening in This Controller

Let me explain what's happening in Listing 3-2.

Line 2 is necessary for Cake to run the controller. Just as it does with the model, Cake is already starting some of its own PHP code in what it calls the *controller*. Next, it moves to any objects that extend this parent class. These will include the application's own controller, or AppController, and any other controller files it finds in the app/controllers folder. All the way down, you need to tell Cake whether you've inserted your own AppController or individual controller file, and you do this by starting a class and extending the previous level of controller. In this case, you created the ItemsController class, and it extends from the AppController.

Line 3 names the controller Items for the same reasons the model also set the object variable to $name earlier.

In line 4, you've called out one of Cake's built-in features: the scaffold. You can include this line in any controller, and Cake will build its own set of HTML forms and tables around what it finds in the database table. In a second, you'll see how helpful this one little string of code can be.

Controller Possibilities

Because the controller controls what happens in the application, it will likely be the most variable of the other resources I've discussed to this point. In a sense, it behaves like the "brain" of the application and coordinates the processes in the models and views. A good MVC application's controller will generally act in this role with most of the custom logic placed here. In Cake, the controller contains a series of functions that are entered like normal PHP functions:

```
function foo() {
...
}
```

Cake's helpers and components can be pulled into a controller and used in the application, as well as third-party components, plugins, and helpers. Later you'll build more advanced controllers that make use of all these possibilities.

Launching the Application

Launching Cake applications is always done by entering the appropriate URL in a web browser. All URLs are sent to the dispatcher or Cake's central routing engine that handles all HTTP requests. The dispatcher parses the URL and resolves it. You can manipulate how the dispatcher does this by changing routes, which is explained in Chapter 10.

How Cake Resolves URLs

By default, the URL structure is delimited by slashes, not the typical messy characters such as the question mark or ampersand that you have undoubtedly seen with many web sites using PHP. There is a growing trend for web sites to be optimized so that they show up as high as possible on the result lists returned by search engines. This has led many developers to forego the traditional way of passing URL routes to a PHP script, instead using slashes to separate URL elements. Usually called *friendly* URLs, these paths are more easily understood by users and search engines, which are themselves beneficial to your application. Friendly URLs also allow Cake to better maintain a consistent reference system within the application, which ultimately makes the programming aspect easier and cleaner for you, the developer.

Cake's default routes follow this pattern:

```
http://localhost/{Application}/{Controller}/{Action}/{Parameter 1}/➥
{Parameter 2, etc.}
```

So, following the Cake defaults, to launch the application, you enter the following in your web browser:

```
http://localhost/todo
```

You should see the same Cake welcome screen that you got after installing Cake. You haven't set up a default or base route for Cake, so it will continue to show the welcome screen by default.

Since you have created the Items controller, to access that area of the application you plug in `items` in the controller spot in the URL:

```
http://localhost/todo/items
```

Creating the Scaffolding

Here is where Cake's scaffolding comes in. Recall that in Listing 3-2, line 4, you called the object variable `$scaffold`. When the dispatcher receives the URL and finds that you are requesting the Items controller, it looks for a default function named `index()`. First, however, it notices that you have told it to render the scaffolding (line 4), and since you haven't specified a function in the controller called `index()` yet, the dispatcher will fetch the built-in views and render a standard list view for the `items` table in the database. After launching the Items controller in the browser, you should get a screen like Figure 3-2.

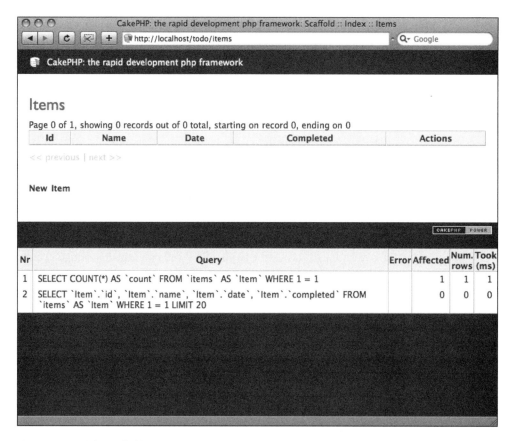

Figure 3-2. *Cake's scaffolding feature rendering a list view of the* items *table*

Notice that no items appear in this list view; you haven't created any yet. Normally, you would have to go into the Items controller, create a new function named add(), and then specify each operation for adding a new record in the items table. But Cake's scaffolding will handle all the CRUD operations for you. You can see the link on the screen named New Item. Click it, and you will have a complete add view generated by the scaffold (see Figure 3-3).

Scaffolding is useful because in one line of code you can translate typical database-handling methods into a web interface. In a short amount of time, you can interact with the database through your Cake application and, consequently, the browser as well. Later, you'll build more dynamic schemes that will use multiple tables simultaneously, and the scaffolding will tell you quickly whether you've effectively linked the associations in the models.

Valuable as it is, Cake's scaffolding does have some limitations. For example, you cannot easily change the look or order of the fields in the forms. To do that, you need to generate a different view file separate from the scaffolding views, which would also require you to write the whole add() and edit() functions in the Items controller. For this and other reasons, the scaffold feature is not intended for production-level output. You will discover more about its utility, however, as you create more elaborate skeletons from which to build more powerful applications.

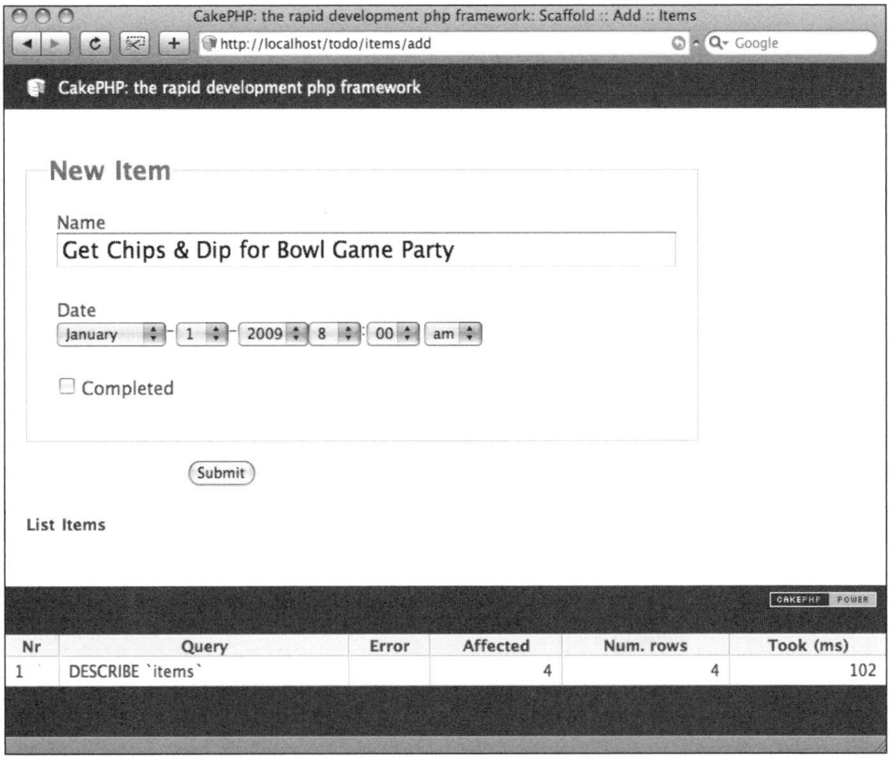

Figure 3-3. *Adding a new item to the database using the scaffolding views and functions*

Summary

In this chapter, you used the scaffolding feature to create a basic to-do list application in Cake. The MVC architecture in Cake made it possible to use a minimal amount of code to get the program running, and thanks to the scaffolding feature, you can even interact with the database without writing any HTML or form processes. Next, you will expand on this application and improve it using other tools, but for now it will be worth it to practice this routine of setting up a quick Cake application with models, controllers, a database table, and a scaffold until you can do this in about five minutes or less.

PART 2

Developing CakePHP Applications

■ ■ ■

CHAPTER 4

Naming Files and Designing the Database

In the previous chapter, I discussed how Cake was able to wrap some standard web functionality around the database structure to produce a to-do list application. Although you could change some things in the application to improve the user experience, overall Cake handles the typical operations of adding, deleting, editing, and viewing records in the database without much code. This is possible because of an important aspect of Cake: *convention.* Because you followed Cake's conventions when naming and setting up the database table, when creating the model and controller files, and when entering the URL in the browser to run the application, Cake was able to piece together your various operations and deliver a handy web program in little time.

Convention Over Configuration

Cake's developers adhered to "convention over configuration" when building the core, meaning they intended not only to provide a framework chock-full of features and functions but to develop an *overall method* for building web applications. In other words, their philosophy is that *how* you go about developing web programs is just as important as *what* you are building. For example, this is why the app folder is structured the way it is—to provide conventions for dividing up the operations of the web application into more standardized areas and to provide conventions for which parts of the application serve which functions. The conventions you learn when using Cake can save you just as much time as the useful tools that come with Cake.

Intercepting Cake

An effective way of visualizing the "convention over configuration" idea is to imagine the frame of a house. None of the appliances, wiring, walls, windows, or doors is present; only a wood frame that delineates the structure of the house is present. If the construction crew was to suddenly assemble the house without your input, they would naturally place doors in certain areas, place windows in other areas, and finish the walls with particular materials.

This is how Cake is assembled when the application launches. It has an overall convention for how it pieces together the application, and knowing that the main objective of the framework is to produce a web-based application, it will automatically go about it in a certain way. In dealing with the controllers, for example, Cake will render its own scaffold or look for specific view files *unless* you intercept it and tell it otherwise.

Other frameworks such as the Zend Framework and Struts go about building applications in a different way. Imagine that the construction crew gave you a catalog of possibilities from which to furnish the house, but in the end, they make you do the assembly work. Some frameworks give you a large array of functions and tools to use in your application but leave the configuration up to you. In a sense, you could use these frameworks in any previously built PHP application because they aren't there to supply you with a specific convention; they are just nice collections of typical web application operations bundled together.

Cake, in a sense, is one large (rather blank) PHP *object*, and your job is to add, here and there, your custom pieces to that object. This object has the capability of providing you with many tools, like the many possible configurations of a house, but by default few of these tools are executed. You draw on them as you extend objects with your own classes and functions.

Because of the convention the Cake developers used to build the framework, there is an expected method by which you extend Cake's objects. From naming tables in the database to coding large chunks of operations, keep in mind that each time you stick to convention, you avoid having to specify with lines of code where the different pieces of your application are located and how they should be assembled.

Starting with the Database

Conventions in Cake begin with the database. If you start with designing how your application will store and work with data, then the rest of the code can more easily fall into place. If you go wrong, however, then you will most certainly discover bugs in the application that will need adjustment to conform to Cake's conventions. Before I show how to build more elaborate Cake applications, I will take the time to nail down Cake's MVC structure and other naming and database conventions.

MVC Default Behaviors

When a Cake application launches, various PHP objects that are already assembled in the Cake libraries are run. The advantage of the MVC structure is that models, views, and controllers are specifically designed for specific operations. Thus, a model, by virtue of being a model and not something else, is automatically expected to do some database operations. These default operations could be mere placeholders, or they could have some default functions, depending on how the framework operates when launched.

Cake automatically assembles an object for each part of the MVC structure. The Controller object automatically behaves a certain way when called, the Model object does as well, and so on. You extend objects in PHP when you create a new instance of a class object and specify that this instance is an extension of an existing object. For example, you can create your own AppController object as an extension of the Controller class object like this:

```
class AppController extends Controller {
```

PHP's syntax is such that you add on extends and the name of the class object to be extended, which in this case is the Controller object. Thus, when the AppController object is called, everything contained in the Controller object is now called as well.

When the controller class object is called, it will automatically look for a model and a view to do its work. You specifically choose the controller to launch by the URL you enter, but you cannot enter a URL to call only a model or a view. Cake's dispatcher will funnel all requests through the `Controller` object, so you must place other objects in the way to intercept the default actions that object will perform when called. If you enter a URL and the dispatcher cannot find a controller object that matches the name in that URL, then the `Controller` object, by default, is set to display an error message. Knowing these default behaviors and knowing where you can intercept them and install your own methods are what coding in Cake is all about.

In the model, for example, each time a record is saved to the database, certain functions are executed. You can intercept this default behavior by entering the `beforeSave()` function in the model with some of your own logic. This intercepts the default `save()` function the `Model` object uses to insert records into the database and allows you to check the data against your own custom parameters before saving them.

As the dispatcher resolves URLs, it will look to files named appropriately, and otherwise it will return errors. When controller actions are run, the `Controller` object looks for specific view files stored in the appropriate area for the controller to execute properly. Throughout the entire Cake application, certain conventions are at work. In a way, the main content of this book is to spell out all these conventions and how to work with them to produce web applications. First I'll describe how to name files and how to name `class` objects in these files appropriately. By placing files in the correct areas with correct names and containing correct `class` names, Cake will know that you are intercepting its default operations and will execute your custom objects instead. The more objects you extend from Cake's default objects, the more elaborate the application.

Naming Conventions

Simply put, if you don't name your files correctly, Cake won't be able to piece the different parts of the application together and will supply you with error messages. Each element of the site must follow certain naming conventions so that when Cake looks for a needed resource, it can find it and run it.

You probably noticed in Chapter 3 that you gave certain names to the model and controller files to make the to-do list application work. I explained that these files have to match up with the table in the database and contain some typical naming schemes when entering PHP code. What if you needed some more elaborate naming schemes to meet the demands of your project? The following are the basic rules for naming files in Cake and how to incorporate more complex names into your Cake application for more custom needs.

Naming Controllers

Each controller name must match a database table name. If you decide to create controllers with names other than tables of the database, you should actually not create a controller but use a component instead (you'll learn more about components in Chapter 11). The names of database tables as well as controllers are lowercase and in plural form. For example, a table containing records for orders in a shopping cart application would be named `orders`. The controller file takes the name of the table it matches and appends an underscore and the word `controller`, and it is a PHP file, so it will carry the `.php` extension. Thus, the Orders controller would be named `orders_controller.php` and would be stored in the `app/controllers` folder.

In the controller file you will need to extend the `AppController` object already being called by Cake when the application is launched. To do so, another important convention is at work. Listing 4-1 shows how to name the controller class in the file and how to extend the `AppController` object.

Listing 4-1. *Inside the Controller*

```
1   <?
2   class RecordsController extends AppController {
3   }
4   ?>
```

Notice that on line 2 in Listing 4-1 I've extended the `AppController` object by starting a new class and naming the class `RecordsController`. The name of the class will always need to match up to the file name of the controller and be camel case[1] with the word `Controller`. If, for example, this controller were for the `orders` table, line 2 would contain the class name `OrdersController`, and the file name would be `orders_controller.php`.

If you follow this convention, Cake will be able to dispatch the request to the correct controller and run the correct action.

Naming Models

Models are named like controllers except they represent interacting with one instance of the database table at a time, so they will take on a singular, not plural, form. Using the earlier shopping cart example, the corresponding model for the `orders` table would be named `order.php` and be stored in the `app/models` folder. Notice that for models, you do not append an underscore plus `model` to the file name.

In Listing 4-2, you can see a similar beginning code structure for the model PHP file that you use in the controller file; I've created a new `class` object that extends the `AppModel` object created by Cake, and I've named it `Record` in conjunction with the naming convention that model names be singular. In the `Order` model, line 2 would change to a class named `Order`, thus linking it to the `orders` database table.

Listing 4-2. *Inside the Model*

```
1   <?
2   class Record extends AppModel {
3   }
4   ?>
```

---

1. Camel case is used frequently in Cake as a convention for naming classes. Sometimes called *medial capitals*, it is the practice of joining words or phrases without spaces and capitalizing them within the compound. Think of the uppercase bumps in the word like humps of a camel.

Naming Views

When the controller renders views, Cake will automatically look for a file with the same name as the action. Views correspond to actions contained in the controller script and are housed in a folder named after the controller. The first step in creating a view to be used as output for a controller script is to create the folder in `app/views` that matches with the name of the controller.

View folders are lowercase and plural just like the naming convention for database tables. For the `orders_controller.php` file, you would create the folder `app/views/orders`.

View files match actions in the controller, so they must be named accordingly. When a controller action is called, Cake will automatically search for a corresponding view following a specific naming scheme. Using the `Orders` example, let's say you wanted the user to be able to see the order before placing it. So, you create an action in the `orders_controller.php` file called `review`. In this action (which is literally a PHP function in the controller script), you pull some variables together and send them to the view following the MVC structure. Cake will automatically search for a view called `app/views/orders/review.ctp` (`.ctp` is the common extension for all Cake views, not `.html` or `.php`).

Table 4-1 contains a breakdown of the naming conventions for model, controller, and view files. Notice that the view files are named after a matching action in the controller and that the folder name containing the views matches the name of the controller.

■**Note** The earliest versions of Cake used the file extension `.thtml` for view files, but this was changed to `.ctp` for CakePHP 1.2. If you do come across older Cake applications, be sure to change these view files' extensions to the now standardized `.ctp` extension.

Table 4-1. *MVC Elements and Their Naming Conventions for the* `records` *Database Table*

Type	File Name	Extension	Class Name	Directory Where Stored
Model	record	.php	Record	app/models
Controller	records_controller	.php	RecordsController	app/controllers
View	{matches action name in controller}	.ctp		app/views/records

More Than One Word in the Name

Perhaps you need to name a database table that uses more than one word. In short, you can use more than one word by separating each word with an underscore. A table, then, containing special orders would be named something like `special_orders`, not `specialorders` or `specialOrders`. But, for Cake to link up to this table, the controllers, models, and views also need to follow suit. Camel-cased titles for the words tell what Cake will seek out when running the controllers, models, and views. See Table 4-2 for an example of what the various names would be for MVC elements matching up with the `list` action for a database table named `special_orders`.

Table 4-2. *MVC Elements' Names for the* `special_orders` *Database Table*

Type	File Name	Class Name	Directory Where Stored
Model	`special_order.php`	`SpecialOrder`	`app/models`
Controller	`special_orders_controller.php`	`SpecialOrdersController`	`app/controllers`
View	`list.ctp`		`app/views/special_orders`

Naming Other Cake Resources

As another matter of convention over configuration, Cake divides up other important resources in much the same way that it does with models, views, and controllers. For instance, if more than one controller needed to use the same actions, then you could create a *component*. The controllers could essentially run an include of the component and run the actions as if they were individually contained in the controller. Other resources act in the same way. A view to be used by multiple views is stored in what's called an *element*, and so on. Each of these resources has its own naming conventions.

Later, you'll make full use of each of these resources. While I'm discussing naming conventions in Cake, it's worth familiarizing yourself with the conventions for other Cake resources.

Components

Component files contain actions or functions that can be used across all the controllers. A component typically aims to provide tools to accomplish a main objective. For example, you may want to organize a set of functions that manage all the e-mail your application must send. Various controllers may need to run an e-mail function here and there, so rather than write the e-mail process into the individual controllers, it's best to house all the e-mailing in a component file. By doing so, you effectively keep all your e-mailing functions in one place in the same manner that by using models you separate out all your database functions.

Components can be fully customized to meet your needs. In fact, a growing repository of third-party components are available on the Web from other Cake developers, which proves helpful in borrowing tasks from other projects and reducing the amount of code you assemble yourself.

The file name of a component can be anything, but like models, views, and controllers, more than one word in the name must be separated by underscores and camel case when naming the `class` object.

Cake comes with a built-in e-mail component, but for the sake of the previous example, if you were to create an e-mail component of your own, you could name the file `email.php` and place it in the `app/controllers/components` directory.

In the file, you would need to create a new component class using the following syntax:

```
class EmailComponent extends Object {
```

Notice that the name of the `class` object is camel cased just as in the controller, and it extends the class `Object`. Later, you'll assemble some customized components to be used in more complex applications.

Helpers

Helpers provide functionality that is used across multiple views. Imagine creating functions in a script that pertain only to final output. You could extend these functions to include various settings that would make the process repeatable throughout the entire application.

Take an HTML link, for example. You could write the link in the view file manually:

```
<a href="/blog/posts/view/55">Read Post 55</a>
```

However, you may want the application to manage the links and dynamically generate the paths. In this case, writing static HTML links would not work. Here's where writing helpers or using one of Cake's built-in helpers can dramatically save you time and effort. A specific link function inside a helper contains a set of parameters that can change depending on the specific attributes of the view (like the text to be linked and the destination of the link). The process of writing the <a> tag around a path, configuring a path to work with Cake's system, and outputting the text to be clicked does not change, so this can be repeated whenever a link needs to be written. Using the HTML helper (which is a default helper in Cake) can accomplish this:

```php
<?php echo $html->link('Read Post 55','/posts/view/55');?>
```

Now, no matter where the Cake application is stored, links created by the $html->link() function will not break because their paths are checked and routed by Cake. If you wanted to alter the display of all links, you could go into the helper and rewrite the function once rather than search for each instance of a link.

Helpers simplify HTML output in significant ways. Imagine reducing to one string of code a complete set of radio buttons or check boxes for an HTML form or truncating news articles with one line. For example, Cake's Form helper can take an array of values (say, $data) and turn out radio buttons ready to be used and submitted back to the controller with one line:

```php
<?php echo $form->radio('data');?>
```

Because helpers are set apart for use in the views, they are stored in the app/views/helpers directory. The file name convention is just like components, and they carry the .php extension. When naming the helper class object, the following syntax is used:

```php
class SpecialHelper extends Helper {
```

Like controllers and components, the name of the helper class is camel case and includes the word Helper, and the class is an extension of the object class Helper. For example, if you were to create a custom helper for e-mailing customers, you might create the app/views/helpers/email.php file and name its class:

```php
class EmailHelper extends Helper {
```

Elements

An element contains presentation output that can be pulled into multiple view files. Anything contained in the element will be displayed in the view depending on where in the view's markup the element is called. Variables can be passed to elements and displayed like how the controller sends variables to views.

Elements are named like controller actions and view files and are stored in the `app/views/elements` directory. For instance, a menu bar could be maintained in an element named `menu.ctp` and called in any of the views. Then, should you need to change a menu item or a link in the menu, rather than change it for every view in the application, you would need to edit only the `menu.ctp` file.

Helpers and elements differ in that helpers work with view logic, whereas elements are more like chunks of HTML that repeat throughout the views. A menu bar would likely require less logic (maybe a couple of variables) and would not contain a series of functions to be rendered. As an element, the menu bar would work well because multiple views would need to use it. Creating pie charts or graphs, however, would require several processes and more logic and therefore would be better suited as a helper than as an element.

Layouts

Many web sites maintain the same overall design from page to page with only specific areas changing content depending on the page. Rather than store in each view file this overall design, you can create a layout file to be used by the entire application or one controller action at a time.

Layouts are stored in the `app/views/layouts` directory and contain presentation output like views and elements. They perform minimal logic and mainly serve to wrap HTML around changing views. A layout's file name can be anything but must be lowercase and have the `.ctp` extension.

Behaviors

When interacting with the database, sometimes the model will need to perform more complex processes than simply adding, updating, or deleting records. In some applications, deleting a record will require performing other manipulations to other tables and records, and so on, with other database operations. Cake resolves this issue with *behaviors*, which are classes that may be called by models when performing model functions.

Behaviors are stored in the `app/models/behaviors` directory and can be named anything following the same rules for naming helper files and components. They must have the `.php` extension. In the file, behavior class names are set with the following syntax:

```
class SpecialBehavior extends ModelBehavior {
```

By using behaviors to store complex or customized model operations, you give the application's models more consistency.

DataSource

In this book I've stuck with MySQL as the main choice for database handling because it is often bundled with PHP. Many applications, however, need to store data in other sources. From PostgreSQL to a customized database engine, Cake is fully capable of handling other data sources. Even creating web services and talking with enterprise APIs such as Facebook or eBay can be handled in Cake. These types of operations are handled with *DataSources*, or, in other words, files that execute functions that talk with a source that stores or supplies data to the application.

The DataSource abstracts the sending, retrieving, saving, and deleting data to the model so that the model really behaves the same regardless of what external source processes the data. Cake comes preinstalled with the following datasources, so you won't have to write from scratch your own if you intend to use one of these to handle your application's data:

- MySQL

- PostgreSQL

- IBM DB2

- Microsoft SQL Server 2000

- Oracle 8

- SQLite

- ADOdb

When creating custom DataSource, make sure the file name is lowercase and has _source.php appended. An XML DataSource could be named, for example, xml_source.php and would be placed in the app/models/datasources directory. Naming the class object in the DataSource file (in this case, for the XML DataSource) is done with the following syntax:

```
class XmlSource extends DataSource {
```

When retrieving or saving data to a source outside your main database configuration source, DataSources can handle all the back-and-forth processing so that the model functions don't have to handle connection or request parameters unique to the DataSource.

Best Practices

Naming conventions in Cake do have specific rules that make it possible for Cake to assemble the various pieces of the application without too much code. Remember the saying "Just because you can doesn't mean you should" when naming files and database tables. The following are some suggestions for best practices when trying to decide upon names for elements of the application.

Keep File Names from Conflicting with Cake Resources

Avoid naming tables in the database that might conflict with a name of a Cake framework element. An example might be naming a table views or controllers.

Other conflicting names include class objects in Cake's libraries such as pages or files. Find a suitable name that can mean something similar such as records or images, or use underscores to add another word to the title such as web_pages or plain_text_files, and this will spare you the trouble of confusing Cake's dispatcher or confusing other developers who might work with your application. Sometimes when looking for help in the Cake community, it will be useful to give specifics. If your names overlap with other Cake objects, you may be asked to clarify.

Use Routes Rather Than Controllers

Some developers create a controller to handle logic alone without connecting it to a database table. They might name a controller `cart` or `blog` to create a separate wing of the application. Or they manipulate the names of their controllers for the sake of friendly URLs. In Cake, controllers are best suited for linking up with specific database tables. For example, you may want to build a blog that has a URL structure that goes something like this:

```
http://localhost/blog/view/5/sep/2008
```

So, how is this URL possible when there is no table named `view` in the database and the controller must match up with a database table?

You can customize how the dispatcher handles all URLs by editing the `app/config/routes.php` file. In this case, it would be best to build your database following convention and then go into the `routes.php` file and create some URL aliases that point to the appropriate controllers. You could create a table named `posts` in the database that stores all the blog posts and write an action in the `posts_controller.php` file that pulls the date from the URL and renders a view for the retrieved post. Then, in `routes.php`, you could write in a route for all URL strings that start with `/view` to point to the Posts controller and pass along the date parameters. If this makes little sense now, don't worry—you'll deal with Cake's routing possibilities in more detail in Chapter 10. Just make sure that you stick to convention first when thinking of how to name your database tables and consequently the controllers and models. Later you can work with routing to ensure that the URLs are structured to your liking.

Name Actions for People, Not Code

Actions appear in controllers and perform a set of operations that follow PHP syntax for functions. They also will link up with a view file to render output to the browser. Knowing how the action name might appear in a URL is important when deciding on how to name functions in the controller. For web sites that aim to be user-friendly and optimized for search engines, their action names might be more important than an internal reference name for the application alone.

A good rule of thumb for naming controller actions is to write names as if you had to spell it out over the phone. E-mail addresses with lots of nonalphanumeric characters (such as underscores and dashes), for instance, are frustrating when spelling them out to someone. Simplicity is best especially when the name will appear in a URL that will be repeated through verbal communication, on paper, or for a search engine.

Be Careful Using PHP Function Names as Action Names

Another important point is that actions can have conflicting names with PHP functions. Naming an action `date`, for instance, would conflict with the PHP `date()` function. Generally, you can get around this problem by naming actions that are specific to the general logic the action will perform. When that logic does coincide with the kind of logic found in other PHP functions, it's only really a matter of trying the action on a case-by-case basis to see whether it conflicts with PHP. Many PHP editing programs highlight PHP functions with a different color, which may also help when trying action names.

Poorly Designed Databases

Ambitious web applications will certainly call for complicated database design. All too often developers try to find a way to fit every piece of data into a field without building associations between tables. Or, rather than store a reference to a record in another table, some developers build scripts that write information into a text field. Worse yet, some developers write a static list in the HTML of the site and change the list manually depending on where the list appears in the application. Not only do these methods make updating the code of the application more cumbersome and less portable, they also don't fit into the paradigm of Cake's rapid development methodology. Poorly designed databases can adversely affect Cake's rapid development qualities and turn up errors or dead ends that lead to time wasted on forcing you to accommodate a bad database.

Why Good Database Design Matters

Much of Cake's rapid development functionality comes from conventions that are tied to how the database is designed. Not only does a good database design matter for the scaffolding feature or the Cake console, but it is the very bread and butter of Cake's data handling. The interactions between different kinds of data will affect the time it will require to use that data throughout the application. In theory, the database should separate data into categories that work off each other, rather than the MVC structure separating roles of operations into different areas.

Cake relies on the process of database normalization for its naming conventions and model functions. Normalization is the technique of designing relational database tables in an effort to minimize duplication and safeguard the database against structural problems. By normalizing your database, you produce an effective schema that improves your Cake application and saves you from data anomalies that can cause data-handling errors.

To contrast poor and good database design or, in other words, to explain why database normalization is so important, I'll discuss a social networking application scenario. For sites that give users web pages of their own, a lot of data will need to be stored. A poor database would have a record for each user's profile and a field for each item in the profile: user's name, e-mail address, home page address, favorite book 1, favorite book 2, image, avatar-sized image, slogan, description, friend 1, friend 2, and so on. When fetching the user's profile in the URL, a bad database wouldn't have any kind of unique ID, so the record would be pulled by the username.

This scenario is problematic because the number of fields is static. The user cannot add more than two books or two friends unless the developer manually adds more fields. Also, the number of fields would get large quickly the more the developer adds functionality to the application. Back-end database maintenance would be frustrating with a high number of fields. Field names such as `favorite_book_1` are clumsy and make it more difficult to organize the code when processing data. Also, without a unique identifier to differentiate the profile records, the possibility exists that the username could get duplicated and thus break the queries that would seek to fetch a user's profile. In theory, without some unique identifier for a record, that record could potentially get forever lost in the database and would not be retrievable.

On the other hand, a good database design would separate different categories of data into different tables. There would be a table for profiles, another for books, and another for users. The users table would store some basic information such as a username and password as well as an e-mail address. As users interact with others through the site, they could select other users to be their friends, and rather than saving that association as a field in the profiles table, another table could store the associations. A profile would be able to display any number of books in the books table by storing the associations in a separate table like the users' friends. In this way, the database stores *associations* as well as individual records. This fact is important for Cake development because of how it separates data into categories and allows for associations to exist between categories. Cake's fundamental design of separating various operations into different areas allows for tighter control of each of these tables in controllers, models, and views of their own.

Feature Creep and Cake

Consider the phenomenon of *feature creep* before designing the database. Feature creep occurs when a project is under way and contributors to the project realize potential for new features based on existing features in the uncompleted project. Before long, the contributors end up requesting so many features that the project becomes much more complicated than at the outset.

Cake will help with feature creep because of the specific areas that are devoted to specific functions. However, if the database is not equipped to handle feature creep, then taking advantage of Cake's flexibility later might not be possible and may necessitate rewriting the application. The trick is to design the database to use associations rather than individual fields for all categories of data. Cake handles associations wonderfully and will dramatically reduce the amount of database querying required to handle complex data structures.

Table Associations

A good web application that illustrates Cake's rapid development functionality and table associations is a blog. Here, you will build a simple blog application using the scaffolding feature to test associations. Later, you'll expand the blog to take on more powerful features. Mastering table associations and how they work in Cake is essential for pulling in advanced features that matter for complex web sites. A simple blog application will help us discuss table associations in an easier way and should help you if you're unfamiliar with table associations to be better equipped to use Cake.

Create a new Cake application in your localhost root named blog. It should have the standard Cake 1.2 libraries and folders inside. As you walk through building this blog, remember how to launch the application in the browser. I'll reference a controller, and that will be executed by calling it in the URL with the correct string, like http://localhost/blog/posts.

The Database Design

Create three tables in the blog's database: posts, comments, and users. Listing 4-3 contains the MySQL query to create fields in the tables.

Listing 4-3. *The SQL Table Structures*

```
CREATE TABLE `posts` (
  `id` int(11) unsigned NOT NULL auto_increment,
  `name` varchar(255) default NULL,
  `date` datetime default NULL,
  `content` text,
  `user_id` int(11) default NULL,
  PRIMARY KEY (`id`)
);

CREATE TABLE `comments` (
  `id` int(11) unsigned NOT NULL auto_increment,
  `name` varchar(100) default NULL,
  `content` text,
  `post_id` int(11) default NULL,
  PRIMARY KEY (`id`)
);

CREATE TABLE `users` (
  `id` int(11) unsigned NOT NULL auto_increment,
  `name` varchar(100) default NULL,
  `email` varchar(150) default NULL,
  `firstname` varchar(60) default NULL,
  `lastname` varchar(60) default NULL,
  PRIMARY KEY (`id`)
);
```

The users table will contain a running list of available authors of blog posts. When a post is created, it will be assigned an author from the users table. Notice that there is a field in the posts table named user_id. This will match up with the id field in the users table, thus linking an author to the post. Also, in the comments table, each comment will be assigned to a post in the same manner. In this case there is a field named post_id, which will match up with the id field in the posts table.

In the models, you will spell out these associations so Cake can pull them together. What's more, you can test how well you've specified the associations using the scaffolding feature. As noted earlier, one main idea in Cake application building is to start with the Cake objects and build out. In general, you will design your database structure first, test their associations in the scaffolding, and then build out with your own code to enhance the application.

"Belongs To"

When associating tables, you need to tell Cake what type of relationship each table has with the others. This blog will have a "belongs to" relationship in a couple of tables. First, since each blog post will have an assigned author, each blog post "belongs to" one user. In other words, the posts table "belongs to" the users table. You have placed a user_id field in the posts table as a way to save this relationship. For each record in the posts table, one of the records from the users table will be saved by assigning one of its IDs to user_id.

To build this relationship into the models, first create the Post model as app/models/
post.php. Listing 4-4 contains the model's code to assign it a "belongs to" relationship with
the User model.

Listing 4-4. *The* Post *Model*

```
1    <?
2    class Post extends AppModel {
3        var $name = 'Post';
4        var $belongsTo = array('User');
5    }
6    ?>
```

Line 4 of Listing 4-4 shows how to enter a "belongs to" relationship in Cake. You do this by
assigning an array of models that are part of the relationship to the current model. The class
object variable Cake uses to build "belongs to" relationships is the var $belongsTo attribute.

In any Cake application, "belongs to" relationships are made by following the code on
line 4. You can add relationships by including them in the array syntax.

className Parameter

A possible key to be included with the $belongsTo settings is className. Simply put, className
is the model to which the current model belongs. In this case, it would be set to User, meaning
the class name of the users table's model. If you decide to abandon Cake's model naming conventions or if there is a complex reason for naming a model other than the standard Cake
convention, then you will need to specify the name in this setting; otherwise, Cake will not
be able to link the association on its own.

foreignKey Parameter

This key sets the foreign key found in the related model. This setting is useful for specifying
multiple "belongs to" relationships.

conditions Parameter

This key contains a SQL string that filters related model records. Generally, it will contain an
equals/not-equals SQL statement for a field (for example, Post.published = 1).

fields Parameter

By default, Cake will return all fields from the associated table. In this case, all fields from the
User record, which is associated with the current post, will be fetched and made available to
the Post model. You can limit this by using the fields key.

You can set these keys to your own values by assigning them as an array to each item in the
$belongsTo array. Listing 4-5 shows the Post "belongs to" relationship with all keys displayed.

Listing 4-5. BelongsTo *Keys Are Assigned to the* Post::User *Relationship*

```
var $belongsTo = array(
    'User'=>array(
        'className'=>'User',
        'foreignKey'=>'user_id',
        'conditions'=>null,
        'fields'=>null
        )
    );
```

"Has One"

Each relationship with association mapping must be specified in both directions. In other words, just saying that posts belong to users is not enough. You must also specify in the User model how users are associated to any other table. In this case, a user will "have many" posts. Three relationships are possible—"has one," "has many," and "has and belongs to many." First I'll discuss the "has one" association.

This relationship is exactly a one-to-one relationship. In applications that assign profiles to users, such as social networking web sites, the "has one" relationship is used. Each user has one profile, and one profile belongs to just one user.

To establish the "has one" relationship, you set the $hasOne attribute like you did with $belongsTo in the Post model (see Listing 4-6).

Listing 4-6. *The* $hasOne *Attribute String That Sets a "Has One" Relationship in the* User *Model*

```
var $hasOne = array('Post');
```

className Parameter

For a "has one" relationship, className should always be set to the model that contains the belongsTo attribute pointing to the current model.

foreignKey, conditions, and fields Parameters

These are similar to the "belongs to" foreignKey, conditions, and fields parameters. Set them to add more specific control to the "has one" relationship.

dependent Parameter

When deleting records in a "has one" relationship, you may want both sides of the association to be deleted. For example, when a user has one profile and the user is deleted, you may want the associated profile to be deleted also. In these cases, the dependent key allows you to do this easily. By default, it is set to false. Set dependent to true to delete records in both tables when the delete action is run through the associated model.

In the blog you are building, you have no need of a "has one" relationship. We will make use of another important relationship in Cake: "has many."

"Has Many"

You've created the Post model; it's time to make the User model. Create the User model in the app/models directory and work in the code shown in Listing 4-7.

Listing 4-7. *The* User *Model*

```
1    <?
2    class User extends AppModel {
3        var $name = 'User';
4        var $hasMany = array('Post');
5    }
6    ?>
```

For your blog, each user will have many posts. Even if a user enters only one post, you would still want the relationship to be capable of saving more than one post per user. By telling the User model that multiple post records are associated with it, and by completing the relationship in the Post model with the belongsTo attribute, Cake can now link the two together.

For more control, you may want to enter more parameters for the "has many" relationship.

className, foreignKey, conditions, and fields Parameters

These parameters specify the same things as described in the "belongs to" relationship earlier.

dependent Parameter

This setting behaves similarly to how it is described for the "has one" relationship. In the "has many" relationship, setting dependent to true will work recursively. In other words, if you set the $hasMany attribute in the User model to dependent=>true, then whenever a user is deleted, *all* posts ever assigned to that user will be deleted as well.

order Parameter

You can control the sorting order of the associated records by entering SQL syntax in this parameter. For example, in the User model, you could set order to Post.datetime ASC, and it would order all associated posts by their date and time in ascending order.

limit Parameter

Some database requests may return a substantial number of associated records. You may want to limit the number of returned records to cut down on server load time. You can do this by setting this parameter to a value representing the maximum number of associated records Cake will fetch from the database.

finderQuery Parameter

To produce even more customized results, you may enter a SQL string in the `finderQuery` key, and it will run when the associated records are queried. You really should need to use this option only if your application requires a high level of database customization. Most of the time, you will be able to work just fine using Cake's built-in model functions.

The "has many" relationship is extremely useful for helping to design effective databases. If you know that you intend to put a select menu in your application for a series of options that will be stored in the database, the "has many" relationship can help you do so without writing a static list in HTML. Instead, you could build a table to store those options and associate them through the models using a "has many" relationship. Then, no matter what may happen with feature creep or with adding or deleting options from the list, you can rest assured the application isn't broken and can handle the changes. It's built on a database, not on static forms, meaning that the application is dynamic and can change easily.

Testing the Associations

An easy way to test the associations in your database is to use the scaffolding feature. You have already created the `Post` and `User` models; now let's see how those associations hold up. You will need to create controllers to run the scaffold.

Create the `posts_controller.php` file in the `app/controllers` directory, and insert the code shown in Listing 4-8.

Listing 4-8. *The Posts Controller File*

```
1    <?
2    class PostsController extends AppController {
3        var $name = 'Posts';
4        var $scaffold;
5    }
6    ?>
```

To test the `User` model, you will also want to build a scaffold around the `users` table. To do this, create the file `app/controllers/users_controller.php` and insert the code shown in Listing 4-9.

Listing 4-9. *The Users Controller File*

```
1    <?
2    class UsersController extends AppController {
3        var $name = 'Users';
4        var $scaffold;
5    }
6    ?>
```

Let's add a couple of test users to the `users` table by launching the Users controller and clicking the Add link. My screen when doing this appears in Figure 4-1; yours should be similar.

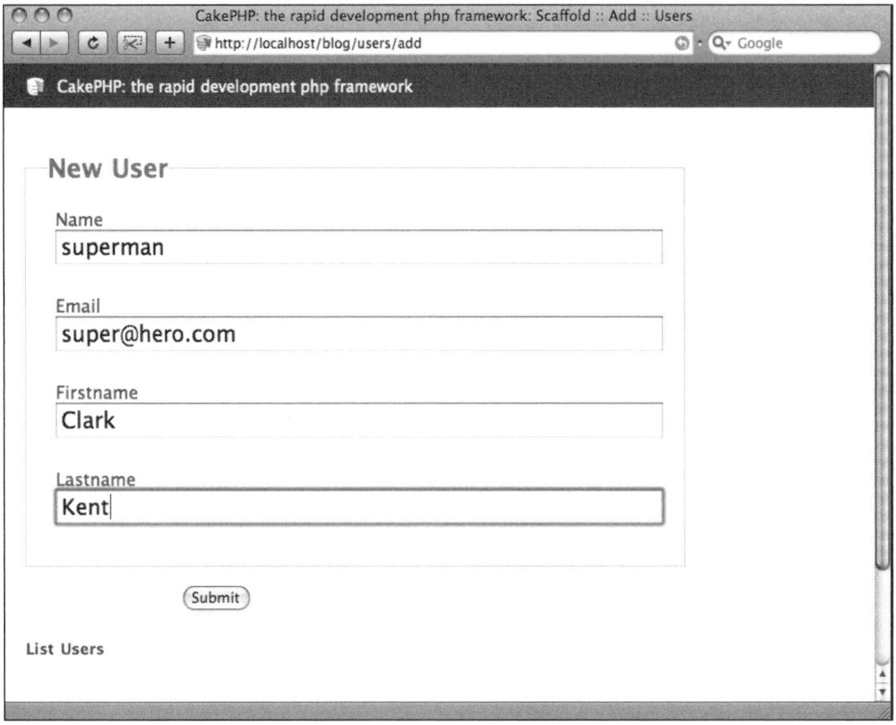

Figure 4-1. *Adding a test user to the database using Cake's scaffolding*

Now that there are a couple of users in the database, you can test whether those users get associated with the posts table. Launch the Posts controller, and click Add to insert a new post. If the association is working right, you should see a select menu that is populated with associated records in the users table; Figure 4-2 shows how this menu appears on the New Post screen.

If the association weren't working correctly, you'd see an empty input text box rather than a select menu for the user. That would indicate that Cake is asking you to fill in the user_id field with your own variable data. Notice that when you save the post, the list screen for the Posts controller displays the name of the user, not an ID number. This is another indication that Cake is picking up the association properly.

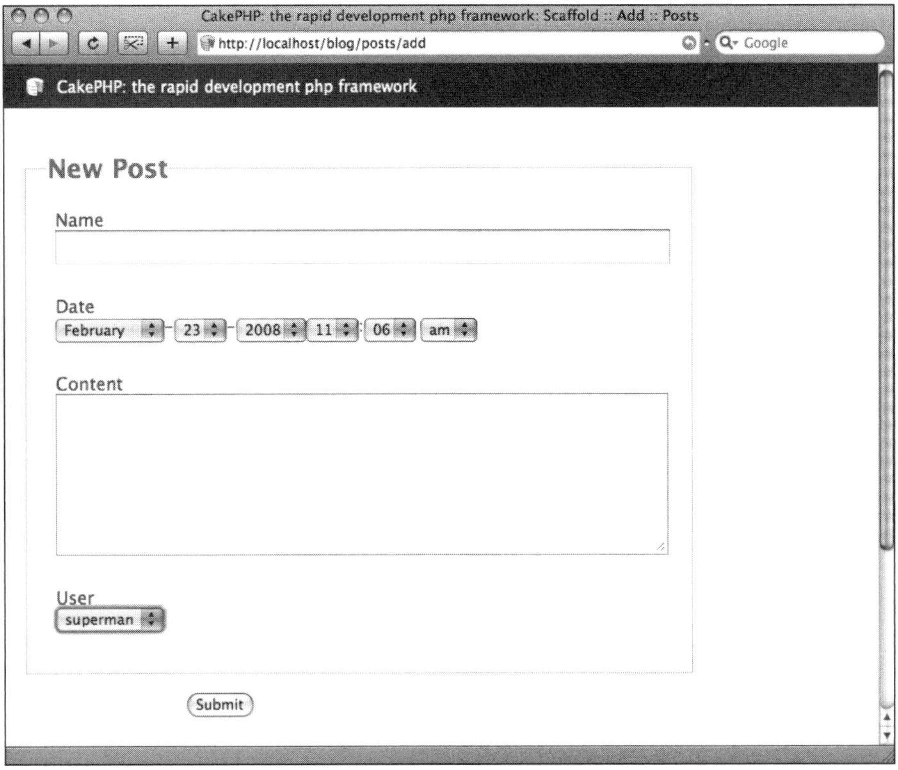

Figure 4-2. *The User menu is populated with actual records from the* users *table.*

Conventions for Establishing Table Associations

As mentioned earlier, you can manually set the foreign key for the relationship. In other words, you can name the fields that store the associated ID however you want. However, Cake does have some naming conventions for working with table associations that make it possible to leave out the foreignKey parameter and other settings, thus reducing the amount of code to build associations.

I have already mentioned that table names in the database ought to be pluralized. For a "has one" or "has many" relationship, you will need to enter a field that will store the associated record's ID value. This field's name follows a naming convention, specifically that it must be named after the model from which the ID comes. You must also append an underscore and id to the field name for Cake to recognize this as the associated foreign key. Notice that when you created the posts table, you followed this convention when adding the user_id field. By doing so, you could leave out the foreignKey parameter when setting the $belongsTo and $hasMany attributes. With the tables being named properly as well as the foreign keys, Cake automatically found the associations and made them available in the scaffolding. No specific code was necessary.

"Has and Belongs to Many"

The final association Cake can recognize for database table relationships is the "has and belongs to many" relationship. This relationship is powerful but also a little difficult to master. The more you experiment with "has and belongs to many" associations, the easier it will be to use them in your applications.

In short, I've already discussed a one-to-one relationship with the hasOne association, and the hasMany association shows you how a one-to-many relationship is managed in Cake. What about a many-to-many relationship?

Many-to-Many Relationships in Cake

Many web sites use tags to order their content. Many blogs, rather than assigning one category to a post, will have a list of tags that can be assigned multiple times to multiple stories, and vice versa. This is a many-to-many relationship between posts and tags. One post can have many tags, and each tag can belong to many posts.

Structurally, the database can handle many-to-many relationships only if there is a third table that saves these associations. In the post-to-tag example, a third table named something like posts_tags would be created. In it would be just two fields: post_id and tag_id. By having a third table, you maintain the flexibility needed to list as many relationships as the application would need to save; there is no limit to the number of associations in either direction because the third table can continually save more records.

As you can imagine, Cake saves a great deal of time in managing this association. Just like the $hasOne and $hasMany attributes, you create a "has and belongs to many" association by entering the $hasAndBelongsToMany attribute in the model.

You can also test "has and belongs to many" associations in the scaffold. Rather than view a select menu for a one-to-many relationship, Cake's scaffolding will render a multiple-select menu. In this way, you can test the association in the same manner that you tested the "has many" relationship earlier.

Applying and Testing This Relationship with the Blog

Let's add a "has and belongs to many" relationship to the blog application. To do this, you will need to create a new table in the database. See Listing 4-10 for the SQL syntax to create the tags table.

Listing 4-10. *The* tags *Table*

```
CREATE TABLE `tags` (
  `id` int(11) unsigned NOT NULL auto_increment,
  `name` varchar(100) default NULL,
  `longname` varchar(255) default NULL,
  PRIMARY KEY (`id`)
);
```

This tags table will hold category tags to better organize your blog posts. The name field will be an alphanumeric field to be used in accessing the tag through the URL. The longname field will store the category's display title for use in links and page headings.

Because the tags table will be linked with posts in a "has and belongs to many" relationship, you must create another table to hold those associations. This table name will follow Cake's naming conventions. For "has and belongs to many" tables, the name must be arranged in alphabetical order with each associated table's name separated by an underscore. Inside the table, you provide the foreign key and associated foreign key as fields with names following the same convention for one-to-many relationships. In this case, the field names will be ordered alphabetically, with post_id first and tag_id second. Use Listing 4-11 to create the new posts_tags table.

Listing 4-11. *The* posts_tags *Table*

```
CREATE TABLE `posts_tags` (
  `id` int(11) unsigned NOT NULL auto_increment,
  `post_id` int(11) unsigned default NULL,
  `tag_id` int(11) unsigned default NULL,
  PRIMARY KEY (`id`)
);
```

The Tag model is absent, so create that next as the app/models/tag.php file. Paste Listing 4-12 into the new Tag model file.

Listing 4-12. *The* Tag *Model*

```
1    <?
2    class Tag extends AppModel {
3        var $name = 'Tag';
4        var $hasAndBelongsToMany = array('Post');
5    }
6    ?>
```

Next, you will have to establish the association in the Post model as well. Adjust this model to reflect the "has and belongs to many" relationship, as shown in Listing 4-13.

Listing 4-13. *The* Post *Model with the* $hasAndBelongsToMany *Attribute Set*

```
1    <?
2    class Post extends AppModel {
3        var $name = 'Post';
4        var $belongsTo = array('User');
5        var $hasAndBelongsToMany = array('Tag');
6    }
7    ?>
```

Last, create the Tags controller with the scaffolding so that you can add tags to test the "has and belongs to many" relationship. Listing 4-14 contains the code for the new Tags controller file.

Listing 4-14. *The Tags Controller*

```
1   <?
2   class TagsController extends AppController {
3       var $name = 'Tags';
4       var $scaffold;
5   }
6   ?>
```

Run the Tags controller to add some placeholder tags for the test. Add more than one to make the test more effective (since the relationship you are testing is many-to-many). Everything is in place for a "has and belongs to many" relationship. Launch the Posts Add action to create a new post, and you should see a multiple-select area populated with the tags' names from the tags table, like Figure 4-3.

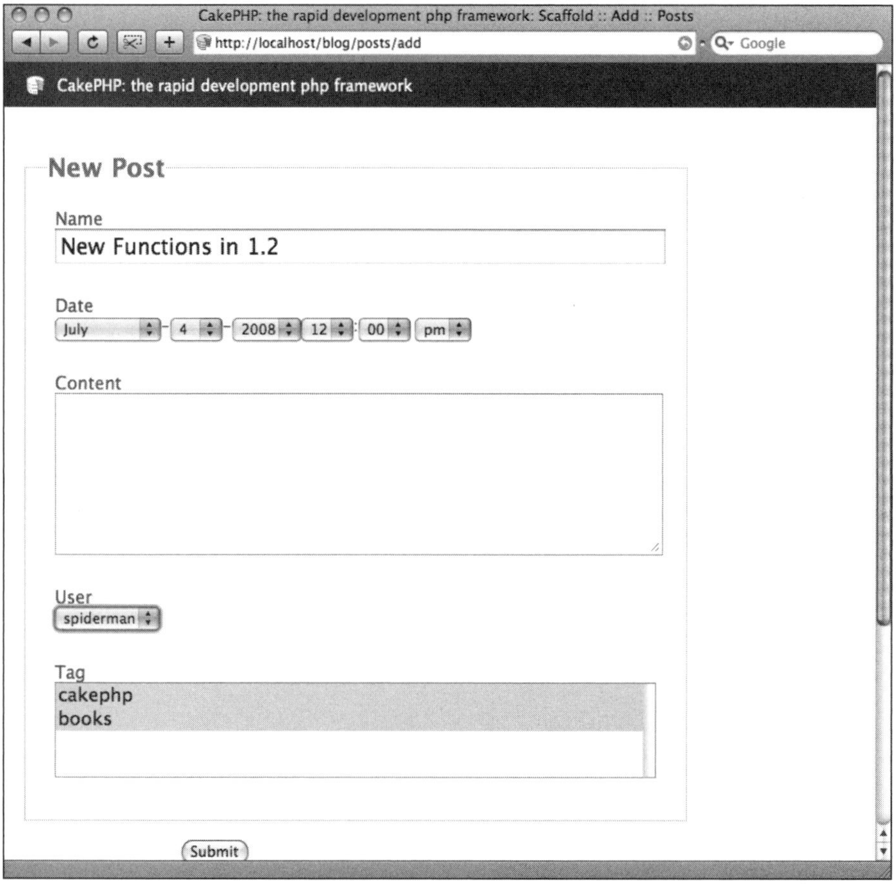

Figure 4-3. *Testing the "has and belongs to many" relationship for tags and posts*

The multiple-select box with the names appearing correctly indicates that Cake has picked up the relationship effectively and is pulling the appropriate data from the `tags` table. To test the relationship going the other direction, create a couple of posts and then access the Tags Add action. You should see there a multiple-select box as well with the associated posts highlighted, as shown in Figure 4-4.

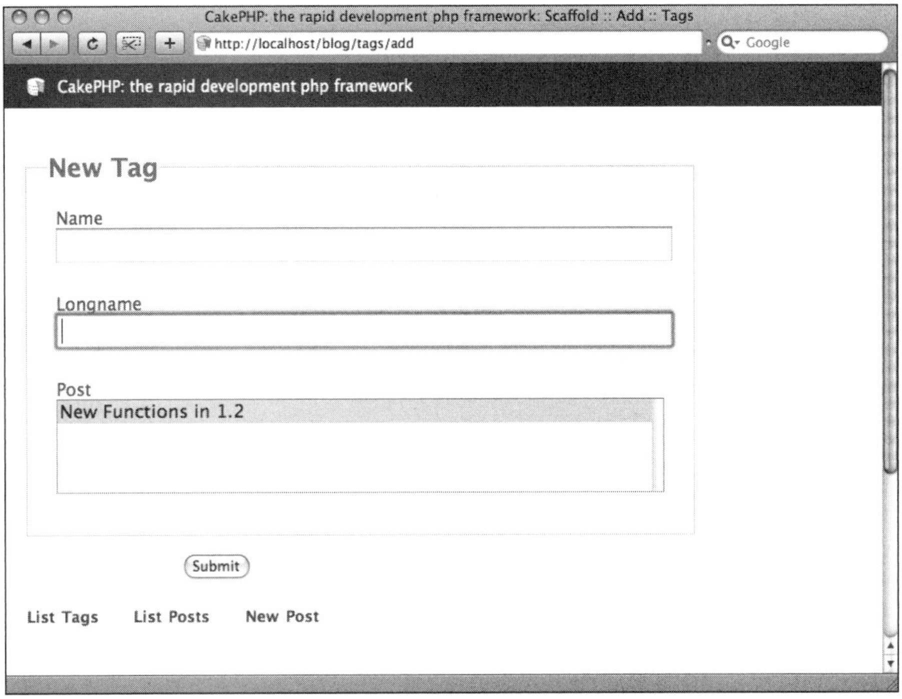

Figure 4-4. *In the Tags Add view, the post's data is displayed in the multiple-select box.*

Both tags and posts have shown the relationship in the scaffolded views. The models are working with each other correctly, so you can now begin manipulating the views to improve the application's design, flow, and features. To provide better control over the "has and belongs to many" relationship, the following parameters are available.

className Parameter

This name corresponds to the associated model. In the `Posts::Tags` example, the `Post` model would need `className` set to `Tag`.

joinTable Parameter

Remember how you created a third table to house all the associations for posts and tags? This is referred to as the *join table* and can be manually set using the `joinTable` parameter. For the blog, you would set this to `posts_tags`, named after the table, not the models.

foreignKey and associationForeignKey Parameters

The current model's key in the join table is `associationForeignKey`, which in this case would be `post_id` for the `Post` model. The `foreignKey` parameter is for the other model, that is, `tag_id` for the `Post` model. Set these for when you must specify multiple "has and belongs to many" relationships in a single model.

conditions, fields, order, and limit Parameters

These parameters behave like all other associations. Set manual SQL conditions, limit the returned fields, set the sorting order of the returned results, and limit the maximum amount of records to be returned with these parameters.

Beyond the Scaffold

Understanding basic installation routines, understanding naming conventions, and using table associations for good database organization will improve your development time and help you get off the ground with your project much more quickly. However, every application will need to move beyond the scaffold before it is ready for deployment. Indeed, the scaffolding feature is really intended for what I covered in this chapter: testing table associations without needing to code any HTML and providing a basic structure to tinker with a few application ideas before getting too deep in programming the site.

Chapter 5 will introduce to you the Bake script, a handy console program that runs much like the scaffold but supplies you with editable code from which you can expand your application. You'll improve the blog and adjust the views to bring it more in line with a production-level Cake application. As always, I recommend you practice using the table associations a few times with other scenarios, bringing in the parameters for each association, and customizing the association to get a feel for the models and good database design. The quicker you can take an application from zero to running the scaffold with advanced table associations, the more comfortable you'll feel with the MVC structure and the fundamental process Cake applications follow.

Table Associations Exercise

You may have noticed that I left the `comments` table out of the tutorial for this chapter. This was to allow you to try building a "has many" relationship for the `posts` and `comments` tables on your own. In this exercise, associate comments with posts by using the appropriate relationship, and test the association using the scaffold. Be sure to check for errors by running the controller from both ends of the association.

Summary

Cake uses naming conventions to simplify building an application. By adhering to the "convention over configuration" paradigm, Cake provides you not only with dozens of useful functions and code-cutting methods but also with an overall method for organizing the resources the application will use. How to name models, views, and controllers, as well as several other Cake resources such as helpers, elements, and components, is an essential aspect of learning Cake. Not only will you need to structure your application following Cake's conventions, but how you design the database also matters for taking advantage of the framework. Database normalization is key to designing a schema that best fits Cake's conventions and is essential for working with the models correctly. When you use the various relationships in your database (one-to-one, one-to-many, and many-to-many), Cake is able to do much of the difficult work in mapping the data and making them available in the application.

CHAPTER 5

■■■

Creating Simple Views and Baking in the Console

So far, you've really only used the scaffolding feature. Although scaffolding can help test associations and get your database working well with Cake, it does not give you much control over design, and the scaffolding does not go beyond simple CRUD operations either. To get into the individual form elements or to change how you want the list view to display the results, you must manually create and edit the views themselves.

Fortunately, Cake comes with some handy console scripts that can help you generate those views, as well as perform other important development tasks. In this chapter, I'll introduce the Bake script, which will essentially run like the scaffold and analyze the database but then provide code to edit. From there you can include your custom logic and add improved actions that go beyond simple CRUD operations. First, let's change the views a little bit for your blog application.

■**Note** All the view files I'll use in this book will run PHP shorthand for the `echo()` function. Your server setup may or may not support this method. If not, be sure to use the longer string `<?php echo();?>` instead of my shorthand `<?= ;?>`. Because the echo command is so common for view files, Cake does come with an echo convenience function that cuts down on characters. Use `e()` to echo and `pr()` for the `print_r()` function if you prefer the Cake convenience functions. Or, you can talk with your hosting provider to make PHP shorthand tags available and stick with the examples as written.

Introducing Layouts

Remember, Cake's framework follows the MVC method: models, views, and controllers. So far, you've become familiar with the model and the controller. Views are separated from the mix to provide for easier handling of output. Cake organizes all the views in the `app/views` folder.

The `views` folder contains the following directories:

- `elements`

- `errors`

- helpers

- layouts

- pages

- scaffolds

The layouts folder contains any overall layout files that are wrapped around your application. You can intercept Cake's default layout for scaffolds, error pages, and any other views by creating your own default layout. Placing a file named default.ctp into the layouts folder tells Cake to apply this layout instead of its own default scaffolding layout. Because it is a layout file, all the surrounding HTML will be applied to all the output.

Writing the default.ctp File

Create app/views/layouts/default.ctp, and place inside it your own HTML/CSS code. Listing 5-1 shows a basic (and boring) HTML layout to demonstrate how layouts work.

Listing 5-1. *A Simple Default Layout*

```
1    <html>
2    <head>
3        <title>My Cake Blog Application</title>
4        <?=$html->css('styles');?>
5    </head>
6    <body>
7        <div id="container">
8        <div id="content">
9            <?=$content_for_layout;?>
10       </div>
11       </div>
12   </body>
13   </html>
```

Most of this is basic HTML code that displays a title called "My Cake Blog Application" in the browser window but does little else. Line 4 of Listing 5-1 is a bit of Cake helper code that will automatically pull in the CSS file named styles.css (you'll create this file in a second).

Line 9 of Listing 5-1 is the key to any layout file in Cake. It's the string that tells Cake where to put all the views. When you launch any controller that hasn't specified another layout file, by default Cake will now swap out $content_for_layout with whatever output you've generated through your controllers, models, and views.

Creating a Style Sheet for the Layout

Public files, or files such as images, JavaScript files, and style sheets that you make available to the general web user are stored in the app/webroot folder. By default, this folder contains placeholders for CSS files, scripts, images, and other public resources. In a production setup, app/webroot will typically serve as the document root. In any case, Cake will internally reference this directory when linking to style sheets, images, JavaScript files, or other public resource files.

Line 4 of Listing 5-1 is Cake helper code that assembles some HTML for you, in this case, a link to a CSS file. This line is pulling the css() function from the HTML helper, which is part of Cake's core libraries and is passing the parameter styles to the function. The HTML helper's css() function knows to look for a styles.css file in the app/webroot/css folder and generate the <link rel="stylesheet" type="text/css" href="/css/styles.css" /> tag for the layout.

By using the HTML helper to build this link, not only is the amount of code entered by hand reduced, but you also ensure that wherever you may run the Cake application, the link will not be broken from inconsistent server setups. Cake comes with many more helpers. Using them can dramatically reduce the amount of code in the application, especially in views and layouts.

As of yet, there is no styles.css file in the app/webroot/css directory. Create that file, but leave it blank. You should get a rather simple view for the blog application (see Figure 5-1).

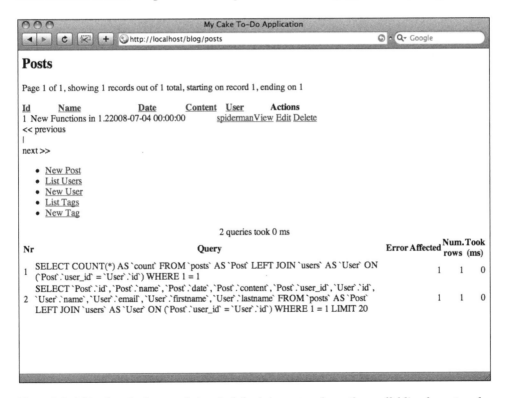

Figure 5-1. *A blank style sheet and simple default layout replaces the scaffolding layout and styles.*

Pretty boring, eh? You can spice this up by simply editing the app/webroot/css/styles.css file. In this file, paste the code shown in Listing 5-2 or do something similar.

Listing 5-2. *Sample CSS Code for the Default Layout*

```
* { font-family: "Lucida Grande",Lucida,sans-serif; }

th {
    font-size: 14px;
    font-weight: bold;
    background-color: #e1e1e1;
    border-bottom: 1px solid #ccc;
    padding: 10px;
}

div.actions ul {
    list-style-type: none;
}
```

Refresh the Posts controller, and you should get some new styles in the display (see Figure 5-2).

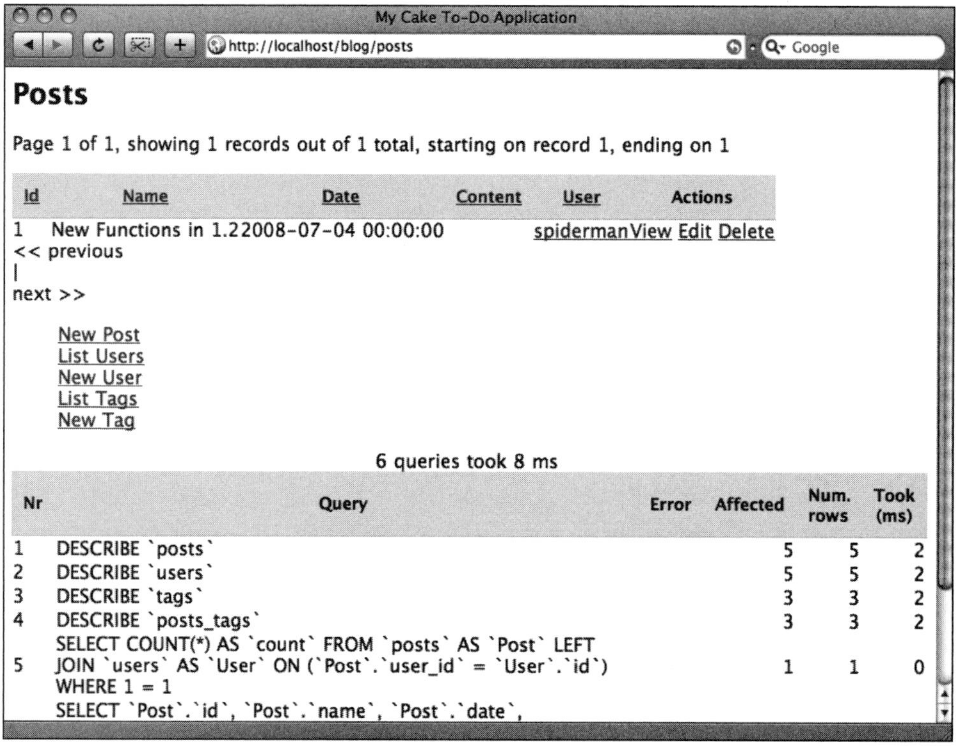

Figure 5-2. *The new styles are reflected in all views.*

You can see that by placing your own styles into the default layout, you can fully edit the design surrounding your application's output. Any views that are rendered, if they follow the default layout, will also be rendered using the same style sheet, so there's no need to duplicate styles or designs.

Return to the `app/views/layouts/default.ctp` file, and change line 4 to the following:

```
<?=$html->css('cake.generic');?>
```

When you refresh the Posts controller screen, you'll notice that Cake's styles have been implemented without the scaffolding's default titles and such. With these style changes, the scaffolding is still generating the individual CRUD operation views but now without Cake's built-in layouts.

Creating Individual Views

What do you do if you want to manipulate the views directly? For example, say you wanted to get rid of the title at the top that reads "Posts" and replace it with "Blog Posts." This is where individual views come in.

Yes, the scaffolding is a nice feature that makes testing code quick and painless, especially if all you want to do is play around with the database to make sure it's working right. But it can't possibly read your mind, and it can create only some generic views. Adding or subtracting from the application output will require you to manually build such output. No worries—this, too, is made much easier through the use of the framework.

Adding Actions to the Controller

To break out of the scaffold, you can delete the `$scaffold` attribute in the controller, or you can intercept the scaffold by adding your own actions instead. Scaffolded actions are specifically named `index()`, `add()`, `edit()`, `view()`, and `delete()`. Inserting an action into the controller bearing any of these names will replace the scaffold for that one action. So, leave the `$scaffold` attribute for all CRUD operations you don't want to code, and generate actions for those you do.

The first, and simplest, action to add is the Index action. All this operation will need to do is fetch all the posts in the database and make them available in the view. The view will then display all the posts as a list. Insert Listing 5-3 into the Posts controller after the `$scaffold` attribute.

Listing 5-3. *The Index Action in the Posts Controller*

```
6    function index() {
7        $this->set('posts',$this->Post->find('all'));
8    }
```

Entering the action into the controller is only half the process. Should you launch the Posts controller, it would display an error message because the controller would send for the view file and there is no Index action view available yet. The next step is to create the corresponding action view by following Cake's conventions. The file will need to be placed in the `app/views/posts` directory and be named after the action. Create the necessary `posts` folder, and place the `index.ctp` file in it. Then paste the view code from Listing 5-4 into this file.

Listing 5-4. *The Index View in the* app/views/posts *Folder*

```
1    <h2>Blog Posts</h2>
2    <table cellpadding="0" cellspacing="0">
3    <tr>
4        <th>ID</th>
5        <th>Name</th>
6        <th>Date</th>
7        <th>Content</th>
8        <th>User</th>
9        <th>Actions</th>
10   </tr>
11   <? foreach($posts as $post): ?>
12   <tr>
13       <td><?=$post['Post']['id'];?></td>
14       <td><?=$post['Post']['name'];?></td>
15       <td><?=$post['Post']['date'];?></td>
16       <td><?=$post['Post']['content'];?></td>
17       <td><?=$post['User']['name'];?></td>
18       <td class="actions">
19           <?=$html->link('View','/posts/view/'.$post['Post']['id']);?>
20           <?=$html->link('Edit','/posts/edit/'.$post['Post']['id']);?>
21           <?=$html->link('Delete','/posts/delete/'.$post['Post']['id'],null,➥
'Are you sure you want to delete #'.$post['Post']['id']);?>
22       </td>
23   </tr>
24   <? endforeach;?>
25   </table>
26   <div class="actions">
27       <ul><li><?=$html->link('New Post','/posts/add');?></li></ul>
28   </div>
```

Essentially, what you have done here is re-create the scaffolding view (assuming you're still using the cake.generic.css file instead of your own). But now that the code is right in front of you, you can toy with any aspect of it and customize it to meet your own needs. Notice on line 1 of Listing 5-4 that I've changed the <h2> tag to read "Blog Posts." In Listing 5-3, the Index action runs a model function that pulls all post records and assigns them to a variable to be used in the view. In line 7 of Listing 5-3, the set() function is a Cake function that assigns a value to a view variable. In this case, the variable will be named posts and will contain the results from the find() function in the Post model.

In line 11 of Listing 5-4, the view file uses the set() function in the controller. Here in the view, posts is now a typical PHP variable named $posts. Line 11 starts a loop through that array variable, which is the equivalent of looping through each record from the database that was fetched in the query. The view simply takes each record's content and displays it in table cells. Each iteration generates a new table row until it reaches the last record in the $posts variable.

Launch the Index action in the Posts controller, and you should see nearly the same screen as the scaffolding view (see Figure 5-3).

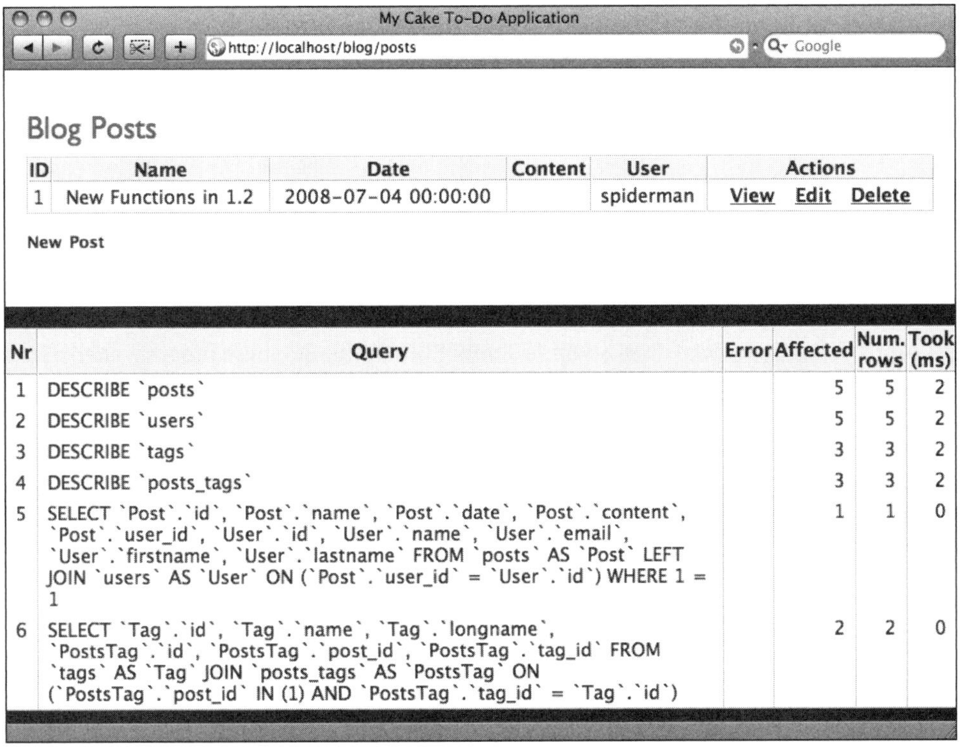

Figure 5-3. *The Index action view rendered by manual, not scaffolded, code.*

The main difference in this example is that you have access to the display code and the action's logic because you have manually supplied the code in the controller and the view file. Creating this code is not challenging, mainly because the Index action required only one line to run the database query and make the results available to the view. More elaborate operations are necessary for the other CRUD operations and will require many more lines of code, both in the controller and in the view. Fortunately, Cake can help generate this code in the console.

Using Bake to Create Views

I've walked you through how to manually create the index view. Actually, though, you should be able to avoid having to type these basic CRUD functions by hand. Included with Cake is a handy console script called the Bake script (the bake.php script, found in the cake/console/ libs folder). Not only will it save you tons of time generating the needed code to build these views, but it will also show you some basic Cake code that will help you understand how Cake uses models, views, and controllers.

Configuring the Console's Profile to Run Bake

However your localhost is set up, you will need a way of running the console to execute Bake. Most Linux setups have a console built into the operating system, and Mac OS X comes bundled with the Terminal application, so if you are running in one of these environments, you shouldn't have to install anything to run shell scripts. For PC users, you may have to install extra software that supports running PHP in the console, such as Cygwin (www.cygwin.com) or MinGW (www.mingw.org). The main requirements for getting Bake to work in your console is that the shell can run PHP and the same database engine you're using for your Cake application.

Many users use helpful programs such as XAMPP, LAMP, or MAMP—personal web server applications that reduce web server setup to a minimum. Although these programs make it possible to essentially click a button to turn on a localhost, they do make things a little bit trickier to get Bake running correctly. Often, the operating system and the web server environments both have shell applications that can conflict with one another when running the console. Whatever your setup looks like, you will likely need to adjust the shell's profile to get Bake working right.

In Mac OS X and some versions of Linux, the command-line console will use a file named .profile, usually invisible in your operating system, when it executes commands. Fortunately, you can add some of your own customized environment settings to tell the console where to go when executing Bake commands.

You can open the .profile file in a number of ways. You can use the following command to edit .profile in the console:

```
vi .profile
```

However, if you're like me, you'd probably rather edit this file in a simple plain-text editor. You will need to locate the profile to open it in your editor, but when saved, Bake should run properly regardless of your localhost settings.

The profile will need the line in Listing 5-5 added to get Bake working properly.

Listing 5-5. *By Entering an Alias into the Profile, You Can Access Bake in the Command Line*

```
alias cake="php ~/Sites/blog/cake/console/cake.php"
```

If you are unfamiliar with console profile aliases, Listing 5-4 may need some explaining. First, a new alias is listed, which in this case is named cake. Now, whenever you type "cake" in the command line of your console, it will execute what is contained within the quotes. The order here is important: the first string is the path to the shell application to be executed when the alias is typed, and the second string is the path to the file to be launched by the shell application. In this case, when "cake" is typed in the console, the shell will run its native PHP shell application. It will also tell PHP to launch the cake/console/cake.php file.

What you enter as the alias here will likely need to be adapted to your own settings, especially if you are running a web server application such as XAMPP. Make sure that the path to PHP points to the PHP application that runs your Cake application. For personal web server users, this will likely be a path to the xampp/php/php5/phpcli.exe file, or something like xampp/xamppfiles/bin/php. Whatever the case, it must be the same command-line PHP application that is used by your localhost root.

Also, the path to Cake's console scripts will change depending on where your application is stored on your localhost. A good rule of thumb here is to make these two paths absolute so that regardless of what environment you're using your console with, it will access the correct applications and scripts.

Launching Bake

With the profile configured correctly, launching Bake is done simply by entering the following in a command line:

```
$ cake bake
```

Two things can happen when Bake is properly launched: it will ask you what you want to bake, or it will ask you where you want a new Cake application copied. If the latter is the case, you will need to specify the path to the blog application to get Bake to work properly with your existing project. To do so, when launching Bake, use the -app parameter to specify the application's path to its app directory. Be sure to include the trailing slash (see Listing 5-6).

■**Note** If you're running your console in Windows, you may need to reference the Cake command using the file name cake.bat instead of the terminal command cake. This will depend on how you've set up your console and how, if any, third-party console applications are configured.

Listing 5-6. *Using the -app Parameter to Point Bake to the Application*

```
$ cake bake -app ~/Sites/blog/app/
```

You can tell whether Bake is working properly with your application when you see the Bake welcome screen (see Figure 5-4).

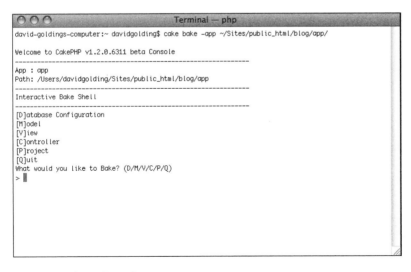

Figure 5-4. *The Bake welcome screen*

Using Bake to Generate CRUD Views

The welcome screen starts by asking what should be baked. Bake can handle creating a handful of application resources:

- Database configuration
- Model
- View
- Controller
- Project

Choosing a database configuration or project will bake either a new `app/config/database.php` file or a new Cake application project. Most of the time, you will use Bake to help create models, views, and controllers. You have already created the Index action in the Posts controller to walk through the steps for manually creating actions and views. With Bake, you will overwrite the Posts controller with a baked controller and then generate the CRUD views.

Bake the Controller First

Select a controller in Bake by typing C in the console. Bake will prompt you to specify from which model to bake, or dynamically write with the Bake script, the new controller (see Figure 5-5). Start with the Posts controller by typing the corresponding number (2).

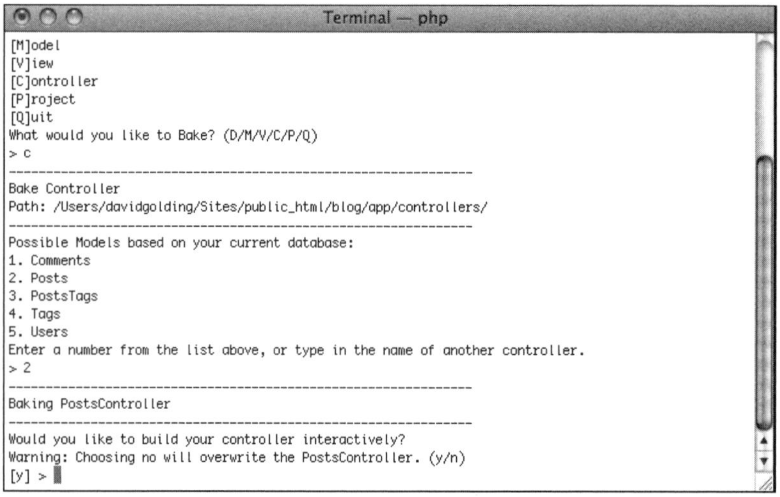

```
[M]odel
[V]iew
[C]ontroller
[P]roject
[Q]uit
What would you like to Bake? (D/M/V/C/P/Q)
> c
---------------------------------------------------------------------
Bake Controller
Path: /Users/davidgolding/Sites/public_html/blog/app/controllers/
---------------------------------------------------------------------
Possible Models based on your current database:
1. Comments
2. Posts
3. PostsTags
4. Tags
5. Users
Enter a number from the list above, or type in the name of another controller.
> 2
---------------------------------------------------------------------
Baking PostsController
---------------------------------------------------------------------
Would you like to build your controller interactively?
Warning: Choosing no will overwrite the PostsController. (y/n)
[y] >
```

Figure 5-5. *To bake a controller, you must specify from which model to build.*

Bake gives you the option of baking the controller interactively. In interactive mode, Bake will walk you through each step of building the controller. With each step you will have the option of modifying the setting to fit your needs. Bypassing interactive mode will produce a default controller and will overwrite any controllers that match the file name of the one Bake builds. Enter interactive mode to bake the controller, and specify these settings:

- Would you like to use scaffolding? [No]

- Would you like to include some basic class methods (index(), add(), view(), edit())? [Yes]

- Would you like to create the methods for admin routing? [No]

- Would you like this controller to use other helpers besides HtmlHelper and FormHelper? [No]

- Would you like this controller to use any components? [No]

- Would you like to use Sessions? [Yes]

Bake will ask you whether creating the Posts controller looks OK; this is an opportunity to start over if somehow during the process you entered the wrong parameter. When you continue, because you have already created a Posts controller, Bake will ask you whether you'd like to overwrite the existing Posts controller. Specify Yes. Finally, Bake will ask whether you want to bake unit test files; specify No.

That's it. The Posts controller will now have the business logic included for the basic class methods (see Listing 5-7).

Listing 5-7. *The Baked Posts Controller*

```php
<?php
class PostsController extends AppController {
    var $name = 'Posts';
    var $helpers = array('Html', 'Form');

    function index() {
        $this->Post->recursive = 0;
        $this->set('posts', $this->paginate());
    }

    function view($id = null) {
        if (!$id) {
            $this->Session->setFlash(__('Invalid Post.', true));
            $this->redirect(array('action'=>'index'));
        }
        $this->set('post', $this->Post->read(null, $id));
    }
```

```
    function add() {
        if (!empty($this->data)) {
            $this->Post->create();
            if ($this->Post->save($this->data)) {
                $this->Session->setFlash(__('The Post has been saved', true));
                $this->redirect(array('action'=>'index'));
            } else {
                 $this->Session->setFlash(__('The Post could not be saved. ➥
Please try again.', true));
            }
        }
        $tags = $this->Post->Tag->find('list');
        $users = $this->Post->User->find('list');
        $this->set(compact('tags', 'users'));
    }

    function edit($id = null) {
        if (!$id && empty($this->data)) {
            $this->Session->setFlash(__('Invalid Post', true));
            $this->redirect(array('action'=>'index'));
        }
        if (!empty($this->data)) {
            if ($this->Post->save($this->data)) {
                $this->Session->setFlash(__('The Post has been saved', true));
                $this->redirect(array('action'=>'index'));
            } else {
                 $this->Session->setFlash(__('The Post could not be saved. ➥
Please try again.', true));
            }
        }
        if (empty($this->data)) {
            $this->data = $this->Post->read(null, $id);
        }
        $tags = $this->Post->Tag->find('list');
        $users = $this->Post->User->find('list');
        $this->set(compact('tags','users'));
    }

    function delete($id = null) {
        if (!$id) {
            $this->Session->setFlash(__('Invalid id for Post', true));
            $this->redirect(array('action'=>'index'));
        }
```

```
    if ($this->Post->del($id)) {
        $this->Session->setFlash(__('Post deleted', true));
        $this->redirect(array('action'=>'index'));
    }
  }

}
?>
```

Bake the Views Second

After the controller is baked, Bake will return to the welcome screen. You can immediately begin baking other resources, and with the controller actions now available for the CRUD operations, you can bake the views.

Select View to bake the views, and choose the Posts controller from which to build them. As before with baking the controller, enter interactive mode and then specify the following settings:

- Would you like to create some scaffolded views (index, add, view, edit) for this controller? [Yes]

- Would you like to create the views for admin routing? [No]

Again, you will be asked whether you want to overwrite the app/views/posts/index.ctp file. Select Yes, and Bake should tell you that the view scaffolding is complete (see Figure 5-6).

Launch the Posts controller, and everything should appear exactly like the scaffolding when the $scaffold attribute is called. Bake provides the same views and functions, but now they are available to you to edit in the controller and the views.

```
 ● ● ●                          Terminal — php
 ---------------------------------------------------------------
 Interactive Bake Shell
 ---------------------------------------------------------------
 [D]atabase Configuration
 [M]odel
 [V]iew
 [C]ontroller
 [P]roject
 [Q]uit
 What would you like to Bake? (D/M/V/C/P/Q)
 > v
 ---------------------------------------------------------------
 Bake View
 Path: /Users/davidgolding/Sites/public_html/blog/app/views/
 ---------------------------------------------------------------
 Possible Models based on your current database:
 1. Comments
 2. Posts
 3. PostsTags
 4. Tags
 5. Users
 Enter a number from the list above, or type in the name of another controller.
 > 2
 Would you like bake to build your views interactively?
 Warning: Choosing no will overwrite Posts views if it exist. (y/n)
 [y] > y
 Would you like to create some scaffolded views (index, add, view, edit) for this controller?
 NOTE: Before doing so, you'll need to create your controller and model classes (including associated
  models). (y/n)
 [n] > y
 Would you like to create the views for admin routing? (y/n)
 [y] > n

 Creating file /Users/davidgolding/Sites/public_html/blog/app/views/posts/index.ctp
 File exists, overwrite? /Users/davidgolding/Sites/public_html/blog/app/views/posts/index.ctp (y/n/q)

 [n] > y
 Wrote /Users/davidgolding/Sites/public_html/blog/app/views/posts/index.ctp

 Creating file /Users/davidgolding/Sites/public_html/blog/app/views/posts/view.ctp
 Wrote /Users/davidgolding/Sites/public_html/blog/app/views/posts/view.ctp

 Creating file /Users/davidgolding/Sites/public_html/blog/app/views/posts/add.ctp
 Wrote /Users/davidgolding/Sites/public_html/blog/app/views/posts/add.ctp

 Creating file /Users/davidgolding/Sites/public_html/blog/app/views/posts/edit.ctp
 Wrote /Users/davidgolding/Sites/public_html/blog/app/views/posts/edit.ctp
 ---------------------------------------------------------------

 View Scaffolding Complete.
 ---------------------------------------------------------------
```

Figure 5-6. *The whole process for baking views off the Posts controller*

Editing Baked Views

Editing the views is a simple task. Open the app/views/posts folder, and you should find the
following baked views:

- add.ctp

- edit.ctp

- index.ctp

- view.ctp

Open the index.ctp file, and you will find all the HTML unique to this view. Change line 2 in this file to the following, and the title on the Index action page will change to "Blog Posts":

```
<h2><? __('Blog Posts');?></h2>
```

You can add to and delete anything from this file to change the Index action view without affecting any of the other actions. For example, the date field is not displayed nicely for the user. You can format this date string to appear more readable by editing it in the view file.

Around line 34 in the app/views/posts/index.ctp file is the date string:

```
<?php echo $post['Post']['date']; ?>
```

Using PHP's date() and strtotime() functions will make this variable display better. Change line 34 to something like the following:

```
<?=date('M jS Y, g:i a',strtotime($post['Post']['date']));?>
```

The date will then read differently for the Index action view (see Figure 5-7).

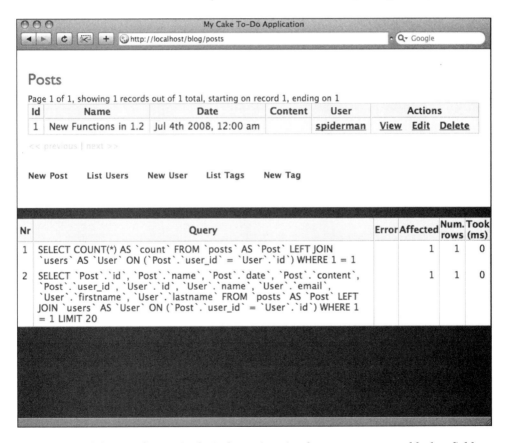

Figure 5-7. *Each listing of a post in the Index action view has a more presentable date field.*

Considering Internationalization

You may have noticed that some text strings in the baked views are encased in a PHP function __(). Simply stated, this function is Cake's method for making views easy to alter dynamically for international web sites. Cake can localize the content encased in this function to the language of the user, but other settings must be entered in the application's controllers and configuration files. If your application has no need of internationalization or localization, then you can avoid using the __() function.

Using Commands for Faster Baking

Some basic commands can make baking Cake resources easier. Simply enter the resource you need to bake after typing the `cake bake` command in the console. Examples include the following:

```
$ cake bake controller
$ cake bake model
$ cake bake view
$ cake bake project
```

You can even enter the name of the resource if you want to bypass interactive mode and just generate the file:

```
$ cake bake controller tags
$ cake bake model comment
```

Don't forget to include the `-app` parameter if your Cake console installation requires you to do so for Bake to access your working application folder:

```
$ cake bake controller tags -app /serverroot/blog/app/
```

Customizing Views

The Bake script cuts down on startup time to get scaffolded views available quickly. By tinkering with the baked view files, you can add onto them your customized elements and forms. In this chapter, you affected only the Index action view and learned to operate the Bake script. Chapter 6 will discuss each line in the baked controllers and views and how to create more advanced web pages. You'll analyze the other CRUD operations and how Cake interacts with user form submissions. Form and HTML helpers that come with Cake will allow you to more effectively administer form fields and submissions with less code than the typical PHP application requires.

Before moving on, practice using Bake with other tables by following this chapter's "Bake More Resources" exercise.

Bake More Resources

In this chapter, you baked the Posts controller and some scaffolded views. Master Bake by generating the controllers for the `tags` and `comments` tables, as well as their models and views. Be sure to try the other Bake commands to improve your development speed and explore the database configuration and project features.

Summary

Layouts in Cake are files that are wrapped around your application. When you create a default layout file, you intercept Cake's default layout for scaffolds, error pages, and any other views. Individual view files are rendered where the `$content_for_layout` variable is echoed in the layout, thus allowing you to create a common interface for multiple views. One of the fastest ways for getting your application off the ground is to use Cake's scaffold and Bake features. By setting up the console to work with Bake, you can generate customized actions and views with simple shell commands, sometimes with only one string of text. Using Bake correctly can speed up development by providing you with basic code that allows you to create, edit, list, and view database records through a web interface. Chapter 6 will examine more closely what is happening in baked elements and will explain how to customize views in Cake.

■ ■ ■

Customizing Views

Using Bake to generate views and controller actions is great for getting an application started quickly. Eventually, though, you will need more customized code to flesh out the application's feature set. For the application to provide much functionality, it will inevitably have some level of user interaction in the form of clicking links and HTML elements, supplying form data, or performing other interactions. As the users interact with the application, they will make requests that operate sequentially through controllers and views. This chapter will go through these sequences and explore the Cake features that give you more fine-tuned control over the user experience.

Handling User Interactions

In general, three kinds of sequences result from a user interacting with a Cake application:

- A simple page request sequence

- A form submission sequence

- An asynchronous (Ajax) sequence

The views and their interaction with the controllers and models will vary depending on the program's processes. When customizing views beyond the Bake or scaffolding views, you will need to keep in mind the kind of process you are building.

A Simple Page Request

Open the app/controllers/posts_controller.php file, and scroll to the View action. It should be similar to Listing 6-1.

Listing 6-1. *The View Action in the Posts Controller*

```
1   function view($id = null) {
2       if (!$id) {
3           $this->Session->setFlash(__('Invalid Post.', true));
4           $this->redirect(array('action'=>'index'));
5       }
6       $this->set('post', $this->Post->read(null, $id));
7   }
```

Processes are usually—if not always—dispatched to the controller. Here, the View action is processed by the controller, and the corresponding view file will be called when the process terminates. The first step of the action is to receive any parameters supplied by the user. Because this is a simple page request sequence, all the user is going to supply is one or two variables that match a record in the database—no form data, no complicated logic tests, just a couple of parameters at most. Line 1 in Listing 6-1 receives the parameter supplied by the user with the function variable $id. This variable is defaulted to null but could very well be changed to an array or have a default value, depending on your application's needs.

In this action, a simple logic test is performed: if the user has not supplied a unique ID of a post to be pulled from the database, return an error; otherwise, read the matching record and forward its contents to the view as a variable. This test is performed on lines 2–6.

Line 3 is executed if the user has not provided an ID value as a parameter. This line uses Cake's Session component, which is a component class that contains several functions for managing and working with sessions. Rather than display a Flash page that renders an error message for the user, the Session component sends a string of text to the view, to be displayed either in the layout or in the individual view file. In this case, the action uses the Session component's setFlash() function. The error string that will be sent is set to "Invalid Post." In the app/views/layouts/default.ctp file, you must include the other end of the Session->setFlash() function, which will receive the error string and display it. Open the default layout, and insert the line in Listing 6-2 somewhere within the <body> element.

Listing 6-2. *Displaying Session Flash Messages*

```
<? $session->flash();?>
```

Now when the error is recognized, line 4 in Listing 6-1 will redirect the user to the Index action in the Posts controller. Because you've included the Session component in the default layout, the error message specified in line 3 will be displayed in the page.

Line 6 in Listing 6-1 passes information from the database to the view using the set() function. This line also includes a model function, read(), which looks up the record that corresponds to the ID supplied by the user and pulls its data. By assigning this model function to the view variable post in the set() function, everything in the record will be made available in the view.

Simple page requests usually behave like this View action. The first step is to retrieve the parameter from the user's link or URL and make it available in the action. The second step is to check for a supplied parameter and supply an error message if the parameter is null. The third step is to fetch the data items that correspond to the request and pass them along to the view. Now with the controller's logic working properly for a simple page request, you can customize the view.

This sequence can include much more than the code I explained earlier. For instance, the action could perform more complex checks on the parameter or work with multiple parameters at a time, run multiple database queries, and then forward those on to the view. In some cases, you may want the action to not even work with the view but forward data to another action. In these scenarios, Cake behaves like a typical PHP script, except when creating the display for the user. Using Cake functions and components, as Bake does with the Session component, takes the place of your own functions or code, but in general the controller will operate as a general PHP script.

A Form Submission Sequence

Handling user form data goes a step beyond a simple page request sequence. In this scenario, a few things will happen in order:

1. The controller action is called, and it determines whether the user is submitting any form data.

2. If there is no form data, the controller instructs the view to display the form. If editing an existing record, the controller may perform a database lookup to propagate the fields in the subsequent view.

3. The user fills out the form and submits it to the controller.

4. This time, the controller finds form data in the request and handles the data. Depending on the results of the action's operation, another view is rendered, usually with a feedback page that alerts the user to a successful submission or a failed one.

To understand the internals of Cake flow, open app/controllers/posts_controller.php, and scroll to the Add action. It should appear similar to Listing 6-3.

Listing 6-3. *The Add Action in the Posts Controller*

```
1    function add() {
2        if (!empty($this->data)) {
3            $this->Post->create();
4            if ($this->Post->save($this->data)) {
5                $this->Session->setFlash(__('The Post has been saved', true));
6                $this->redirect(array('action'=>'index'));
7            } else {
8                $this->Session->setFlash(__('The Post could not be saved. ➡
     Please try again.', true));
9            }
10       }
11       $tags = $this->Post->Tag->find('list');
12       $users = $this->Post->User->find('list');
13       $this->set(compact('tags', 'users'));
14   }
```

The Add action behaves like the outline earlier: in line 2 of Listing 6-3, it checks for any user form data with a simple logic test and then saves the data to the database (if present); otherwise, it returns an error to the user and renders the Add view.

$this->data

Cake handles form data for you and sticks to convention when doing so. All the form fields supplied to the controller will automatically be formatted in an array with naming conventions that dictate where in the array the data will be stored. The form will always be parsed and organized following the MVC structure. For an example, observe Listing 6-4.

Listing 6-4. *A Simple Form*

```
<?=$form->create('Posts');?>
<?=$form->input('name');?>
<?=$form->input('content',array('type'=>'textarea','rows'=>4,'cols'=>40));?>
<?=$form->end('Submit');?>
```

Though I haven't yet discussed it, Listing 6-4 uses the Form helper, which I will use more extensively later. In short, the Form helper runs functions in the view that determine how to display a chunk of HTML code. The input() function in the Form helper is useful because it takes the name provided (which corresponds to fields in the database) and renders an HTML <input type="text"/> element with all the appropriate names and values for Cake to parse the data automatically. If you were to take a peek at the page source in the browser, this view would output the following:

```
<form method="post" action="/blog/posts/add">
<input type="text" name="data[Post][name]" id="PostName"/>
<textarea name="data[Post][content]" cols="40" rows="4" id="PostContent"></textarea>
<input type="submit" value="Submit"/>
</form>
```

When the user fills out the form and submits it, Cake places the form data into the $this->data array like this:

```
Array (
    [Post] => Array (
        [name] => Title Entered in the Name Field
        [content] => All the content provided in the <textarea> field.
    )
)
```

When working with associated models, $this->data may also include those fields as well. In the case of the Post model, you have already built an association between posts and tags for the blog. When done correctly, the form will pass along associated fields to $this->data nicely:

```
Array (
    [Post] => Array (
        [name] => Title Entered in the Name Field
        [content] => All the content provided in the <textarea> field.
    )
    [Tag] => Array (
        [Tag] => Array (
            [0] => 1
            [1] => 56
        )
    )
)
```

In the $this->data['Tag']['Tag'] array, each selected item's ID is placed as a separate element in the array, since the Tag model is associated with the Post model as a "has and belongs to many" relationship.

User form submissions can get more complex quickly. Also in the posts' Add action is a datetime field. Working with dates and times can be rather cumbersome; differentiating between months, days, minutes, and hours can be a nightmare considering each has a specific set of numbers by which it may be represented (for example, one month may have 30 days, another may have 31, and February changes between 28 and 29 days every four years). When used in conjunction with the Form helper, $this->data can dramatically shave off code for dealing with dates and times. When done correctly in the view with the Form helper, Cake parses a form containing dates and times for the $this->data array like so:

```
Array (
    [Post] => Array (
        [date] => Array (
            [month] => 07
            [day] => 04
            [year] => 2008
            [hour] => 12
            [min] => 00
            [meridian] => pm
        )
    )
)
```

Whether in the view or the controller, you can pull user-submitted data from $this->data like any PHP array. For example, checking for the year can easily be done by examining the $this->data['Post']['date']['year'] value. Or, you can fetch the meridian by calling the $this->data['Post']['date']['meridian'] value. Dates and times in Cake are all the more attractive when considering that in the view all the necessary date and time fields are supplied with a single line:

```
<?=$form->input('date');?>
```

Back in line 2 of Listing 6-3, the Add action checks for a user submission by looking at the $this->data array: if it is empty, then the user has not submitted anything; if not, a form has been submitted, and the action must handle the data.

Lines 3–6 in Listing 6-3 save the data to the database, provided a test of $this->data has passed successfully. The rest of the action behaves like a simple page request. If no data has been supplied, the action pulls some associated data from the Tag and User models and passes it along to the view.

Saving Forms

When $this->data is formatted according to Cake's conventions (which is mostly managed by implementing the Form helper in the view), saving data is easy. Cake performs saves through the use of the create() and save() model functions.

■**Note** The distinction between a *model function*—either a function written in the model class or a cus-tomized function stored in the model file—and other functions (such as controller actions, for instance) is that they are always executed through the model. This means that to launch a model function, you must always do so through the model class. In this case, the Post model saves the data, so the model functions have names like $this->Post->save(), not just $this->save(). Other model functions such as read() and find() will always be run similarly, through a specified model. Hence, the syntax goes $this followed by the model, followed by the function, with the function's parameters housed in the parentheses.

The create() function inserts a new record into the table. Because this model function flows from a specified model, it will insert into said model. In line 3 of Listing 6-3, the create() function is being called from the Post model, so the new row will be inserted in the posts table. Running the save() function immediately following the create() function will propagate whatever is passed for saving to the new row. Line 4 in Listing 6-3 sends the preformatted $this->data array. The save() function is already built to parse and save the array, so no other data handling is needed.

In short, the first step for adding a new record is to create a new row with the create() model function, and the second step is to save $this->data by passing it through the save() model function. The baked Add action goes beyond just saving the data by checking for an error in the process. You could intercept the save function by entering some logic in the beforeSave() model action. If this action returns false, then in the controller (line 4 in Listing 6-3, for example) the save() model function also returns false. The controller can then use the Session component to display an error message or perform other operations in response to a failed save in the model.

Saving form data for a specific ID is done by setting the model ID variable, as in the following example:

```
$this->Post->id = $id;
$this->Post->save($this->data);
```

This is usually necessary only for updating a record. When creating a new record, use the create() model function.

Filling Form Fields for Editing or Updating

The form submission sequence may also include editing records in the database or previously saved data. In this instance, the controller will need to include a few more operations than the Add action does. Open the app/controllers/posts_controller.php file and scroll to the Edit action. It should include code similar to Listing 6-5.

Listing 6-5. *The Edit Action in the Posts Controller*

```
1    function edit($id = null) {
2        if (!$id && empty($this->data)) {
3            $this->Session->setFlash(__('Invalid Post', true));
4            $this->redirect(array('action'=>'index'));
5        }
6        if (!empty($this->data)) {
7            if ($this->Post->save($this->data)) {
8                $this->Session->setFlash(__('The Post has been saved', true));
9                $this->redirect(array('action'=>'index'));
10           } else {
11               $this->Session->setFlash(__('The Post could not be saved. ➥
     Please try again.', true));
12           }
13       }
14       if (empty($this->data)) {
15           $this->data = $this->Post->read(null, $id);
16       }
17       $tags = $this->Post->Tag->find('list');
18       $users = $this->Post->User->find('list');
19       $this->set(compact('tags','users'));
20   }
```

This action is more or less the combination of the Add and View actions. Editing requires both a simple page request (the record or data source to be edited) and a form submission process, which is included in the baked Edit action. The action performs three logic tests. First, has the user supplied a record ID alone? Second, has the user provided any form data? Third, has the user provided neither a form submission nor a record ID? These tests are found in three chunks of code, namely, lines 2–5, 6–13, and 14–16.

Notice that on line 15, $this->data is equal to the result of the read() model action. In other words, the read() function result follows the same formatting rules as form submissions in the controller. Going in both directions, either reading a database record and making it available in the view or sending form data from the view to the controller, Cake will format the arrays in the same manner.

An Asynchronous Sequence

Asynchronous processes occur when the user makes a request through a web page and the server responds without exiting or refreshing the current page. In other words, from the user's perspective, the request is processed by the server in the background without any interference with the current display. Usually, a specific HTML element is updated by the server instead of the whole web page. Asynchronous HTTP requests have become popular in recent years as enterprise-level web sites have made better use of JavaScript and XML. Most developers refer to any asynchronous server responses as *Ajax* operations, even though Ajax started as an acronym meaning Asynchronous JavaScript And XML.

Recently, several open source Ajax frameworks have appeared, making asynchronous operations easier to manage. Cake comes with an Ajax helper designed to facilitate asynchronous user sequences. With tools such as these, working with the server without reloading the entire web page has never been easier. The simple page request and form submission sequences can be made to work asynchronously in Cake, but JavaScript methods must be used to accomplish the correct HTTP response.

For Ajax to work, the default behavior of the web browser must be manipulated by JavaScript. For example, when clicking a link or a form button, the web browser automatically sends an HTTP request synchronously and waits for a new web page to be returned by the server. This behavior is suppressed by JavaScript; the form button in this example uses JavaScript to send the HTTP request without the browser refreshing or waiting for a new page. JavaScript also handles receiving the server's response and determines where to display the outcome of the user's request. Because Ajax relies on JavaScript, the asynchronous sequence in Cake begins with the view file.

In the view, whichever HTML elements send or receive Ajax requests must include the correct JavaScript code. If you use an Ajax framework, then the layout will generally include the links to the framework's libraries. An Ajax link, for instance, might use the `onClick` HTML attribute with JavaScript code that follows the framework's methods rather than use the synchronous `href` attribute. However the Ajax framework prepares and handles asynchronous processes, the URLs it uses will generally follow the pattern used by Cake. In the view file, the Ajax forms or links will consequently point to a controller just like synchronous forms and links.

The controller, however, does need to perform a slightly different operation for Ajax to work in Cake. Assume that all the JavaScript is in place to send an asynchronous request to a Cake controller. In this sense, the controller will behave the same as if the request were made in a typical fashion. By default, however, Cake will render the corresponding view file, depending on which action is being run. The `render()` function makes it possible to intercept the default view render and tell Cake that it must behave asynchronously.

Simply put the `render()` function in the action where you would normally allow the controller to terminate and output the view. Be sure to include the Ajax parameter in the function so that Cake knows to render the view asynchronously:

```
$this->render('add','ajax');
```

Later, we'll deal with more advanced Ajax methods, which will require extensive editing in the views. For now, be aware that the asynchronous sequence is an option in Cake and is handled almost identically to the other two responses.

Writing Individual View Files

With the controller logic in hand, next the individual view files must handle user interaction sequences properly. Open the `app/views/posts/view.ctp` file. Scroll to lines 1–30; they should appear like the code in Listing 6-6.

Listing 6-6. *The View Action View File, Lines 1–30*

```
1     <div class="posts view">
2     <h2><?php  __('Post');?></h2>
3         <dl><?php $i = 0; $class = ' class="altrow"';?>
4             <dt<?php if ($i % 2 == 0) echo $class;?>><?php __('Id'); ?></dt>
5             <dd<?php if ($i++ % 2 == 0) echo $class;?>>
6                 <?php echo $post['Post']['id']; ?>
7                  
8             </dd>
9             <dt<?php if ($i % 2 == 0) echo $class;?>><?php __('Name'); ?></dt>
10             <dd<?php if ($i++ % 2 == 0) echo $class;?>>
11                 <?php echo $post['Post']['name']; ?>
12                  
13             </dd>
14             <dt<?php if ($i % 2 == 0) echo $class;?>><?php __('Date'); ?></dt>
15             <dd<?php if ($i++ % 2 == 0) echo $class;?>>
16                 <?php echo $post['Post']['date']; ?>
17                  
18             </dd>
19             <dt<?php if ($i % 2 == 0) echo $class;?>><?php __('Content'); ?></dt>
20             <dd<?php if ($i++ % 2 == 0) echo $class;?>>
21                 <?php echo $post['Post']['content']; ?>
22                  
23             </dd>
24             <dt<?php if ($i % 2 == 0) echo $class;?>><?php __('User'); ?></dt>
25             <dd<?php if ($i++ % 2 == 0) echo $class;?>>
26                 <?php echo $html->link($post['User']['name'], ➥
array('controller'=>'users', 'action'=>'view', $post['User']['id'])); ?>
27                  
28             </dd>
29         </dl>
30     </div>
```

The View action, in short, is a simple page request. The user will have asked for a specific record to be displayed, and this view file is meant to do that in an organized fashion. Most of what is being rendered in these lines is HTML. Line 1 creates a new <div> element, and line 30 closes it. Some important Cake operations are at work here, however, that correspond with the data provided in the controller. Recall that in Listing 6-1's line 6, the View action performs a read() model function and assigns the result to a variable named post with the set() function. This variable is now available in the View view as $post and can be displayed throughout the view however you please.

Bake provided you with a series of HTML tags surrounding instances of the $post variable that serve to display the contents of the returned record nicely. Notice that $post is formatted like $this->data. It contains an array of model names with nested arrays that match the fields in their respective tables. Notice how line 26 displays data from an associated model. In this

case, posts have been associated with users, and when the controller performed the read()
function, it noticed the association and supplied the related records as well. All of these data
are available in the $post array.

Using the Debug Function

Often you will want to view the contents of these data arrays. Cake's debug() function provides
a detailed and nicely formatted view of a specified array. In this view file, insert the following
line, which uses the debug() function:

```
<? debug($post);?>
```

When you refresh the View action, you ought to see a bright yellow box containing a print-
out of the contents of the $post variable (see Figure 6-1).

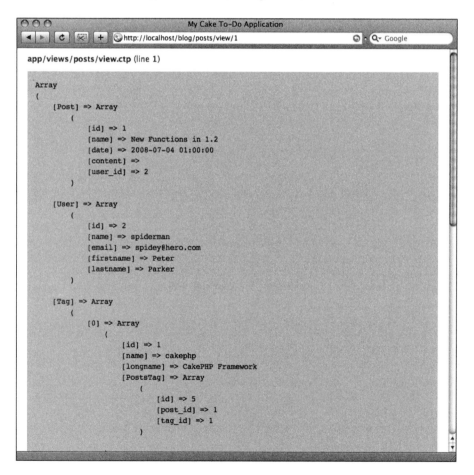

Figure 6-1. *The* debug() *function displaying the contents of the* $post *variable*

Each model is keyed in the array by its name and has related records attached. Not only has Cake provided you with the contents of the post record the user requested but also with the records from associated models. Say you wanted to display the name of the assigned user of this blog post by the title of the post. You could do this by performing an echo() function of the correct array, key, and value:

```
<h2><?=$post['User']['firstname'].' '.$post['User']['lastname'];?></h2>
```

The debug() function helps you figure out during the development process what exactly is being tossed around in the view. It can be used with any array. Of course, other array display functions can be used, such as the print_r() function native to PHP or Cake's convenience function pr().

Customizing the View File from Scratch

Bake has provided you with a fabulous start to this simple page request. Let's go from scratch and simplify the view so as to make it more readable for a site visitor. In your blog application, this view will be a simple story display like other blogs or newspaper sites. You won't need to display fields such as the ID or the author's ID, even though those may be useful for constructing links that point to other actions or controllers.

Edit the app/views/posts/view.ctp file by deleting the baked code and inserting the code in Listing 6-7.

Listing 6-7. *A Simplified View*

```
1    <h1><?=$post['Post']['name'];?></h1>
2    <p>Author: <?=$post['User']['firstname'];?> <?=$post['User']['lastname'];?></p>
3    <p>Date Published: <?=$post['Post']['date'];?></p>
4    <hr/>
5    <p><?=$post['Post']['content'];?></p>
```

Listing 6-7 is very simplified code, but starting small helps you include other useful features as you go along. Line 1 displays the post's title as an <h1> element. Lines 2–3 display the associated user's first name and last name as well as the post's date in separate <p> tags. Finally, line 5 displays the textual content of the post. The $post variable still contains the other array data you could use, but only a couple of fields in the view have been called out.

The HTML Helper

Suppose you wanted the title of the post to be a link to itself, just for consistency throughout the application. In this case, the built-in HTML helper could be used to generate the appropriate links for you. Change line 1 in the View view file to Listing 6-8.

Listing 6-8. *The HTML Helper and Its* link() *Function*

```
<?=$html->link('<h1>'.$post['Post']['name'].'</h1>','/posts/view/'.$post['Post']➡
['id'],null,null,false);?>
```

Each parameter in the link() function is separated like other PHP function parameters. Between commas, and when necessary, with arrays, you pass along your own variables and settings to the helper function, and it returns some HTML to be displayed. You won't need to use every parameter, so in these cases you can enter a null value. In Listing 6-8, you've called out the link() function in the HTML helper by first calling the $html object. With this particular helper, most of its functions will require you to perform an echo() function, which you've done with the shorthand operator <?= rather than spelling out the function. The final parameter in the function corresponds to the link() function's escaping feature. In this case, you've set it to false so that the function ignores escaping the greater-than and less-than symbols as HTML entities.

The first parameter in the HTML helper's link() function is the text to be displayed. The second parameter is the URL, following the application's routes, that will be placed in the link. Notice that you've used the $post variable to supply the title and the current ID to make this link operable and correspond to the user's request.

For a simple page request, not much more is needed other than to display the contents of passed arrays. Form submission processes, however, will require more detail. As already mentioned, Cake has supplied helpers that help with this.

Customizing an HTML Form

Listing 6-4 describes a basic Cake form that uses the Form helper to render form elements. How you customize these features will require consistency and understanding of how the Form helper works.

Open the app/views/posts/add.ctp file. Its contents should match the baked code in Listing 6-9.

Listing 6-9. *The Baked Contents of the Posts Add View File*

```
1     <div class="posts form">
2         <?php echo $form->create('Post');?>
3         <fieldset>
4          <legend><?php __('Add Post');?></legend>
5         <?php
6             echo $form->input('name');
7             echo $form->input('date');
8             echo $form->input('content');
9             echo $form->input('user_id');
10             echo $form->input('Tag');
11         ?>
12         </fieldset>
13         <?php echo $form->end('Submit');?>
14     </div>
15     <div class="actions">
16         <ul>
17             <li><?php echo $html->link(__('List Posts', true), ➥
       array('action'=>'index'));?></li>
18             <li><?php echo $html->link(__('List Users', true), ➥
array('controller'=> 'users', 'action'=>'index')); ?> </li>
```

```
19                <li><?php echo $html->link(__('New User', true), ➡
array('controller'=> 'users', 'action'=>'add')); ?> </li>
20                <li><?php echo $html->link(__('List Tags', true), ➡
array('controller'=> 'tags', 'action'=>'index')); ?> </li>
21                <li><?php echo $html->link(__('New Tag', true), ➡
array('controller'=>'tags', 'action'=>'add')); ?> </li>
22        </ul>
23    </div>
```

Lines 15–23 contain links to various actions that all use the HTML helper's link() function. Lines 2–13 contain the form and its fields that make the action possible. As the application talks back and forth between the view and the controller, the Form helper intercepts all
the data being tossed around and analyzes each piece of data to determine how it ought to be
displayed in the form. As long as $this->data remains consistent with Cake's default construc-
tion, the Form helper will be able to keep up. Sometimes the application's design will require
some added settings to make the Form helper work properly, but for the most part, it works
wonderfully with $this->data and saves you a lot of headaches. Say goodbye to that old PHP
$_POST array!

As done with the View view, let's rebuild the Add view from scratch. Replace the contents
of the app/views/posts/add.ctp file with Listing 6-10.

Listing 6-10. *Some Minimal Code for the Add Action*

```
<div class="posts form">
<?=$form->create('Post');?>
    <fieldset>
        <legend>Add Post</legend>
    <?
        e($form->input('name'));
        e($form->input('date'));
        e($form->input('content'));
       e($form->input('User'));
        e($form->input('Tag'));
    ?>
    </fieldset>
<?=$form->end('Submit');?>
</div>
```

This code resembles what was already supplied by Bake but uses the e() convenience
function (which is identical to echo()) and trims out the action links. Notice that the input()
function is at work for each of the fields and the Form helper automatically recognizes what
type of data will be contained in each field. For the associated models, the model's name (for
example, User and Tag) was provided, and the Form helper assumes that the field is an association and builds off the relationship. Automatically, you're given a select menu for the user
and a multiple-select for the tag.

To customize the form elements, the available options in the Form helper functions must
be used. An example is adding some parameters to the input() function. Currently the Tag

input element is a multiple-select menu that contains a list of tags found in the $this->data array. Changing this to multiple check boxes would normally take several lines of HTML tags to render each individual check box. With the Form helper, you can customize the form to handle multiple check boxes with one string of code (see Listing 6-11).

Listing 6-11. *The Form Helper's* input() *Function Rendering Multiple Check Boxes Instead of a Multiple Select Menu*

```
echo $form->input('Tag',array('type'=>'select','multiple'=>'checkbox'));
```

The first parameter for the input() function is the name of the model or current model's field. The second parameter is an array containing several options as keys and their specific settings as values. Notice that you've told the Form helper to render an input element using the data housed in the Tag key in the $this->data array and that this element must be a select type but use checkbox for the multiple options instead of the default. Refresh the Add action, and you should see the simplified form with the customized check boxes. Cake formats the data the same, regardless of the type of HTML elements, and since the controller is already set to save the data it receives from the view, the Add action continues to work properly.

Using Other Helpers

Cake comes preinstalled with several helpers:

- Ajax
- Cache
- Form
- HTML
- JavaScript
- Number
- Paginator
- RSS
- Session
- Text
- Time
- XML

Each of these helpers contains several functions that simplify handling data and displaying content. Each helper will operate under the same basic syntax—an object available in the view as a variable plus its function with its parameters supplied in the parentheses. Third-party helpers are also available on the Internet, many of them through Cake's official Bakery (http://bakery.cakephp.org). To make the helper available, besides the HTML and Form helpers, you must specify in the controller that the helper is being used. You do this by populating the helper settings array with the corresponding helper's class name:

```
var $helpers = array('Ajax','Session','Time');
```

By placing this string up by where the var $name and var $scaffold attributes are called, Cake is able to begin a new instance of the helper class object and make it available in the view. Using more helpers adds to the customization possibilities in your arsenal. The more familiar you are with Cake's helpers, the more options you will have when customizing your views.

Readable Dates and Times

Practice using helpers in your views by trying the Time helper. Remember to set the $helpers attribute in the controller to include the Time helper first. Then in the Posts View view, use the nice() function to make the $post['Post']['date'] value more readable. Hint: you'll need to pass the variable to the function for it to work properly.

Summary

Users will most often interact with your Cake application in one of three ways: by making a simple page request, by submitting a form of some kind, or by sending page or form requests asynchronously (also described as *Ajax processes*). Controllers and views work together in Cake to handle these types of sequences. When customizing the view with which the user will interact, you will also work in the controller to provide the necessary logic to process the user's requests. The controller will use functions such as set() and render() to call out the view and provide it with the necessary parameters and variables. Standardized arrays such as $this->data make handling user form data much easier as the controller parses data rendered in the view and runs it through the model. This chapter explained how $this->data is formatted by Cake as well as its interaction with the Form helper. Expanding the capabilities of controllers and models comes next—Chapter 7 will describe how to customize controllers and models to perform more complex operations.

CHAPTER 7

■■■

Working with Controllers and Models

A single operation in Cake will generally invoke multiple MVC elements and will work in those elements simultaneously. For instance, in the previous chapter, you used the Form helper both to receive fetched data from the controller and model, and to send user form data to the controller for processing. Changing something in the controller can affect how the Form helper behaves, which is most noticeable when manipulating something like the $this->data variable.

As I discuss more advanced ways of developing controllers and models in this chapter, don't forget that changes to the view may be necessary for the operation or customization to work correctly. For example, managing sessions is such an integrated process that you may spend equal time in the view (creating login screens and displaying a session's status), the controller (performing session logic to determine aspects of the session), and the model (saving session data in the database). To work an overall session operation into the application, in other words, will mean editing and testing actions in the controller, model functions, and views together.

Building an Extensive Blog

The classic tutorial for frameworks has been to build a blog. On Cake's official web site, there is an entire blog application tutorial. However, you need a thorough explanation of *what* is happening, not just a walk-through of *how* to build the program. So, how this tutorial differs from others is that I will systematically explain every line of code in this application. You should be able to master the concepts, not just the steps. With such mastery, you should be able to wrap your head around a lot of the features Cake has to offer and understand how to incorporate them into your own customized applications.

The blog program you've been working with has already allowed you to explore the scaffolding, Bake, and helper features Cake has to offer. To make the blog more powerful, you'll need to deal with models, views, and controllers simultaneously. Now that you've been introduced to various starting points and key concepts, it's time to discuss application building in more detail. Let's begin with controllers and models, the lifeblood of any Cake application.

The extensive blog you will build will include these advanced features:

- Articles that run through a wiki processor that turns content into HTML elements

- Reader comments with community voting

- Routes that create date-friendly URLs

- An admin area where the site administrator can add stories

- User management for multiple authors

- Category sorting for organizing posts dynamically

- A sitewide menu system for navigating through categories and articles

Features such as these will not be too difficult to produce but will make full use of all the controllers, models, and views. In this tutorial, you'll approach one feature at a time and build it into the application. Along the way, I'll continue to explain important concepts for developing in Cake. First I'll discuss controller actions in general, and then I'll show how to build some custom actions.

Working with Actions

You have already built and worked with actions in Cake. In the following extensive blog application, you will build a host of actions, each for a specific function in the site. Rules for developing actions follow the pattern of typical PHP functions.

In Listing 7-1, I've created a basic controller action named foo. Notice that it follows the typical function syntax in PHP. Controller actions behave somewhat differently from typical PHP functions, however. For instance, when the action is launched by Cake, it will also automatically render a corresponding view or produce an error. Only if the action is called by another action in the application will it be capable of returning a value without displaying a view.

Listing 7-1. *A Basic Controller Action*

```
function foo($bar = null) {
    $this->set('output',$bar);
}
```

Using Variables in Actions

Passed function variables can be initiated and receive default values by naming and setting variables in the parentheses of the action. These variables are available throughout the action. Global variables, however, to be used by all actions in a controller can be created within the controller class as class attributes:

```
var $myVar = 'Variable value';
```

Now, in any of the controller actions, I could use the $myVar attribute by placing $this-> before it:

```
function foo($bar = null) {
    $bar = $this->myVar;
    $this->set('output',$bar);
}
```

Be sure when creating your own class attributes that they don't conflict with other Cake properties like $scaffold or $helpers.

Other local variables can be called within the action as in other PHP scripts:

```
function foo() {
    $bar = 'hello world';
    $this->set('output',$bar);
}
```

Requesting Actions

In your Posts controller, suppose you needed to fetch a list of tags from the Tags controller. Conventionally, you do this through the model, especially since what you are trying to accomplish is a database query of some kind. But to illustrate how controller actions can talk to one another, let's run this query through the controllers instead of the models.

In the Posts controller in one of the actions, I could pass along a list of tags to the view by using the set() and requestAction() functions, like so:

```
$this->set('tags',$this->requestAction('/tags/getList'));
```

The requestAction() function is pointing to the Tags controller's getList() action, which hasn't been produced yet. For the $tags variable in the Posts controller's view to be formatted with data, the getList() action in the Tags controller will need to run a return of some data, *not* point to the view (which it will do by default). If you leave out a return in the getList() action, then the Tags controller will by default try to render a view in the app/views/tags directory named getlist.ctp.

So, for this to work properly, the getList() action will need to look something like this:

```
function getList() {
    return $this->Tag->find('list');
}
```

Sometimes there is just no way around using the requestAction() function. Most of the time, however, you should be able to use a component, model, or other element to navigate your code. When needing to launch another action with its views and everything else, use the redirect() function instead of requestAction(). Requesting actions as opposed to redirecting is reserved for performing logic in another controller and pulling its results to the current controller, not for simply launching another action elsewhere in the application. In short, the redirect() function causes another browser request and changes the URL, while requestAction() works internally to launch specific actions.

How Callback Actions Work in the Controller

Controller callbacks make it possible to perform logic before or after launching an action. For example, say you launched the View action in the Posts controller. Before the View action is run by the controller, certain callbacks are checked for any content. By placing code in these callback actions, you can perform some logic for any and all actions before the action is executed, after it is executed, or just before the view is rendered. Let's say you wanted to restrict access to the View action; you could accomplish this in a callback action.

beforeFilter

The beforeFilter() callback action is called before every action is executed. It is entered like any other action, as a PHP function, and interrupts processing controller logic in the requested action. To block users from accessing a certain area of the site, the beforeFilter() action can check the session for information.

   This particular callback example in Listing 7-2 ensures that for the View action, the user must be logged in; otherwise, it redirects the user to a login action (more on these possibilities later). This is just one example of using a callback to interrupt launching an action in the controller.

Listing 7-2. *The* beforeFilter() *Callback Aaction*

```
function beforeFilter() {
    if ($this->action == 'view') {
        if (!$this->Session->check('User')) {
            $this->redirect('/users/login');
        }
    }
}
```

afterFilter

Just like the beforeFilter() callback action, afterFilter() performs logic after every action is called.

beforeRender

This callback action performs logic between the execution of the requested action's logic and the rendering of the view output for all actions. Like beforeFilter() and afterFilter(), beforeRender() can be made to apply to a specific action by using the $this->action variable.

Customizing the Controller for the Blog

Currently, the Posts controller already contains the typical CRUD actions as supplied by Bake. The first screen in the application at which the user will arrive will be the Index action of this controller (Listing 7-3). Let's customize this screen to list five blog posts with their content and author information. First, you will need to take a look at the index() action and make it perform the logic needed for the Index view to display properly.

Listing 7-3. *The Index Action in the Posts Controller*

```
1    function index() {
2        $this->Post->recursive = 0;
3        $this->set('posts', $this->paginate());
4    }
```

Recursive

Line 2 of Listing 7-3 sets the Post model's recursive attribute to 0. This attribute affects how Cake pulls data from the table. Remember that posts are associated with tags and users. When the Post model runs a query to pull posts from the database, it will also fetch associated records from the tags and users tables. The recursive attribute tells the model how far to look when pulling those associated records. If users were to have an association with another table and the recursive attribute were set to a value greater than 1, then the model would pull not only the associated user records but their associated tables' records as well.

In the Index action, the recursive attribute is set to zero, which means that beyond the initial level of associations, Cake will ignore other records. Table 7-1 outlines the possible recursive values and their results.

Table 7-1. *Possible Recursive Values*

Value	Result
−1	Returns only the current model and ignores all associations
0	Returns the current model plus its owner(s)
1	Returns the current model and its owner plus their associated models
2	Returns the current model, its owner, their associated models, and the associated models of any associations

Pagination

Line 3 of Listing 7-3 uses the paginate() controller function. This allows the Paginator helper to simplify column sorting and multiple pages of data. Essentially, the paginate() function performs a find() model function but also analyzes the result and passes some important pagination parameters to the view. Then, in the view, the Paginator helper takes those parameters and constructs multiple pages and column sorting. If the paginate() function is not run in the controller, the Paginator helper would break in the view. If pagination is an important element of the application, then leave the paginate() function here. However, for this blog, I will remove the Paginator helper from the view, so the paginate() function can also be removed from the Index action.

The find() Function

You can actually cut down the code for the Index action by using the find() function instead of paginate(), as shown in Listing 7-4.

Listing 7-4. *The Revised Index Action*

```
1    function index() {
2        $this->set('posts',$this->Post->find('all'));
3    }
```

Notice that line 2 runs the model function find() through the Post model. This function is one of the more powerful features in Cake. It allows you to run a series of important database queries without constructing any SQL strings. In fact, if you were to switch the data source to something other than SQL, the find() function could still run data queries in the syntax of the data source. The parameters of the find() action include more than just query strings. With this function you can order the results, limit the number of returned rows, set the recursive value, and more.

The parameters for the find() function are displayed in Table 7-2. A find() operation that uses all the parameters would look something like this:

```
$this->Post->find('all',array('conditions'=>➥
array('User.id'=>1),'fields'=>'Post.name','order'=>➥
'Post.id ASC','limit'=>10,'recursive'=>0));
```

In this example, the Post model would run a query searching for all posts associated with the user with an ID equal to 1. It would also return only the name field and would order the results array by the posts' IDs in ascending order. The returned array would have a maximum of ten results, and the query would pull from the first set of ten in the batch. Lastly, the recursive value is set to 0, forcing the query to supply only the Post model data and its owner model.

Table 7-2. *Parameters Available in the* find() *Model Function*

Name	Default Value	Details
type	'first'	Can be all, first, or list; determines what type of find operation to perform
conditions	null	Array containing the find conditions as key and value
fields	null	Array specifying from which fields to retrieve data
order	null	Ordering conditions; used to specify by which field to order the result set; field name must be followed by either ASC or DESC
page	null	Page number for using paged data
limit	null	The limit of results to be calculated per page
offset	null	The SQL offset value
recursive	1	Recursive value for associated models; can be overridden by the recursive attribute

This example shows one way of notating parameters in the find() function. Simply put, the parameters in the function are stored in an array and follow the type of find action to be performed. Another way of listing the parameters in find() is like this:

```
find( type[string], parameters[array] )
```

In other words, all of the find parameters are stored in the `parameters` array, and the type of find (`all`, `first`, or `list`) is passed in `type`.

When not specifying the type of find operation, `find()` will perform the `first` type by default. When you need to fetch only the first record of a result set and you want to specify more complicated conditions, then you can use an alternate notation method that leaves out the `type` parameter altogether. In this case, each parameter is entered in `find()` between parentheses, not in a `parameters` array as in the notation explained earlier. The `find()` function would then take on settings in this fashion:

```
find( conditions[array], fields[mixed], order[string], recursive[int] )
```

If I were to fetch the first post of the entire table but ordered by `date`, I could use `find()` like this:

```
$this->Post->find(null,null,'date DESC');
```

Manipulating these parameters in the `find()` function and using these two ways of notating find conditions allows you to perform more complex database queries and trim the data set to exactly what results you need. This saves you from having to run loops through data where you can provide an array with specific conditions and the model returns data set for you, already formatted to be handled in the controller and view.

Setting Find Conditions

Find conditions are formatted as an array. The key corresponds to the field to be searched, and the value represents the value to be found in the field. Notice that the field provided in the find condition is structured differently than a typical SQL query string. The associated model (in this case `User`) followed by a period and the field name tells the `find()` function to run the query through the associated model, not the `Post` model. In other words, search in the associated table for fields named `id` with the value 1.

Using arrays for find conditions is probably the more efficient way of putting together your queries. By default, the query will search for values equal to what is entered in the array. To search for the field with values not equal to a certain value, simply add `<>` before the expression:

```
$this->Post->find('all',array('conditions'=>array('User.id'=>'<> 1')));
```

Cake parses other SQL expressions, which include `LIKE`, `BETWEEN`, and `REGEX`, but you must have a space between the operator and the value. You can search for date or datetime fields by enclosing the field name in the SQL `DATE()` parameter.

Setting Multiple Conditions

Cake supports multiple conditions. By using the array to format the conditions, multiple searches are easily managed:

```
$this->Post->find('all',array('conditions'=>➥
array('User.id'=>1,'DATE(Post.date)'=>'CURDATE()')));
```

The default way of pulling the conditions into a single query is by using the AND boolean operator. In other words, the previous example will tell the model to find all posts owned by the user with an ID of 1 *and* all posts with a date equal to today.

Suppose you need to perform a multiple condition query with the OR operator instead. You do this by setting the condition's array as the value in an array with the key or like so:

```
$this->Post->find('all',array('conditions'=>array(
    'or'=>array(
        'User.id'=>1,'DATE(Post.date)'=>'CURDATE()'
    )
)));
```

All valid SQL boolean operations can be used in place of OR in this example. These include AND, OR, NOT, or XOR.

You can also have Cake search for multiple values in a field. Simply attach an array to a field key with all the possible values for which to search:

```
$this->Post->find('all',array('conditions'=>array('User.id'=>array(1,2,5,10))));
```

Displaying the Most Recent Posts

As the posts table grows, the results returned by the current find() function in the Index action will grow as well. To guarantee that the server load is not compromised down the road and because you need only the five most recent posts, you can customize the find conditions to return only five records and not (potentially) hundreds.

The easiest way to do this is to set the limit to 5 and order the results by creation date, descending:

```
$this->Post->find('all',array('order'=>'date DESC','limit'=>5,'recursive'=>0));
```

Now, the find() function will pull all Post records and their owners (in this case User records associated with the post), sort by the date field with the most recent first, and limit the results to five.

The example database is structured with an auto_increment in the ID field, meaning that the ID field not only identifies records by a unique value but also tells you the order of creation. Because, in theory, the administrator could manipulate the date field but not the ID field, it may be worthwhile in some instances to order by ID rather than by date. This, though, is at the discretion of the client or developer. In this blog, we'll trust that the date assigned to the post will determine when the post appears in the site.

Insert the new conditions into the find() function in line 2 of Listing 7-4 and replace the Index action with the resulting code.

Adjusting the Index View

The Index view will need to be adjusted as well, if only to remove administrative actions from the reach of the user. Go into the app/views/posts/index.ctp file and insert the following code, or work in your own customized view code that displays the content in a more storylike form:

```
<? foreach($posts as $post): ?>
<div class="story">
    <?=$html->link('<h1>'.$post['Post']['name'].'</h1>','/posts/view/'.➥
$post['Post']['id'],null,null,false);?>
    <p>
        Posted <?=date('M jS Y, g:i a',strtotime($post['Post']['date']));?>
    </p>
    <p>
      <b>By <?=$post['User']['firstname'];?> <?=$post['User']['lastname'];?>➥
</b>
    </p>
    <br/>
    <p><?=$post['Post']['content'];?></p>
</div>
<? endforeach; ?>
```

The View Action

The exercise you just completed made it possible for the user to click the title of each post in the Index view, which would take them to the View action for that post. The View action should already contain the baked code shown in Listing 7-5.

Listing 7-5. *The View Action in the Posts Controller*

```
1    function view($id = null) {
2        if (!$id) {
3            $this->Session->setFlash(__('Invalid Post.', true));
4            $this->redirect(array('action'=>'index'));
5        }
6        $this->set('post', $this->Post->read(null, $id));
7    }
```

Line 6 of Listing 7-5 shows the use of the read() function. This is similar to the find() function I have already discussed, but it does have some unique qualities that are especially useful for simple page requests.

The read() Function

In short, the read() function reads the contents of a particular record. It differs from find() in that it does not include the recursive parameter. See Table 7-3 for parameters available in the read() model function.

Table 7-3. *Parameters, in Order, Available in the* read() *Model Function*

Name	Type	Default Value	Explanation
fields	Mixed	null	String value for a single field name or an array of field names
id	Integer	null	ID of record to be read

The View action's use of the read() function is appropriate for the task at hand; leave it the same. Lines 3–4 of Listing 7-5 contain functions for setting an error message through the Session component and for redirecting the user in the event of an error.

The setFlash() Function

In Chapter 6 I discussed the setFlash() function, but only in basic terms. This function can go beyond displaying a mere error message. Table 7-4 lists its parameters.

Table 7-4. *Parameters, in Order, Available in the* setFlash() *Function in the Session Component*

Name	Type	Default Value	Explanation
message	String	null	The message to be made available in the $session->flash() function in the layout
layout	String	default	The layout in which to place the flash message; this can switch the <div> container element in which the flash is displayed from the default to another customized one
params	Array	null	Parameters to be passed to the layout as view variables
key	String	flash	A way to distinguish various flash message types for multiple flash messages

By default, the $session->flash() function in the layout, when it receives a flash message from the setFlash() function, will display the message inside a standardized HTML string:

```
<div id="flashMessage" class="message">Invalid post.</div>
```

To customize the HTML wrapped around the flash message, you can add a new layout file in the app/views/layouts folder and set the layout parameter in the setFlash() function. For example, you could create a custom flash layout named flash.ctp in the layouts directory with the following single line of code:

```
<div class="error_message"><?=$content_for_layout;?></div>
```

Then, in the setFlash() function, you can pass the new layout parameter like so:

```
$this->Session->setFlash('Invalid Post.','flash');
```

When the flash message is displayed, it *will not* replace the whole layout for the view. The entire contents of the new flash layout file will be placed where the $session->flash() function appears in the layout. Then, where $content_for_layout appears in the flash.ctp file, the flash message will be inserted. Setting the layout parameter allows full customization of how the flash messages are displayed, but it will require creating a separate layout file to hold that custom HTML.

If, for some reason, the flash needed to contain more specifics regarding the error, you could pass along variables to the layout by adding them in the third slot of the function as an array:

```
$this->Session->setFlash('Invalid post.','flash',array('story'=>$id));
```

In the `app/views/layouts/flash.ctp` file, the variable passed through the previous `setFlash()` function will be available as `$story`, which behaves like passed variables in view files through the `set()` controller function.

The key parameter in `setFlash()` makes it possible to have flash messages appear in different areas of the layout. For instance, the `app/views/layouts/default.ctp` file could contain two `flash()` functions differentiated by the key:

```
<div id="top">
<? $session->flash('top');?>
</div>
<div id="bottom">
<? $session->flash('bottom');?>
</div>
```

Now when the controller fires a flash message with `setFlash()`, you can specify where you want the message to appear. Using the key in a flash message like this:

```
$this->Session->setFlash('Invalid post.',null,null,'bottom');
```

tells the Session component to match the message with the `flash()` function with the parameter set to `bottom`.

Line 3 of Listing 7-5 needs to display a basic flash message only in the event of an error, so I won't add any more parameters to the `setFlash()` function. But you can, of course, make the message say anything you want. Simply change the first parameter to your own error message.

The redirect() Function

Line 4 of Listing 7-5 redirects the user in the event of an error. You can do this by using the `redirect()` controller function. The available parameters for `redirect()` are listed in Table 7-5.

Table 7-5. *Parameters, in Order, Available in the* `redirect()` *Controller Function*

Name	Type	Default Value	Explanation
url	Mixed	null	A string or array pointing to another site or location in the application.
status	Integer	null	The HTTP status code, if desired (for example, 404 or 500 error codes).
exit	Boolean	true	If true, the PHP exit() function will be called after the redirect.

■**Caution** If the exit parameter in this function is set to `false`, Cake will continue to execute code in the controller following the redirect. Only when the exit parameter is set to true, meaning the PHP `exit()` function is called and thus terminating script execution, will all other processes be stopped after the redirect. This may have unintended consequences since the user's browser will request a new page but an old script may continue to run.

The URL parameter for the `redirect()` function can be set up as an array. Notice in line 4 of Listing 7-5 that the array has a key and value corresponding to locations in the Cake application. The available keys for use in this function correspond with Cake's router arguments. For example, the array would redirect the user to the Index action in the Users controller:

```
array('controller'=>'users','action'=>'index')
```

Single strings are also possible in the URL parameter. These follow the same URL structure used in the web browser to access areas of the Cake application. This same path shown in the previous array could be formatted as a string like so:

```
'/users/index'
```

Other Cake functions can help with the URL parameter. One example is the `referer()` function. By placing `$this->referer()` in the URL parameter, Cake will redirect to the referring page of the current action.

The status parameter allows you to pass an HTTP status code as part of the server response. One of the most frequent error responses from the server is a 404 Not Found error. Sometimes you may want the `redirect()` function to be used for unresolved URLs. In these cases, using 404 as an integer in the status parameter allows the application to respond to the error like a typical 404 server response. All the HTTP status codes are available.

In line 4 of Listing 7-5, you're assuming that the user accesses the View action from the Index action, so in the event of an error, you'll redirect them back to this action.

Customizing the Post Display

The View view will need to be adjusted for the same reasons you adjusted the Index view. You may also want to tweak this view to make the posts easier to read. Previously, you simplified this view. In this exercise, try embellishing the View view with your own design. Be sure to make the story readable and have good layout. You may even want to play with the `app/webroot/css` folder and add your own styles. The following is some minimal code to start with that belongs in the `app/views/posts/view.ctp` file:

```
<?=$html->link('<h1>'.$post['Post']['name'].'</h1>','/posts/view/'.$post['Post']➡
['id'],null,null,false);?>
<p>Author: <?=$post['User']['firstname'];?> <?=$post['User']['lastname'];?></p>
<p>Date Published: <?=$post['Post']['date'];?></p>
<hr/>
<p><?=$post['Post']['content'];?></p>
```

Creating a Model for the Blog

The Add and Edit actions in the Posts controller use important model functions. You can extend the interactions these actions have with the Post and related models by adding new functions in the model. In Chapter 6, you customized some CRUD views and learned about submitting forms. Now you'll take a look at the model functions and extend them. You'll begin with the Add and Edit actions in the Posts controller, examine their logic, and see how they relate to extending the Post model.

The Add Action

The Index and View actions interact with the model with a simple database query. For the Add action to work properly, however, sending data to the model is required. By using callbacks such as the controller's beforeFilter() and afterFilter() functions, you can intercept database saving, run data validation checks, and more. Let's first examine the Add action in the controller. Open the app/controllers/posts_controller.php file, and scroll to the Add action (see Listing 7-6).

Listing 7-6. *The Add Action in the Posts Controller*

```
1    function add() {
2        if (!empty($this->data)) {
3            $this->Post->create();
4            if ($this->Post->save($this->data)) {
5                $this->Session->setFlash(__('The Post has been saved', true));
6                $this->redirect(array('action'=>'index'));
7            } else {
8                $this->Session->setFlash(__('The Post could not be saved. ➥
Please, try again.',true));
9            }
10        }
11        $tags = $this->Post->Tag->find('list');
12        $users = $this->Post->User->find('list');
13        $this->set(compact('tags', 'users'));
14    }
```

Most of the logic in this action resembles the commands discussed in the "Customizing the Controller for the Blog" section of this chapter. Where this action differs is in its use of model functions. In Chapter 6, I briefly discussed the save() function; now I'll explain this model function more carefully.

The save() Function

As previously mentioned, the save() function takes a formatted array (usually the automatically formatted $this->data array) and saves its values to matching fields in the database. Some other parameters are available for this function that allow for data validation and specifying to which fields the data will be saved (see Table 7-6).

Table 7-6. *Parameters, in Order, Available in the* save() *Model Function*

Name	Type	Default Value	Explanation
data	Array	null	The data, keyed by field and value, to be saved to the database
validate	Boolean	true	Triggers data validation as specified in the corresponding model
fieldList	Array	null	A list of fields to which data is allowed to be written

The save() function returns either a true or false depending on the success of the save. For example, when data validation occurs and fails a test (as specified in the model), the model will return false. In the controller, processes such as flash messaging or reacting to a failed validation in other methods can be specified.

Notice that Line 4 in Listing 7-6 already is made to handle a returned result of the save() function. In other words, line 4 fires off lines 5–6 if the save() function returns true. To run a validation test, you don't have to use the controller (in fact, you should avoid using the controller); you can run validations in the model alone.

Validating Data

Perhaps one of the most cumbersome tasks in web development is running data validation tests on user-submitted forms. One reason why this can be such a detailed task is that users really can throw just about anything at the application when you give them an open field. How is the application supposed to know how to deal with an infinite number of textual variations the user could provide? Rather than get pulled into a long and grueling conversation about regular expressions, Cake lets you tackle this problem in much less technical terms.

The first step to setting up data validation for user-submitted forms, as in the Add action, is to open the model and begin defining validation rules. Go to the app/models/post.php file. It should appear like the code in Listing 7-7.

Listing 7-7. *The Post Model*

```
1   <?
2   class Post extends AppModel {
3       var $name = 'Post';
4       var $belongsTo = array('User');
5       var $hasAndBelongsToMany = array('Tag');
6   }
7   ?>
```

You have already built the model's associations with the User and Tag models. Begin building your validation rules by inserting a new line between lines 5 and 6.

```
var $validate = array();
```

So far, no rules have been entered in the $validate attribute array. To create a validation rule, simply key the array to correspond to fields and their rules. If any of the rules are not met during a save, the model will then return an error to the controller and exit the save process.

The posts table will receive data for the name, date, and content fields and will receive the ID for the associated User model. You can validate the type of data being supplied for each of these fields by providing a key for each and a rule in the $validate array. Here is where the type of field in the database will help you determine the kinds of data you want to store. The name field is a standard varchar field, so you may want to validate that the only characters to be stored here are alphanumeric. Simply add the following string to the $validate array:

```
var $validate = array('name'=>'alphaNumeric');
```

You could continue the array for all the other fields with rules that match their field types like so:

```
var $validate = array(
    'name'=>'alphaNumeric',
    'date'=>'date',
    'content'=>null
);
```

Using Multiple Validations

Many more validation possibilities exist. You may need to check the length of the supplied string, or the symbols used, or even apply multiple rules to a single field. The model can accommodate more options simply by extending each field with its own array. Each item in this array will contain a key that matches an available option and the value you supply for validation.

Required Fields

To require a field, use the `required` boolean option:

```
var $validate = array('name'=>array('required'=>true));
```

In this example, if the user submitted a null value for `name`, then the model would fail during validation. Thus, the `save()` function in the controller would return `false`, telling the controller that nothing was saved to the database.

Another important point about this parameter is that it will continue to invalidate if no index for the field is found in the data array. For instance, `$this->data` is the array with keys and values that get saved, and if no key exists for the field name to be validated, `required` will also invalidate.

You may have constructed the database in such a way that a field may need to remain empty, but not trigger an invalidation response if the key is missing from the data array. To do this, use the `allowEmpty` parameter. By setting this parameter to `false`, you are essentially saying "Do not allow this field to contain empty characters like spaces, tabs, and so on." The catch is that this parameter is called into the validation only if there exists a key for the field in the data array.

Setting Error Messages During Validation

You can customize the invalidation error message to be used by the controller and/or displayed in the view. You do this with the `message` key:

```
var $validate = array(
    'name'=>array(
        'rule'=>'alphaNumeric',
        'message'=>'The Title of the Post can only contain alphanumeric characters'
    )
);
```

To display this error message in the view, be sure to include the Form helper's `error()` function:

```
<?=$form->input('name');
<?=$form->error('name');
```

Create or Update?

Two possibilities exist for saving data: creating a new record or updating one. Sometimes you may need validation to occur only during an update process and not when creating a new record, or vice versa. To distinguish which type of save needs validating, use the on parameter:

```
var $validate = array(
    'name'=>array(
        'rule'=>'alphaNumeric',
        'message'=>'The Title of the Post can only contain alphanumeric characters',
        'on'=>'create'
    )
);
```

The available options for the on key are create and update.

Using Built-in Validation Rules

Several built-in validation rules reduce certain data-checking processes to a single parameter. Table 7-7 lists the available rules.

Table 7-7. *Built-in Rules*

Value	Rule	Example
alphaNumeric	Field must contain only letters and numbers	`'rule'=>'alphaNumeric'`
between	Length of field must be between supplied values	`'rule'=>array('between',10,20)`
blank	Field must be left blank or contain only whitespace characters	`'rule'=>'blank'`
cc	Field must be a valid credit card number	`'rule'=>array('cc','fast')`
comparison	Field's numeric value is compared to a supplied value	`'rule'=>array('comparison', '>=',21)`
date	Field must contain a valid date string	`'rule'=>'date'`
decimal	Field must be a valid decimal number	`'rule'=>'decimal'`
email	Field must be a valid e-mail address	`'rule'=>'email'`
equalTo	Field must equal the supplied value	`'rule'=>array('equalTo','www')`
extension	Field must contain the supplied file extension suffix	`'rule'=>array('extension','jpg')`

Value	Rule	Example
ip	Field must be a valid IPv4 address	`'rule'=>'ip'`
minLength	Field must have length at least as long as supplied value	`'rule'=>array('minLength',12)`
maxLength	Field must be shorter in length than supplied value	`'rule'=>array('maxLength',30)`
money	Field must contain a valid monetary amount	`'rule'=>array('money','left')`
numeric	Field must be a valid number	`'rule'=>'numeric'`
phone	Field must be a valid phone number	`'rule'=>array('phone',null,'us')`
postal	Field must be valid ZIP code	`'rule'=>array('postal',null,'uk')`
range	Field must be between supplied values	`'rule'=>array('range',0,100)`
ssn	Field must be a valid Social Security number	`'rule'=>array'ssn',null,'us')`
url	Field must be a valid web address	`'rule'=>'url'`

With all these validation rules, you also have the option of specifying your own regular expressions to fine-tune the validation. If, for instance, your site must validate ZIP codes for a country other than the United States, Canada, and the United Kingdom, you can supply your own regular expression based on the postal code criteria of that country. Some of these expressions can be entered in the parameter's array (like postal), but all custom validations can be specified with the custom parameter:

```
'rule'=>array('custom','/[a-z0-9]{12,}$/i')
```

Using Multiple Rules

Each field can have multiple validation rules. Simply follow the array syntax to extend the field's rules to include more than one. For each rule, you can use the validation parameters discussed earlier. Listing 7-8 shows your Post model with a variety of validation settings.

Listing 7-8. *Various Validation Rules for the* Post *Model*

```
1    var $validate = array(
2        'name'=>array(
3            'alphaNumeric'=>array(
4                'rule'=>'alphaNumeric',
5                'required'=>true,
6                'message'=>'The Title may not contain any symbols'
7            ),
8            'maxLength'=>array(
9                'rule'=>array('maxLength',80),
10                'message'=>'The Title must not exceed 80 characters'
```

```
11                )
12            ),
13            'date'=>array(
14                'rule'=>'date',
15                'required'=>true,
16                'message'=>'You must supply a valid date'
17            ),
18            'content'=>array(
19                'required'=>true
20            )
21        );
```

Notice that, on lines 3 and 8 of Listing 7-8, a separate rule was assigned to the name field. The benefit of having more than one rule in this array rather than creating one custom regular expression to cover both rules is that the error messages you forward to the browser can be specific to the cause of the invalidation. Using multiple rules also allows you to take advantage of Cake's built-in rules and save time.

Go ahead and add Listing 7-8 to the Post model just below the model associations. Now the form submission process has validation handling included in the model. You could have run some cumbersome validation logic in the controller, but this would have gone beyond Cake's MVC architecture. By running data validation through the model, more streamlined functions and methods are available to you.

Error Messages in the View

For the error messages used in lines 6, 10, and 16 of Listing 7-8 to be visible to the user, you will need to prepare the views with the Form helper. By using the error() function, create error message placeholders in the app/views/posts/add.ctp and edit.ctp views. Make sure the supplied parameter matches the given field, such as $form->error('name') for the name field.

Writing Custom Model Functions

Suppose you wanted to enter a URL that would fetch not only a post by its ID but all posts for a given year. This type of process would likely require a few lines of logic to run the query, depending on the URL supplied by the user. All too often, beginners to Cake try to perform this logic in the controller, resulting in large controllers throughout the application. Because this is a process that deals specifically with data, you should run this function in the model.

Open the Post model, and insert Listing 7-9 after the recently added data validation attribute.

Listing 7-9. *The Custom* findByYear() *Function in the* Post *Model*

```
1   function findByYear($year=null) {
2       $date = $year.'-01-01 00:00:00';
3       $end_date = $year.'-12-31 23:59:59';
4       return $this->find('all',array('conditions'=>array('DATE(Post.date)'=>➥
'>'.$date,'DATE(Post.date)'=>'<'.$end_date)));
5   }
```

In the controller, you'll use this function so it will pass the $year variable supplied by the user. Lines 2–3 of Listing 7-9 initialize variables for the start and end dates of the year that will match the datetime field in the database. Line 4 performs the query and searches all records whose date fields match the range between $date and $end_date. It also uses return to pass the results back to the controller.

This function is held by the model, but the model itself won't execute the function. The controller will do that. So in the Posts controller, insert a new action called read(). Use Listing 7-10 to include the model function you just created.

Listing 7-10. *The Read Action in the Posts Controller*

```
1   function read($year=null) {
2       if (!$year) {
3           $this->Session->setFlash('Please supply a year');
4           $this->redirect(array('action'=>'index'));
5       }
6       $this->set('posts',$this->Post->findByYear($year));
7   }
```

Most of this logic is taken from the View action and uses the Session component and the redirect() function to run an error test on the $year variable passed in the URL. Line 6 is the key to your custom model function. Notice that the function is called like the find() function, except it matches the custom function you added to the Post model. The results returned from the function are passed right on to the view by using the set() function.

Now, to test your new function, you'll need to create the Read view file. Create this file, and add the debug() function to view the contents of the $posts variable. Launch the action by supplying a year in the URL, like so:

```
http://localhost/posts/read/2008
```

Your result should include an array something like Listing 7-11.

Listing 7-11. *The Returned Array from the* findByYear()·*Function for One Record*

```
Array
(
    [0] => Array
        (
            [Post] => Array
                (
                    [id] => 1
                    [name] => New Functions in 1.2
                    [date] => 2008-01-01 00:00:00
                    [content] => No content yet.
                    [user_id] => 1
                )

            [User] => Array
                (
                    [id] => 1
                    [name] => spiderman
                    [email] => spidey@hero.com
                    [firstname] => Peter
                    [lastname] => Parker
                )

            [Tag] => Array
                (
                    [0] => Array
                        (
                            [id] => 1
                            [name] => cakephp
                            [longname] => CakePHP Framework
                            [PostsTag] => Array
                                (
                                    [id] => 1
                                    [post_id] => 1
                                    [tag_id] => 1
                                )

                        )

                )

        )

)
```

Each record in the database that contains a date value matching the given year will now appear in this view. You accomplished a couple of important things here. First, you followed strict convention by placing the extended logic in a custom function in the Post model rather than using the controller. You also used variables in the right places to allow the user to specify any year in the URL. The application can dynamically handle whatever value is supplied, and you can even extend your function to run a test on a valid year, if you want, without affecting the controller or the view.

Trimming Results

Imagine that you ran the same query used in the previous section but for a large database with thousands of stored records. All the associated models would get pulled into the array and make for a substantially large process. Early on you won't notice the load your customized code could impose on the server, because you're usually dealing only with test data and in low quantities. But what if you were to launch the application on an extremely busy web site? Quite possibly the application could overload the server when searching for all the associations. For this reason, Cake has provided some functions that can help trim results by killing associations on the fly.

The unbindModel() Function

In Listing 7-11, several lines of code were returned to describe the associated models in the array. Remember, this is just one record. All these lines would be multiplied not only by the number of records returned but also by how many associated tags are assigned to each record. There's a possibility of loading redundant data, especially when you run queries on "has and belongs to many" associations.

The unbindModel() model function allows you to temporarily kill the "has and belongs to many" relationship the Post model shares with the Tag model. In the findByYear() function in the Post model, you can run this function before the database query, and the results will change dramatically. Listing 7-12 shows how to insert this function in the findByYear() function.

Listing 7-12. *Using the* unbindModel() *Function to Trim Results and Server Load*

```
1    function findByYear($year=null) {
2        $date = $year.'-01-01 00:00:00';
3        $end_date = $year.'-12-31 23:59:59';
4        $this->unbindModel(array('hasAndBelongsToMany'=>array('Tag')));
5        return $this->find('all',array('conditions'=>array('DATE(Post.date)'=>➥
'>'.$date,'DATE(Post.date)'=>'<'.$end_date)));
6    }
```

Line 4 in Listing 7-12 shows how to use the unbindModel() function to kill the hasAndBelongsToMany association. One important aspect of this function is that it is run only once; in other words, once line 5 has done its find() query, the association will resume for all other succeeding model functions.

Now reload the Read action and take a look at the resulting array:

```
Array
(
    [0] => Array
        (
            [Post] => Array
                (
                    [id] => 1
                    [name] => New Functions in 1.2
                    [date] => 2008-01-01 00:00:00
                    [content] => No content yet.
                    [user_id] => 1
                )

            [User] => Array
                (
                    [id] => 1
                    [name] => spiderman
                    [email] => spidey@hero.com
                    [firstname] => Peter
                    [lastname] => Parker
                )
        )
)
```

The entire Tag association is left out *when the query was run*, meaning that the server load was reduced by how much it would take to retrieve all the Tag model's associated records. You also have a leaner array that contains only what is needed, which recalls the philosophy that Cake is supposed to trim fat, not add it.

The unbindModel() function accepts two arrays: one containing all the associations to unbind and another for the models themselves. Notice that line 4 of Listing 7-12 has an array that contains the "has and belongs to many" relationship, and this relationship is assigned an array for all models that might have that association. You can specify one or more models to be unbound from the current model by extending the array.

The bindModel() Function

Just as the unbindModel() function helps you kill associations on the fly, the bindModel() allows you to assign associations as well. Again, this function operates for just one query and then ceases to affect other succeeding model functions.

This function follows the same syntax as the unbindModel() function and contains two arrays: one for the association to be bound to the current model and another for the models to be assigned to the association.

```
$this->bindModel(array('hasMany'=>array('Tag')));
```

The Read View

Right now, the Read view contains only the `debug()` function to show you the contents of the `$posts` array. Using Cake's HTML helper as well as any other custom HTML, make a view to wrap around this array.

Summary

The MVC structure can be tricky for some, but you should feel comfortable with Cake's use of this kind of architecture. You explored adding your own customized functions to models and controllers to extend the application and explored the logic that comes from baked actions and views. In the following chapters, you'll dive in and make something of your blog application. Along the way, you'll pull in other useful built-in helpers, and in Part 3, you'll use other customizable areas that will improve the power of your application. If you think you have the hang of working in models, views, and controllers, then congratulations—you've overcome the hardest part of learning Cake.

CHAPTER 8

■■■

Implementing Ajax Features

In recent years Ajax has become a more common method for handling requests among popular web sites. In short, Ajax makes it possible for the user to interact with the web site without waiting for the page to load or refresh. By working with HTTP requests this way, the web site behaves more like a desktop application. Methods that were thought to be impossible for web browsers have not only changed the Internet landscape but are turning the tides on software development. Many developers call this phenomenon the rise of "Web 2.0." However, building a rich Web 2.0 application is no simple task and usually requires a heavy dose of JavaScript. With Cake's help, you can bring common Ajax procedures into an application without much headache, and the amount of JavaScript you will have to use is minimized.

In this chapter, you will use the Ajax helper to build a comments section for your extensive blog application. Users will be able to add comments and vote other users' comments up or down, all without waiting for the page to reload or refresh. Along the way, I'll mention the possibilities of the Ajax helper and also introduce some Ajax methods that go beyond the scope of this helper. This chapter won't dive into all the possibilities Ajax provides, simply because that could be a book all by itself, but it will explain how Ajax can work in a Cake application and open up the door to other more complex methods you can try on your own. Let's first examine how Ajax is supposed to work and then use it to improve your blog.

How Ajax Works

In Chapter 6 I discussed asynchronous sequences and how Cake uses the render() function to pull a view without loading the whole page. In your blog application, you'll use Ajax to manage comment submissions in this way, meaning that the user will submit a comment, and they will see the comment post to the page instantly. In other words, the comments form will disappear, the text of the comment will appear below any other previously posted comments, and everything else on the page will remain in place. Figure 8-1 shows how Ajax works behind the scenes to add comments to a given post.

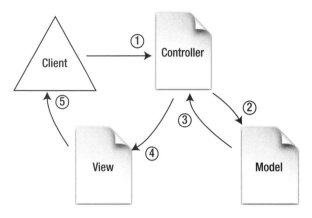

Figure 8-1. *The Ajax flow for submitting a comment asynchronously*

This figure looks almost identical to a typical flow in Cake. But it does differ in a couple of important ways:

1. When the form is submitted to the controller in this step, it is done using the Ajax helper. This means that the form data is collected by a JavaScript function and passed to the controller without changing the state of the browser.

2. The controller handles the form data as it would a typical response. It sends data to be saved to the model and checks for invalidations.

3. The model saves the data in the database and returns a successful response.

4. Rather than display the view normally, the controller uses the render() function to pass the output along as an Ajax response. The view file is fetched normally, but its contents are rendered in the waiting HTML element. In other words, the Ajax helper observes the response and places whatever is returned in a specified HTML element (for example, a <div> or <span> element).

5. The view is sent back to the client and, thanks to JavaScript, is displayed within the page, not replacing the whole page as a normal HTTP response would do.

In the blog application, the user will enter some data into a couple of form fields and then click Submit. The form will be passed along in the background because the Ajax helper intercepts the HTTP request and, with the help of JavaScript, does all the server-side processing without refreshing the page. You will render the view inside the web page rather than replace the page because you will tell the Ajax helper where in the page to update once the server responds. This area will be the whole comments section, allowing you to dynamically add the user's comment to the rest of the post's comments without refreshing the browser.

Working with Ajax Frameworks

Just as Cake helps reduce the amount of PHP code needed to run a script, some Ajax frameworks cut down on the amount of JavaScript needed to perform Ajax methods. These frameworks are worthwhile because tackling Ajax can be extremely complex. It's better to take advantage of open source Ajax frameworks than pull open that 500-page JavaScript primer.

Some of the most popular Ajax frameworks include the following:

- Prototype (www.prototypejs.org)

- jQuery (www.jquery.com)

- Adobe Spry (http://labs.adobe.com/technologies/spry)

- MooTools (www.mootools.net)

Any of these frameworks can be used in Cake, but the Ajax helper currently works only with Prototype. Later, I'll use jQuery to run some Ajax methods in Cake, but it will be done without the Ajax helper.

Using the Ajax Helper

Cake comes standard with the Ajax helper—a nifty set of methods for simplifying the code you enter in the view to make Ajax requests work properly. Like other helpers, it has more than a dozen useful functions (see Table 8-1) that can be called to reduce a process usually to a single string.

Table 8-1. *Functions in the Ajax Helper*

Function	Description
afterRender()	Includes code blocks after a view has been rendered
autoComplete()	Creates an autocomplete text field
div()	Creates a <div> element for Ajax updates
divEnd()	Closes an Ajaxed <div> element
drag()	Creates a draggable element; requires the Scriptaculous animation libraries
drop()	Creates a droppable element; requires Scriptaculous
dropRemote()	Creates an area that triggers an Ajax response when a draggable is dropped onto it
editor()	Creates an editor control that is swapped for the element when triggered by the user; requires Scriptaculous
form()	Creates a form element that runs in the background when submitted
isAjax()	Returns true if the current request is a Prototype update
link()	Creates a link to run an Ajax call
observeField()	Triggers an Ajax response when the observed field is changed
observeForm()	Observes a form and triggers an Ajax response when changed
remoteFunction()	Creates Ajax functions to be run, usually in conjunction with a link() event
remoteTimer()	Triggers an Ajax response at a specified time interval
slider()	Creates a slider control; requires Scriptaculous
sortable()	Makes lists or other objects sortable; requires Scriptaculous
submit()	Renders a form submit button that triggers an Ajax form submission

Like all other helpers, the Ajax helper must be initialized in the controller by including it as a value in the var $helpers array:

```
var $helpers = array('Html','Form','Ajax');
```

Then, in the view, the Ajax helper functions are called by using the $ajax object. For example:

```
$ajax->submit();
```

Of course, parameters are passed to the function, depending on the function being used.

```
$ajax->submit('Submit',array('url'=>'/comments/add','update'=>'comments_add'));
```

Preparing the Ajax Helper

Before you can use the Ajax helper, one or two important steps must be taken that are unique to this helper. Because it depends on Prototype, you must ensure that Prototype JavaScript files are included in each page. You will also need to make these scripts accessible for all the views that could potentially use the Ajax helper.

Installing Prototype

Download the latest version of Prototype from www.prototypejs.org/download. You should end up with a JavaScript file named something like prototype-1.x.x.x.js. Place this file in the app/webroot/js folder. It is now accessible by the whole application. To finish installing Prototype, you need to edit the default layout. Somewhere between the <head> tags in the app/views/layouts/default.ctp file, include the following line:

```
$javascript->link(array('prototype'));
```

Here, you are using the JavaScript helper to produce a link to the JavaScript file. These links appear something like this to include the script in the web page:

```
<script type="text/javascript" src="/js/prototype.js"></script>
```

Of course, the JavaScript helper automatically produces the correct URL to the JavaScript file.

Including the JavaScript Helper in the App Controller File

If you went ahead and refreshed the application, you may have noticed the following error:

```
Undefined variable: javascript [APP/views/layouts/default.ctp, line 5]
```

This error occurs whenever the helper is not initialized properly. In this case, you're trying to use a helper in the layout file, and since the default layout is meant to be called for all controllers, you will need to initialize the JavaScript helper in all controllers.

There is a way around going into each controller individually. By creating your own App controller file, you can place functions to be used by all controllers in it and thereby cut down on redundant code. To do this, however, there are some conventions to be used so that Cake can recognize the App controller.

The location of the App controller is `app/app_controller.php`. Like other controllers, the file must include the proper PHP code to create a new instance of the App controller object:

```
<?
class AppController extends Controller {
}
?>
```

Making Helpers Available for the Whole Application

In the App controller, you can also include any helpers that may be used in any or all controllers. This is done, as in an individual controller, by assigning a list of helpers in the array of the var `$helpers` attribute.

For the sake of your blog application, let's go ahead and include all the helpers you will need to use. Insert the following line into line 3 of the new App controller:

```
var $helpers = array('Html','Form','Ajax','Javascript');
```

The `$javascript->link()` function in the default layout file should now work properly. Generally, when using helpers in layouts, you should use the App controller to include those helpers; it will save you from having to do helper includes in every controller.

Adding Comments to the Blog

Before you can use the Ajax helper to handle user comments, you will need to create the table to store the comments in the database. Make the new table with the name `comments` in the database, and create the fields shown in Listing 8-1.

Listing 8-1. *SQL for Creating the* `comments` *Table*

```
CREATE TABLE `comments` (
    `id` int(11) unsigned NOT NULL auto_increment,
    `name` varchar(255) default NULL,
    `content` text,
    `post_id` int(11) unsigned,
    PRIMARY KEY (`id`)
);
```

Next, create the `Comment` model with the code shown in Listing 8-2.

Listing 8-2. *The* `Comment` *Model*

```
<?
class Comment extends AppModel {
    var $name = 'Comment';
    var $belongsTo = array('Post');
}
?>
```

Notice that this model has the `belongsTo` association with the `Post` model. To bind this association, you will need to edit the `Post` model to include the "has many" relationship. Open the `Post` model, and insert the following line to complete the association:

```
var $hasMany = array('Comment');
```

For good measure, create the Comments controller in `app/controllers/comments_controller.php`, and paste in the code shown in Listing 8-3.

Listing 8-3. *The Comments Controller*

```
<?
class CommentsController extends AppController {
    var $name = 'Comments';
}
?>
```

The Comments controller, as well as the matching table and model, are now prepared properly for use in the application. Now you can work comments into the blog by inserting some Ajax helper code in the Posts views and controller.

Working Ajax into the View

Using the Ajax helper requires that the Prototype framework be included in the web page. You've done this by installing the Prototype script in the `app/webroot/js` folder and also providing a link to that file in the `app/views/layouts/default.ctp` file. You've also made the helper available in the App controller. Working Ajax into the individual view that will be using the helper is now easy to do.

Displaying Comments

Remember that the Ajax output will be inserted into an HTML element of your choosing. Whatever element you use in the view to handle this output is where all the action will take place. `<div>` and `<span>` elements are for any generic block-level or inline content, respectively. Let's create a `<div>` to handle all the Ajax output for comments in the Posts view. Open `app/views/posts/view.ctp`, and at the bottom of the file create the `<div>` to be the target of the Ajax handling.

In Listing 8-4, I've left space on line 9 for an iteration of comments as well as an Ajax form to submit a new comment. To pull associated comments and make them available here, you will need to edit the View action in the Posts controller.

Listing 8-4. *Adding the Comments Section to the Posts View*

```
6     <hr/>
7     <h2>Comments</h2>
8     <div id="comments">
9
10    </div>
```

Listing 8-5 is almost the same as before, except I've tweaked the lines after line 6. Line 7 fetches the requested post record, and line 8 fetches the comments associated with the current post. Line 9 uses the set() function to pass those variables along to the view.

Listing 8-5. *The Adjusted View Action to Provide Associated Comments for the View*

```
1    function view($id = null) {
2        if (!$id) {
3            $this->Session->setFlash('Invalid Post');
4            $this->redirect(array('action'=>'index'));
5
6        }
7        $post = $this->Post->read(null,$id);
8        $comments = $this->Post->Comment->find('all',array('conditions'=>array(➥
'Post.id'=>$id)));
9        $this->set(compact('post','comments'));
10    }
```

Back at line 9 of Listing 8-4, you can now plug in a loop to display the contents of the $comments array (see Listing 8-6).

Listing 8-6. *The Comments Loop in the Posts View*

```
9    <? foreach($comments as $comment): ?>
10    <div class="comment">
11        <p><b><?=$comment['Comment']['name'];?></b></p>
12        <p><?=$comment['Comment']['content'];?></p>
13    </div>
14    <? endforeach;?>
```

The loop follows the conventional structure of the find() results in line 8 of Listing 8-5. Notice on line 11 in Listing 8-6 that the array is formatted to include the Comment key, which corresponds to the name of the Comment model and the name and content keys, which match up with fields in the table. I've also used lines 10 and 13 to instantiate a <div> element to be designed with CSS for better display.

In the database, create some test comments and refresh this post. You should get a similar screen to Figure 8-2.

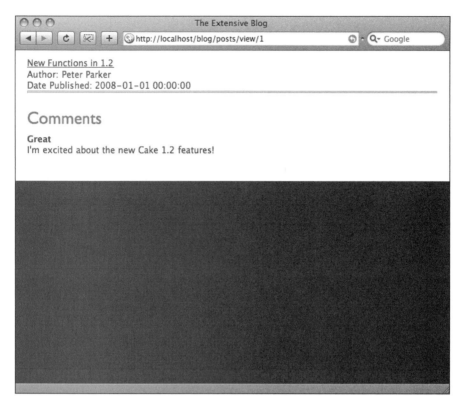

Figure 8-2. *Comments now displayed in the Posts view*

Using an Ajax Form

Now after line 14 in the `app/views/posts/view.ctp` file, you can include a form for adding comments. When doing so, you'll use the Ajax helper so that when the user submits a comment, it updates the `<div id="comments">` element without refreshing the whole screen.

To work Ajax into this view, insert the Ajax form shown in Listing 8-7 into the view file.

Listing 8-7. *The Add Comments Form*

```
15    <?=$ajax->form('/comments/add','post',array('update'=>'comments'));?>
16    <?=$form->input('Comment.name');?>
17    <?=$form->input('Comment.content');?>
18    <?=$form->input('Comment.post_id',array('type'=>'hidden','value'=>➡
$post['Post']['id']));?>
19    <?=$form->end('Add Comment');?>
```

Line 15 in Listing 8-7 does all the Ajax magic for you. Notice that the parameters you are supplying in the $ajax->form() function tell it to first send the form data to the Add action in the Comments controller.

The second parameter specifies what method to use when sending the form data. This is currently set to post but could be changed to get if desired.

The third parameter is the options array containing keys and values that correspond to possible features in the function. Here, you've assigned the value comments to the key update. What this means is that the $ajax->form() will update the <div> with the ID of comments. You have already created the <div id="comments"> on line 8 of the view file.

Lines 16–19 work like typical Cake form elements; they use the Form helper to create fields that correspond to fields in the comments table. Notice that I've included the model name in the field (Comment.) to specify that these fields are part of the Comment model, not the current Post model.

The only thing tricky about lines 16–19 is how the current post ID is passed to the Comments controller on line 18. Simply put, you made a hidden form element named after the post_id field in the comments table and assigned it the value contained in the $post['Post']['id'] variable.

That's all there is to it! When users come to a post in the blog, they will see a list of comments previously submitted as well as a set of form fields with which to supply their own comment. When the user clicks Add Comment, the form will submit in the background.

At this point, there is only one problem—the Comments controller is not yet ready to handle the submitted form. The next step is to work Ajax into this controller by tweaking the Add action.

Working Ajax into the Controller

The current Comments controller contains nothing but the $name attribute. Let's add the Add action to it, but with Ajax in mind (see Listing 8-8).

Listing 8-8. *The Add Action in the Comments Controller*

```
1    function add() {
2        if (!empty($this->data)) {
3            $this->Comment->create();
4            if ($this->Comment->save($this->data)) {
5                $comments = $this->Comment->find('all',array('conditions'=>➥
array('post_id'=>$this->data['Comment']['post_id']),'recursive'=>-1);
6                $this->set(compact('comments'));
7                $this->render('add_success','ajax');
8            } else {
9                $this->render('add_failure','ajax');
10           }
11       }
12   }
```

Lines 1–4 of Listing 8-8 are just like the baked Add action: they check for supplied data found in the parsed $this->data array, they create a new record in the database if data has been supplied, and they run the save() function in the model to insert the data into the new database record and check for a successful result from the model. Lines 5–7 are executed when a successful save has occurred, and line 9 is called only upon a failed save. (You could, if you wanted, run data validation in the model, and the controller would be prepared to handle the results.)

So, assuming that the supplied comment was saved successfully, then you would want to fetch all the comments in the database, including the newly added one, and display them in the <div id="comments"> element. Therefore, you must run a database query to pull the comments and pass that along to the view. Line 5 does this with the find() function; it pulls all comments with a post_id equal to the value supplied in the hidden form element you created in line 18 of Listing 8-7. I've also set the recursive value to -1 so that each comment in the resulting array doesn't include the entire contents of the associated post; you want the comments themselves without their associations. Line 6 passes the results of the find() function to the view.

Rendering for Ajax

The secret of making Ajax work in the controller is nothing more than using the render() function to bypass the typical view-rendering mechanism in the MVC structure of Cake applications. In line 7 of Listing 8-8, you use the render() function, with a second parameter to specify that the output is of the Ajax type. By including this parameter, you instruct Cake to disable its viewing mechanism and send only the view's output (not the layout as well) to the waiting JavaScript event. You must create a corresponding view file in the app/views/comments folder to be used by the controller and displayed in the <div id="comments"> element back in the Posts view.

Create the app/views/comments/add_success.ctp file. This file will be rendered to complete the Ajax form submission, so it will need to also iterate through the $comments array as does the app/views/posts/view.ctp file. Paste Listing 8-9 into the add_success.ctp file.

Listing 8-9. *The* add_success.ctp *File*

```
<? foreach ($comments as $comment): ?>
<div class="comment">
<p><b><?=$comment['Comment']['name'];?></b></p>
<p><?=$comment['Comment']['content'];?></p>
</div>
<? endforeach;?>
```

You should now be able to add comments to a post without the page being reloaded, like you see in Figure 8-3.

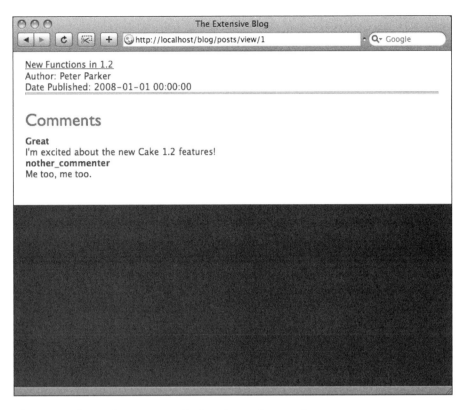

Figure 8-3. *The Post's comments displayed asynchronously*

Line 9 of Listing 8-8 calls for another view file in case an error occurs during the form submission. To accommodate this, create `app/views/comments/app_failure.ctp`, and insert some kind of error message there:

```
<p><b>Sorry, but your comment could not be added to this post. Please try again➥
later.</b></p>
```

You could also include the form in case the user wanted to immediately try again. In this case, the code would the same as Listing 8-7.

Using Other Ajax Helper Functions

Sometimes you may need to use a different method for submitting forms with Ajax. Or, depending on the task, you may not even need to submit a form but perform another process with Ajax. There are a variety of other Ajax helper methods for these needs.

The submit() Function

In Listing 8-7, you created an Ajax form using the `$ajax->form()` function. Another way of submitting a form with Ajax is by using the `$ajax->submit()` function. This method will work almost exactly as the `form()` function does, except that in the view you make the submit button—rather than observing a change event in the form—trigger the Ajax process.

Two lines in Listing 8-7 will need to change: the form tag itself and the submit button. See Listing 8-10 for how I've changed these tags from how they appear in Listing 8-7 to use the `$ajax->submit()` function.

Listing 8-10. *Using the* `$ajax->submit()` *Function to Submit a Form in the Background*

```
15    <?=$form->create('Comment',array('action'=>'add','onSubmit'=>'return ➥
false;'));?>
16    <?=$form->input('Comment.name');?>
17    <?=$form->input('Comment.content');?>
18    <?=$form->input('Comment.post_id',array('type'=>'hidden','value'=>$post➥
['Post']['id']));?>
19    <?=$ajax->submit('Add Comment',array('url'=>'/comments/add','update'=>➥
'comments'));?>
20    </form>
```

Note that line 15 of Listing 8-10 has changed from the `$ajax->form()` function to the `$form->create()` function. You've added the `onSubmit` key in the options array and passed the value `return false;` to this attribute. This will keep the form from sending a synchronous HTTP request when a form event occurs.

All but lines 19–20 have remained the same as before. The `$ajax->submit()` function is similar to the `$ajax->form()` function in that it uses an options array to pass some important parameters. These parameters specify where to send the form (the `url` parameter) and which HTML element receives the Ajax response (the `update` parameter). Line 20 is simply closing out the form.

When used in this way the same Ajax process is accomplished, but with the `$ajax->submit()` function. Some customized JavaScript functions may interrupt the form observe event, and in these cases using the `$ajax->submit()` function may prevent those hiccups. Other advantages of using the `$ajax->submit()` function over the `$ajax->form()` function include the ability to use multiple Ajax events within a form. With the `$ajax->form()` function, some Ajax calls such as autofill can trigger the JavaScript event observation. When using multiple Ajax calls within a form, the `$ajax->submit()` function usually bypasses any conflicts that could occur with `$ajax->form()`.

The link() Function

Many Ajax methods don't require any form data. The simplest Ajax call is one that simply sends a parameter to a script and returns a response in the background. These types of Ajax processes can be managed with the `$ajax->link()` function. You can build this function into the blog by creating a community voting mechanism for each comment.

Add the votes field in the comments table with this SQL:

```
ALTER TABLE `comments` ADD `votes` int(11) DEFAULT '0' ;
```

You'll add an Ajax link in each comment box that, when clicked, will either add 1 to the value in votes or subtract 1 from it. The new total will be sent back to the browser and updated in the comment box.

Copying Some Helper CSS

The design of the voting links will need to be crafted in the CSS files the application is currently using. Without some CSS to help you out here, the tool will look confusing and will also get in the way of understanding the $ajax->link() function, so let's add some CSS to improve the design. I've provided some styles in Listing 8-11 you can use if you'd like.

Listing 8-11. *CSS Markup for the Voting Tool*

```css
.comment {
    border: 1px solid #ccc;
    border-width: 1px 0px 0px 0;
    clear: both;
    width: 500px;
}

.comment p {
    float: left;
    clear: left;
}

.vote {
    width: 50px;
    height: 20px;
    background-color: #fffdc3;
    text-align: center;
    font-size: 16px;
    font-weight: bold;
    padding: 15px 0 15px 0;
    float: right;
}

.cast_vote {
    height: 50px;
    float: right;
}

.cast_vote ul {
    list-style-type: none;
}
```

```
.cast_vote ul li {
    font-size: 9px;
    margin: 5px 0 5px 0;
}
```

If you wanted to tinker with this design to fit your own style, by all means do so. But the CSS in Listing 8-11 should at least help you see the various elements at work in the voting feature.

Using the link() Function in the View

Next, inside the `<div class="comment">` element in the `app/views/posts/view.ctp` file, you will need to supply some code to display the voting links and total votes. Starting on line 11, insert the lines shown in Listing 8-12.

Listing 8-12. *The View Code to Display Voting Links and Total Votes*

```
11    <div id="vote_<?=$comment['Comment']['id'];?>">
12        <div class="cast_vote">
13            <ul>
14            <?=$ajax->link('<li>up</li>','/comments/vote/up/'.$comment➥
['Comment']['id'],array('update'=>'vote_'.$comment['Comment']['id']),null,false);?>
15            <?=$ajax->link('<li>down</li>','/comments/vote/down/'.$comment➥
['Comment']['id'],array('update'=>'vote_'.$comment['Comment']['id']),null,false);?>
16            </ul>
17        </div>
18        <div class="vote"><?=$comment['Comment']['votes'];?></div>
19    </div>
```

Line 11 of Listing 8-12 appends the comment's unique ID to vote_ to provide you with a uniquely identified `<div>` element to update. The Add Comments form already will perform some Ajax, so to avoid any collisions in updating elements, I've ensured that the ID of each comment is unique.

Most of the markup in Listing 8-12 is to organize the design of the feature so as to be accessible to the user and so it can be changed to fit the design of your own site. But the `$ajax->link()` function has been included in lines 14 and 15. It behaves similarly to the `$html->link()` function used in baked views, with the first parameter being the text to be displayed and the second parameter being the `href` attribute. The `href` is set to a controller action you haven't created yet called Up or Down and passes along through the URL the comment ID to receive the vote. When this link is clicked, rather than perform a standard HTTP link request, Cake will provide some Prototype functions to perform the request in the background and receive the response. Notice that in the options array of this function you've set the update element to the same value as line 11: vote_ and then the unique ID of the comment.

Creating Voting Actions in the Controller and Model

The Vote action, which is referenced in lines 14–15 of Listing 8-12, doesn't exist yet; let's create it in the Comments controller. This action will be rather simple: add or subtract 1 from the votes field in the comments table and return a total votes value to the view. Of course, this action will use the render() function to render the views in Ajax mode.

Use Listing 8-13 to add the Vote action to the Comments controller.

Listing 8-13. *The Vote Actions in the Comments Controller*

```
1    function vote($type=null,$id=null) {
2        if ($id) {
3            $votes = $this->Comment->vote($type,$id);
4            $this->set(compact('votes'));
5            $this->render('votes','ajax');
6        }
7    }
```

Recall that one Cake best practice is to make the model "fatter" than the controller if possible; that is, you should add code to the model instead of the controller if possible. I've put this principle to work in line 3 of Listing 8-13 by creating my own model function vote(), and I've passed the parameters supplied in the $ajax->link() functions of lines 14–15 of Listing 8-12. This function will do all the work with the database to both fetch the votes and update the number of votes for the comment. It will need to know whether it is a vote up or down and which comment to update, which has been passed through the controller variables $type and $id.

Listing 8-14 contains the model function vote(), which will do the database work to make the vote happen. Add this to the Comment model after the other attributes and associations.

Listing 8-14. *The* vote() *Model Function in the Comment Model*

```
1    function vote($type=null,$id=null) {
2        if (!$id) {
3            return "-";
4        } else {
5            $votes = $this->read(null,$id);
6            $votes = ($type == 'up' ? $votes['Comment']['votes']+1 : $votes➡
['Comment']['votes']-1);
7            $this->id = $id;
8            $this->saveField('votes',$votes);
9            return $votes;
10        }
11    }
```

Line 5 of Listing 8-14 pulls the number of votes for the supplied comment ID from the database. Line 6 adds or subtracts 1 from the total depending on the type of vote. Lines 7–8 save the result to the database using the saveField() function. This function allows you to update only one field (or column) in the row rather than format the whole `$this->data` array for the more common `save()` function. Of course, you need to tell the model which record to update, and this is done at line 7 by setting the ID attribute. Finally, at line 9, the new total is returned to the controller to be displayed in the view.

Creating the Votes View

The last step is to create the view to be rendered by the controller action in line 5 of Listing 8-13. This will be simple enough: it will only need to display the passed value inside the same `<div>` element used in the Posts view. Listing 8-15 contains the code for the `app/views/comments/votes.ctp` file.

Listing 8-15. *Displaying the New Total with the Votes View*

```
<div class="vote"><?=$votes;?></div>
```

Go ahead and refresh the Posts view, and click the Ajax links to vote comments up and down. The total number of votes should automatically change in the background without any page reloads, and this was all done without submitting any forms, like in Figure 8-4. Using the `$ajax->link()` function allows you to do similar asynchronous tasks easily in a way that's often easier and more fun for the user. And it sure beats trying to code by hand all the JavaScript that makes this possible.

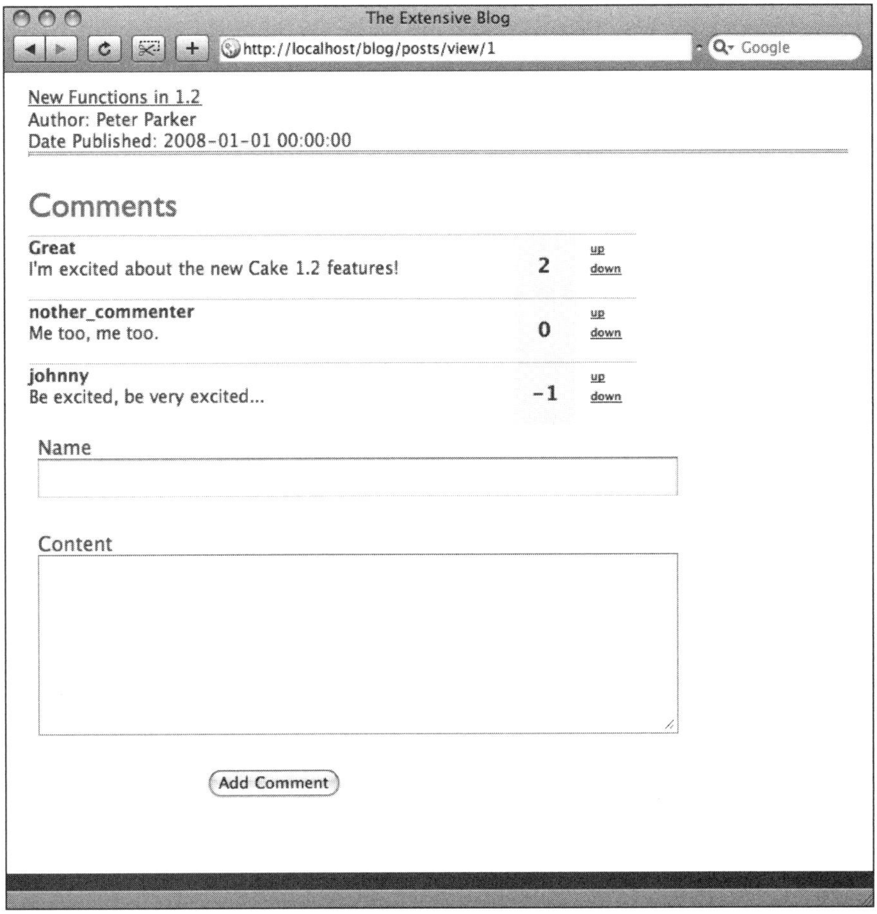

Figure 8-4. *Ajax voting is now working in the comments section.*

Doing More with the Ajax Helper

You have barely scratched the surface of the possibilities that the Ajax helper opens up. As you can see in Table 8-1, the Ajax helper includes much more than the form(), submit(), and link() functions. True, these functions are useful because they allow you to discuss the main concepts of using Ajax in a Cake application. What about using Ajax with animation frameworks? Or building fancy Web 2.0 features such as a drag-and-drop shopping cart or a slider tool that adjusts sizes of HTML elements? When considering how you want to bring Ajax into your Cake application, remember some of these fundamental steps.

Passing JavaScript with the Options Array

Look for the options array in various helper functions, even in non-Ajax helpers when bringing in more complex or customized JavaScript functions. By using this array, you can pass on JavaScript functions to the HTML element being rendered by the helper that work with more complex Ajax methods. For instance, if I wanted to craft my own JavaScript function, I could call that function with the options array like this:

```
$form->input('OK',array('type'=>'button','onSubmit'=>'alert(\'Hello World\');'));
```

Not only did I pass along the parameter saying what type of form input field the helper should render (in this case an HTML button), but I also assigned the JavaScript `alert()` function to the element by keying the HTML attribute `onSubmit` and giving it a value.

Using the options array is generally more effective than using raw HTML. Usually the helpers can provide a uniform linking system or display mechanism that cuts down on the headache of keeping the application consistent. Also, getting used to the look and flow of helper strings can be more aesthetic for the eyes, especially if you favor PHP syntax over HTML markup. Probably the most important reason for sticking with helpers, even for custom JavaScript and Ajax calls, is to prevent duct-taping your application. In other words, you're working in Cake, and the framework is strong enough to lessen your code. Too often developers settle for a hack or for a deprecated method to get a complex process working right. Don't overlook how Cake's helpers can contribute to your process. You'll find more features than you might have been expecting to help you through the challenge.

Prototype vs. jQuery

In recent months, the jQuery framework has increased in popularity and in functionality. Many Cake developers have begged for Cake to be rewritten around this framework rather than Prototype. At the time of writing, rumors are floating around that jQuery will eventually replace Prototype in the Ajax helper. Whatever the case, the Ajax helper is destined to go on working the same way; you just may need to install a different library in the `app/webroot/js` folder.

Regardless of the direction Cake will take, both frameworks offer some important features that every serious Ajax developer will want to consider. Again, you can pull in their functions by using the options array in various helper functions. For example, using jQuery's form plugin, I can upload a file with the Form helper:

```
<?=$form->button('Upload',array('onClick'=>'$(\'#storyEditForm\').ajaxSubmit({➥
target: \'#storyTextUpload\',url: \'".$html->url('/stories/text').'\'}); return➥
false;'));?>
```

There's definitely more to this function than what is included here, but this example does illustrate how to assign a jQuery function to the `onClick` event in the `$form->button()` function. Provided that my controllers are using the `render()` function in Ajax mode, Cake can run its logic through the MVC structure as normal and still use an Ajax library outside the Ajax helper.

Uploading Files with jQuery

We couldn't possibly explore every possible Ajax method available in Cake. However, one of the most common needs of web applications is some kind of file upload. This task can be rather cumbersome, especially when you want to manage file uploads with Ajax. Many of the Ajax frameworks don't support file input elements because of the way they serialize HTML forms. JavaScript can't place the file contents into a string, which is how many of these frameworks submit form data. Fortunately, jQuery's Form plugin can handle file uploads, making it possible to integrate uploading with Ajax.

Because jQuery currently is not part of the default Ajax helper, adding a file upload feature to your blog will demonstrate how to incorporate a non-Prototype framework into Cake.

Installing jQuery and the Form Plugin

Remember that you must install the JavaScript libraries to be called manually. Download the latest version of jQuery as well as the Form plugin. The following links should help in locating those files:

- *jQuery*: http://docs.jquery.com/Downloading_jQuery

- *Form plugin*: http://jqueryjs.googlecode.com/svn/trunk/plugins/form/
  jquery.form.js

Next, you have to place the necessary files into the app/webroot/js directory and make them available in the default layout. The trouble is that jQuery may conflict with Prototype, which you have used to provide the comments voting and submissions, so let's add some logic to the default layout to detect whether it's running the Posts Add action or something else.

Open the default layout (app/views/layouts/default.ctp), and replace the JavaScript helper line referencing Prototype with the following line:

```
<?=($this->params['controller'] == 'posts' && $this->params['action'] == ➥
'add' ? $javascript->link(array('jquery.js','jquery.form.js')) : $javascript->➥
link('prototype'));?>
```

Now when the Posts Add action is fired, jQuery will be initialized, not Prototype. But Prototype will remain the default script for all other actions, thus not conflicting with the comments section.

Creating the Posts Add Action

Perhaps an author of the blog has already typed a post in a plain-text file and wants to upload it to the blog. Let's create a file upload mechanism that can analyze a plain-text file and insert it into the Content field in the Posts Add action to facilitate creating new posts.

Open the app/views/posts/add.ctp file (which should have already been baked) and replace its contents with Listing 8-16.

Listing 8-16. *The File Upload Feature in the Add Action*

```
1     <div class="posts form">
2       <?=$form->create('Post',array('name'=>'postAddForm','id'=>'postAddForm',➥
'type'=>'file'));?>
3         <fieldset>
4             <legend>Add Post</legend>
5             <?=$form->input('name');?>
6             <?=$form->input('date');?>
7             <?=$form->input('content');?>
8         <div id="postTextUpload">
9             <?=$form->input('content', array('label'=>'Content ','rows'=>'15',➥
'cols'=>'75'));?>
10              <?=$form->input('upload_text',array('label'=>'Upload Text File ',➥
'type'=>'file'));?>
11              <?=$form->button('Upload Text',array('onClick'=>➥
'$(\'#postAddForm\').ajaxSubmit({target: \'#postTextUpload\',➥
url: \"'.$html->url('/posts/text').'\'});return false;'));?>
12          </div>
13          <?=$form->input('User');?>
14          <?=$form->input('Tag',array('type'=>'select','multiple'=>'checkbox'));?>
15        </fieldset>
16      <?=$form->end('Submit');?>
17    </div>
```

Line 2 of Listing 8-15 assigns the form the ID of postAddForm, which will be needed for jQuery to collect the form data. This line also sets the type attribute to file so that the form includes the enctype="multipart/form-data" attribute for the form submission to work correctly.

Notice that I've wrapped a <div> element around the Content field starting on line 8 so that I can replace the current field with a filled one after the file is uploaded.

Line 10 contains the actual file input field. With the Form helper, you need specify only that the input type is equal to file to render a file input field.

Line 11 is where all the Ajax happens. By setting the onClick attribute to a jQuery-formatted string containing all the necessary code, the Form helper will be able to render a button containing the necessary JavaScript to execute an Ajax method through jQuery. This syntax follows the form submission method used in the jQuery Form plugin.

Creating the Posts Controller Text Action

When the file is chosen and the user clicks the Upload Text button, jQuery will submit the whole form to the text action in the Posts controller because of the URL parameter you wrote in the onClick event.

So, in the app/controllers/posts_controller.php file, you'll need to include the function shown in Listing 8-17.

Listing 8-17. *The Text Action in the Posts Controller*

```
1    function text() {
2        if (!$this->data['Post']['upload_text']) {
3            $this->set('error','You must select a text (.txt) file before you ➥
can upload.');
4            $this->render('text','ajax');
5        } else {
6            App::import('Core','File');
7            $file =& new File($this->data['Post']['upload_text']['tmp_name']);
8            if ($this->data['Post']['upload_text']['type'] != 'text/plain') {
9                $this->set('error','You may only upload text (.txt) files.');
10                $this->render('text','ajax');
11            } else {
12                $data = h($file->read());
13                $file->close();
14                $this->set('text',$data);
15                $this->render('text','ajax');
16            }
17        }
18    }
```

Line 2 of Listing 8-17 checks for any contents in the upload_file field. File uploads will still be automatically parsed by Cake, which is more secure than using the PHP $_FILES array. To facilitate file handling, Cake's core includes a series of File class functions. But to use these functions in the controller, since they're not component classes, helpers, or other Cake elements, you must instantiate a new File class; this is done in line 6 with the App::import() function. On line 7, the File utility is assigned to $file as a class object; now, throughout the action, the $file object will provide you with Cake's core File functions. Also, the $file object will represent the uploaded file itself, so when you have to maneuver through the upload, it will be much easier to save the data to the server.

Line 8 checks to see whether the file is the right MIME type ("text/plain" for plain-text files). Lines 12–15 handle the file itself. Now, in this action, you need only to retrieve the contents of the file and make them available in the Contents field. So line 12 just reads the file and places the contents in the $data variable. Line 13 closes out the file, and lines 14–15 make the $data variable available in the app/views/posts/text.ctp view file. Line 15 takes care to render the view in Ajax mode so as to not trigger Cake's synchronous rendering engine.

All that's left is to swap out the Content field with a new propagated one; this is done in the Text view file, which you haven't created yet.

Writing the Text View

Create the app/views/posts/text.ctp file, and paste Listing 8-18 into it.

Listing 8-18. *The Text View File*

```
1    <? if (!empty($error)): ?>
2        <p><?=$error;?></p>
3        <?=$form->input('Post.content', array('label'=>'Content','rows'=>'15',➥
'cols'=>'75'));?>
4    <? else: ?>
5        <p>Upload successful</p>
6        <?=$form->input('Post.content',array('label'=>'Current Text ',➥
'value'=>$text,'rows'=>'15','cols'=>'75'));?>
7    <? endif;?>
8    <?=$form->input('Post.upload_text',array('label'=>'Upload Text File ', ➥
'type'=>'file'));?>
9    <?=$form->button('Upload Text',array('onClick'=>'$(\'#postAddForm\')➥
.ajaxSubmit({target: \'#postTextUpload\',url: \"'.$html->url('/posts/text')➥
.'\'}); return false;'));?>
```

Listing 8-16 mimics the Posts Add view, except that it adds an error check (and displays the error message) and supplies the Content field with the file upload contents (available in the $text array from the controller).

Now you should be able to upload the contents of a plain-text file and make them available instantly in the Add action without reloading the page. Thanks to jQuery and its Form plugin, you can do this in Ajax. Unfortunately, the Ajax helper doesn't allow for jQuery functions or file uploads yet, so you had to provide the JavaScript functions to make it happen in the onClick attribute.

More Ajax Features

The world of Ajax is continually expanding. Several open source projects have made previously expensive or complex libraries available to the masses. As Ajax methods continue to improve, you can rest assured that Cake's structure will remain open to Ajax and allow those methods to be brought into your Cake applications. Hard-coding the onClick and other DOM events certainly extends the capabilities of the Cake application, but by practicing with other Ajax helper functions, you can take care of most common Ajax processes with Cake.

Summary

In this chapter, we discussed how Cake simplifies Ajax methods with its built-in Ajax helper. You built a comments feature into your blog application that allows the user to add a comment to a blog post and also provides users with a way to vote on those comments. Currently, Cake's Ajax helper is built on the Prototype JavaScript library, and this chapter explained how to work Prototype into your Cake application. Using other Ajax frameworks like jQuery is also possible in Cake but is done outside the Ajax helper for most methods. I showed how to use jQuery to upload a text file, which is just one feature you could add from another Ajax framework. The Ajax helper is just one of the many helpers available in Cake. Chapter 9 will explain helpers in more detail, including the HTML and Form helpers, as well as how to create a custom helper of your own.

PART 3

■ ■ ■

Advanced CakePHP

In Part 2, you began building a blog application, and along the way I discussed some key fundamentals—how to build controllers, models, and views, as well as where to use helpers to streamline development. Using and customizing other advanced features such as helpers, behaviors, DataSources, and components allows you to take advantage not only of Cake's efficient structure but of its cutting-edge functionality as well. In this part, you will build your own features and explore advanced built-in functions.

CHAPTER 9

■■■

Helpers

In the previous chapters, you capitalized on some of Cake's built-in helpers to dramatically improve and speed up the development of some typical web application processes. Using the Ajax helper, you added some flare to the process of submitting and voting on the blog's comments. The Form helper facilitated data handling and form submissions, and the HTML helper condensed the amount of markup you wrote by hand in the views and managed the links throughout the site to prevent any breaks. In this chapter, you will explore built-in helper functions in depth and even build a couple of your own. First, I'll briefly discuss installing helpers.

Installing Helpers

You have already used some built-in helpers and made them available to the application by entering their names in the var $helpers array in the controller or App controller. When installing third-party helpers or creating your own, you must take the following steps to ensure the helpers work properly:

1. Every helper file should go in the app/views/helpers directory.

2. Include the helper's class name in the var $helpers array in either the App controller or in a specific controller in whose views the helper may be called.

3. When using the helper in the view, make sure you call the helper's class object correctly (that is, use the $ajax variable to call the Ajax helper object). Don't create local variables in the view that might conflict with available helper objects.

In Chapter 8, you created the App controller file to make some helpers available to the whole application. This is generally good practice when most of the controllers in the application use a set of helpers because it allows you to use one string of code in one location rather than spelling out the helper includes in various places. You may ask, why not include all the built-in helpers in the App controller by default rather than having to go through this extra step? The answer is that, by so doing, you compromise the load time of the application. It's better to use the App controller to specify helpers that all or most controllers use most often, rather than include them all at the outset and bog down the application.

If, for example, only one controller in the application uses the Time helper, then it's best to include this helper in that controller alone. Helpers such as HTML, Form, and Ajax are best called in the App controller because of their common use throughout the application. When a helper is called in the App controller, the helper object will be created and loaded into the server memory for each action the application performs. That can add up quickly if too many helpers are called for the whole site.

Because PHP code is parsed and compiled each time it is accessed, anything you can do to reduce the amount of code will help site performance. Using code only where it is needed will also help you when troubleshooting. Including too many helpers in the App controller increases server load and may necessitate adjusting PHP settings or using a runtime accelerator with PHP.

Using Cake's Built-in Helpers

One of the most attractive qualities of Cake is its collection of helpers. Tasks such as rendering RSS feeds, managing form submissions, truncating and highlighting text, and performing Ajax methods are all simplified by helpers. Cake provides a large assortment of web-specific functions that can save you hours of headaches; knowing what is available in Cake's built-in helpers is key to building advanced Cake applications.

■**Note** Rather than inundate the chapter with long explanatory tables, I've opted for a more "dictionary" approach to explaining the helpers and their functions. Each function will have its own set of parameters that are called by populating the parameter in the view. Each parameter is separated from the previous one by a comma and includes in brackets the type of data specified in the parameter. Beneath each description, I include each parameter's default value. Leaving the parameter blank, or entering `null` in its place, means that the default value for that parameter will be used when the function is executed.

Explain Every Helper Function?

This chapter could get very boring very fast. Listing all the possible helper functions would make for a very long list indeed and would turn this chapter, more or less, into API documentation. (If API documentation is what you want, then by all means check out Cake's online API at `http://api.cakephp.org`. It's kept up-to-date and contains resource links to the source code itself for each function.) I will explain the functions in detail rather than reprinting the API documentation. The fact remains that some helpers are used so frequently that, for most developers, leaving out a detailed survey of Cake's built-in helper functions would hinder your progress in really using what Cake has to offer. Therefore, I will only highlight the HTML and Form helpers in detail, since these are fundamentally necessary for anything to happen in even the most basic Cake application.

Don't be afraid to try these functions on your own; most of the time, they're rather straightforward, and since they don't manipulate your database, you can't inflict any permanent damage on your application. Usually the more helpers you use, the more time you save, so it's worth practicing. A common pitfall for inexperienced Cake developers is to be unaware of helper functions so they resort to building their own processes or custom helpers to perform tasks that have already been standardized in a helper function. (I have certainly been guilty of this—I once wrote an entire console script to automate building views before I realized that Cake already came with Bake!)

Let's move on to the HTML and Form helpers. You should already be acquainted with them since you have used them previously; but they do offer more features than those mentioned so far.

Working with the HTML Helper

You have already used the HTML helper, and this is perhaps the easiest one to master. Using the HTML helper provides some advantages:

- Often the amount of HTML markup you must enter in the view is reduced by sticking to the helper.

- HTML output can be managed dynamically rather than manually by passing along variables to the helper. You won't have to write your own methods for common tasks that are already available through the HTML helper.

- Have I overstated the advantage of managing links? I'll say it again: this helper saves you the migraine headache of sifting through and testing all the possible broken links should you change a domain name, change a URL scheme, or move to a different hosting provider. This cannot be overstated—especially since one of the biggest challenges for new web developers is making their applications portable.

- For some users, reading through PHP is easier than reading HTML. At the very least, those who favor PHP's syntax to HTML markup will find the HTML helper a better method for coding the views.

The HTML helper is called in the view by using the $html object. This helper is one of two that is automatically included in the whole Cake application without having to use the var $helpers array in the controller. However, once you add more helpers to the application, it's not a bad idea to spell out the HTML helper in the var $helpers array; this way, no matter what future version of Cake the application may run on, the helper will be called appropriately. A more verbose $helpers property also ensures that other developers involved on the project know precisely which helpers are at work in the view.

▋Caution The HTML helper is specified in title case like all other helpers in the var $helpers array. This means that using var $helpers = array('HTML'); with all capitals will not work properly; it must be done with Html like so: var $helpers = array('Html');.

In the following sections I've included descriptions of most of the HTML helper functions and how to use them. As you come across opportunities to use them in your applications, be sure to maintain consistency; you could always write HTML by hand, which could bypass some of the advantages of using the HTML helper.

charset

This function outputs the HTML `<meta>` tag, specifying the character set for the page. Using this function generally occurs in a layout file.

`charset( charset[string] )`

> `charset = null`: The character set to be used in the `<meta>` tag

For example, the following:

`<?=$html->charset('UTF-16');?>`

will output this:

`<meta http-equiv="Content-Type" content="text/html; charset=UTF-16"/>`

The default character set can be specified in the `app/config/core.php` file. Change the `App.encoding` setting on or near line 47 following the standard HTML character set specifications. (For your information, a list of registered character set values is available from the World Wide Web Consortium at `www.w3.org/International/O-charset-lang.html`.) The `App.encoding` value is originally set to `UTF-8`.

CSS

This function outputs a tag for including a style sheet. Generally, CSS files are stored in the `app/webroot/css` directory and are made available by using the CSS function as described in this section. A `<link>` or `<style>` tag is returned depending on the values specified in the parameters.

`css( path[mixed], rel[string], attributes[array], inline[bool] )`

> `path`: The name of the style sheet (excluding the `.css` extension) or an array of multiple style sheets in the `app/webroot/css` directory.

> `rel = 'stylesheet'`: The `rel` attribute; if set to `import`, then the function will return the `@import` link in the `<style>` tags rather than the `<link rel='stylesheet'>` tag.

> `attributes`: Contains any HTML attributes to be included in the `<link>` or `<style>` tag; arranged as keys named for the attribute and values to be assigned to the attribute.

> `inline = true`: If set to `false`, the result will be placed in the `<head>` element of the page; otherwise, the function will output inline.

Using the `attributes` array, you can specify a style sheet for printing or screen output like so:

`<?=$html->css('cake.generic.print',null,array('media'=>'print'));?>`

or like so:

`<?=$html->css('cake.generic.screen',null,array('media'=>'screen'));?>`

Multiple style sheets can be called by passing an array in the path parameter:

```
<?=$html->css(array('reset','type','layout'));?>
```

The CSS function is generally used in layouts but can also be called in individual view files.

div

This function returns a formatted `<div>` tag. Its use is rather straightforward and basic, given that `<div>` tags are meant to be wrappers for HTML styles and layout or placeholders for JavaScript actions.

div(class[string], text[string], attributes[array], escape[bool])

class = null: The name of the `class` attribute for the tag.

text = null: The text to appear inside the `<div>` element.

attributes: Contains any HTML attributes to be included in the tag; arranged as keys named for the attribute and values to be assigned to the attribute.

escape = false: If set to `true`, the contents of the `text` parameter will be escaped for HTML.

Say I wanted to create a uniquely designed tab or page element to be displayed as a `<div>` element. The `$html->div()` function could be used thusly:

```
<?=$html->div('tab','Home');?>
```

to output the following:

```
<div class="tab">Home</div>
```

If a passed variable contained the contents of the `<div>` tag, I could easily display the variable with slightly less code than if I were to use only HTML markup. The `div()` function as follows:

```
<?=$html->div('story',$story['Story']['contents']);?>
```

uses a few less characters than does this:

```
<div class="story"><?=$story['Story']['contents'];?></div>
```

This function is generally used as a convenience wrapper for displaying `<div>` tags and allows you to stick with PHP instead of HTML if you choose.

docType

Like the `$html->charset()` function, this function is used mainly in layouts to avoid entering the long standards-compliant HTML document type string.

docType(type[string])

type = 'xhtml-strict': The document type to be used in the docType declaration

For possible document types to be used in the type parameter, see Table 9-1.

Table 9-1. *Possible Document Types to Be Used with the* $html->docType() *Function*

Parameter Value	Document Type
html4-strict	HTML 4.0 Strict
html4-trans	HTML 4.0 Transitional
html4-frame	HTML 4.0 Frameset
xhtml-strict	XHTML 1.0 Strict
xhtml-trans	XHTML 1.0 Transitional
xhtml-frame	XHTML 1.0 Frameset
xhtml11	XHTML 1.1

By entering the following in the layout file:

```
<?=$html->docType('xhtml-strict');?>
```

the document type declaration is produced as the following string:

```
<!DOCTYPE html PUBLIC "-//W3C//DTD XHTML 1.0 Strict//EN" "http://www.w3.org/TR/➥
xhtml1/DTD/xhtml1-strict.dtd">
```

image

Managing images can be a tedious task for elaborate web sites. The $html->image() function helps with graphics management by simplifying the rendering of image tags and using a standardized internal path scheme to reference the files. This function dynamically outputs an <img> tag.

image(path[string], attributes[array])

path: The path to the image file

attributes: An array of keys and values corresponding with HTML attributes to be included in the <img> tag

The path to the image file can be constructed in one of three ways. First, if you enter only a file name, this function will automatically output the path relative to the app/webroot/img directory. For instance, to display the file app/webroot/img/title.jpg, only the file name title.jpg is needed in the path parameter.

```
<?=$html->image('title.jpg');?>
```

Second, if you enter a full link to an external image file, the `$html->image()` function will reference the file directly with no path manipulation. An image available at www.mydomain.com/images/title.jpg could be accessed by this function with this:

```
<?=$html->image('www.mydomain.com/images/title.jpg');?>
```

Finally, the path can be made relative to the app/webroot directory by starting with a forward slash:

```
<?=$html->image('/img/gallery/title.jpg');?>
```

Like other helper functions, HTML attributes can be passed through this function using the `attributes` array. For example, the following:

```
<?=$html->image('title.jpg',array('alt'=>'My Homepage','class'=>'title');?>
```

outputs the following:

```
<img src="/blog/img/title.jpg" alt="My Homepage" class="title" />
```

link

Using the `$html->link()` function helps with maintaining consistent links and also is a convenience wrapper for the common `<a>` tag. This function outputs an `<a>` anchor tag.

link(title[string], url[mixed], attributes[array], confirmMessage[string], ➥ escapeTitle[bool])

title: The content to be linked; may include HTML tags, but the `escapeTitle` parameter must be set to `false` to display correctly.

url = null: If an array, this will cause the link to point to controllers and actions; as a path relative to Cake, it will be parsed as an internal link; as an absolute URL, it will be passed as it is.

attributes: The parameter through which to pass HTML attributes to be included with the tag.

confirmMessage = false: When set, this message will be displayed in a JavaScript alert dialog box; if the user proceeds, the link will be activated.

escapeTitle = true: By default, any symbols will be escaped for HTML; when set to `false`, the string supplied in `title` will be passed along as entered.

This function is rather simple: provide the content to be linked, and tell Cake where to send the user when clicked. I discussed basic inline links with the `$html->link()` function when I showed how to bake some views. These are simple enough—linking the string "Add a Post" to the Posts Add action is done with the following code:

```
<?=$html->link('Add a Post','/posts/add');?>
```

But you can use an alternate method for producing this same link by entering an array in the url parameter, like so:

```
<?=$html->link('Add a Post',array('controller'=>'posts','action'=>'add'));?>
```

Of course, entering an absolute URL into the url parameter will send the user off site:

```
<?=$html->link('Check out the Bakery','http://bakery.cakephp.org');?>
```

You can include a confirmation message to be displayed as a JavaScript alert dialog box by entering a string in the confirmMessage parameter. For instance, say you wanted to alert the user before deleting records from the database. You could do this by entering the confirm message in the $html->link() function:

```
 <?=$html->link('Delete','/posts/delete/'.$post['Post']['id'],null,'Are you sure➥
you want to delete this post?');?>
```

When this is clicked, a box will appear asking the user "Are you sure you want to delete this post?" If the user clicks Proceed, then the link will be activated.

You can include HTML tags in this function by setting the escapeTitle parameter to false. Even other helper functions that output HTML can be included in the title parameter, like so:

```
<?=$html->link($html->image('title.jpg'),'/',null,null,false);?>
```

meta

$html->meta() outputs <meta> tags, which can be used for specifying a site description or other <meta> tags. It can also output <link> tags for RSS feeds and a site favicon.

meta(type[string], url[mixed], attributes[array], inline[bool])

type = null: The type of <meta> tag to be produced; this can be set to any string, but some built-in strings are also available (rss, atom, icon, keywords, and description).

url = null: If an array, this will cause the link to point to controllers and actions; as a path relative to Cake, it will be parsed as an internal link; as an absolute URL, it will be passed as is.

attributes: Parameter for passing along HTML attributes and their values.

inline = true: If set to false, the tag will appear within the <head> tags of the layout.

If the type parameter is set to either rss, atom, or icon, then the corresponding MIME type will be returned. For instance, the following:

```
<?=$html->meta('icon');?>
```

returns these strings:

```
<link href="/blog/favicon.ico" type="image/x-icon" rel="icon"/>
<link href="/blog/favicon.ico" type="image/x-icon" rel="shortcut icon"/>
```

nestedList

`$html->nestedList()` displays an array as a nested list. This can be very helpful when debugging.

nestedList(list[array], attributes[array], itemAttributes[array], tag[string])

> `list`: The elements to list

> `attributes`: The HTML attributes to be passed to the list tag

> `itemAttributes = null`: The HTML attributes to be passed to the individual item (`<li>`) tags

> `tag = 'ul'`: The type of list tag to be used, either ordered or unordered lists (`<ol>` or `<ul>` tags by entering `ol` or `ul`)

For each array and nested array passed in the `list` parameter, a new list tag will be called (that is, for unordered lists, a new `<ul>` tag will be returned with the contents of the nested array parsed with `<li>` tags). The array can contain as many levels as desired. For instance, say the `$posts` variable has the following array contents:

```
$posts = array(
    'Post 1'=>array(
        'Jan 1, 2008',
        'No Author'),
    'Post 2'=>array(
        'Jan 2, 2008',
        'Administrator')
);
```

By placing this array in the `list` parameter of the `$html->nestedList()` function, the following HTML would be returned:

```
<ul>
    <li>Post 1
        <ul>
            <li>Jan 1, 2008</li>
            <li>No Author</li>
        </ul>
    </li>
    <li>Post 2
        <ul>
            <li>Jan 2, 2008</li>
            <li>Administrator</li>
        </ul>
    </li>
</ul>
```

This function works well with lists pulled from the database using the `find('list')` or `generateList()` model function.

para

Simply put, this is a convenience function for wrapping the paragraph tag around a chunk of text. It can be useful in simplifying HTML escaping for content that may contain nonalphanumeric characters.

`para( class[string], text[string], attributes[array], escape[bool] )`

> class: The CSS class name of the <p> tag
>
> text: The content to appear inside the <p> element
>
> attributes: HTML attributes to be passed and displayed in the tag
>
> escape = false: When set to true, the content will be HTML-escaped
>
> The following test string:

```
<?=$html->para(null,'This is a test for the $html->para() function',null,true);?>
```

will return the following when run through the $html->para() function:

```
<p>This is a test for the $html-&gt;para() function</p>
```

style

The $html->style() function is a convenience wrapper for inserting styles into HTML elements. For instance, a particular element may need to have some inline styles assigned to it with the style attribute. This function allows you to specify those styles in PHP instead of CSS.

`style( data[array], inline[bool] )`

> data: CSS settings arranged as an array
>
> inline = true: If set to false, each CSS element will be separated by a hard return; if true, the CSS will be returned as a single string.

A Cake application may use the database to manage CSS styles. A model for a CSS table could fetch the styles and provide them as an array to be used in the view. To simplify parsing through this array, the $html->style() function could save some time. Say I've got some CSS stored like the following array:

```
$styles = array(
    'p_bold'=>array(
        'font-size'=>'1.0 em',
        'font-weight'=>'bold'
    )
    'p_italic'=>array(
        'font-style'=>'italic'
    )
);
```

Then, by using the $html->styles() function, I can reduce fetching these styles to a single function. In conjunction with the $html->para() function and assuming this $styles variable is available in the view, notice how the styles() function conveniently handles dynamic CSS:

```
<?=$html->para(null,'Paragraph Text',array('style'=>$html->styles($styles➥
['p_bold'])));?>
```

This line would return the following HTML:

```
<p style="font-size:1.0em; font-weight:bold">Paragraph Text</p>
```

This function can also simplify loops through elements that use database-driven styles. Just make sure the keys in the styles array are formatted correctly by following the previous example.

tableHeaders and tableCells

These functions display a table. Also, a common feature of tabular displays is alternating rows. Rather than build PHP formulas for alternating through table rows, the $html->tableCells() function can automatically attach a CSS class or HTML attributes to odd and even rows. Similar to other convenience wrappers, both the $html->tableHeaders() and $html->tableCells() functions make displaying dynamic content in HTML much easier to manage.

tableHeaders(names[array], trAttributes[array], thAttributes[array])

names: Array of names for the table's columns

trAttributes = null: HTML attributes to be passed to the <tr> tag

thAttributes = null: HTML attributes to be passed to the <th> tag

tableCells(data[array], oddTrAttributes[array], evenTrAttributes[array],➥
useCount[bool])

data: Table data arranged as rows and columns in an array

oddTrAttributes = null: HTML attributes to be passed to odd rows

evenTrAttributes = null: HTML attributes to be passed to even rows

useCount = false: If true, adds the class name column- plus the number of the row to the <tr> element

The $html->tableHeaders() function renders only the header row inside a table. Be sure to enter the <table> element tags by hand as HTML and include these table functions inside this element. The returned HTML contains both the <th> and <tr> tags, so to pass HTML attributes to one or both of these, use the trAttributes and thAttributes parameters, respectively. The following line:

```
<?=$html->tableHeaders(array('1','2'),array('class'=>'row'),array('class'=>➥
'header'));?>
```

will return the following:

```
<tr class="row"><th class="header">1</th> <th class="header">2</th></tr>
```

The names array for the $html->tableHeaders() function is formatted with only the names themselves without any nested arrays. However, the data array for the $html->tableCells() function must include nested arrays ordered by column for each row. For example, the following array is formatted for use in the $html->tableCells() function:

```
$cells = array(
    'row1'=>array(
        'column1','column2','column3'
    ),
    'row2'=>array(
        'column1','column2','column3'
    )
);
```

The actual text contained in the row keys (for example, row1 and row2) will not be displayed in the HTML output:

```
<tr>
    <td>column1</td>
    <td>column2</td>
    <td>column3</td>
</tr>
<tr>
    <td>column1</td>
    <td>column2</td>
    <td>column3</td>
</tr>
```

addCrumb and getCrumbs

$html->addCrumb() and $html->getCrumbs functions render breadcrumbs (for example, home->about->mailing address). These functions manage a breadcrumbs array and make it available to each view. The $html->addCrumb() function adds a link to the breadcrumbs array, and the $html->getCrumbs() function fetches and displays the array.

addCrumb(name[string], link[mixed], attributes[array])

name: The text to be displayed

link = null: Can be keyed in an array (for example, array('controller'=>'posts','action'=>'add')) or entered as a string (for example, '/posts/add'); if left blank, no link will be rendered around the text

attributes: HTML attributes to be passed to the <a> tag of the crumb

Adding the home page of the site to the breadcrumbs array, for example, is simple using this function:

```
<?=$html->addCrumb('Home','/');?>
```

To display the breadcrumbs, however, you must use the `$html->getCrumbs()` function. Some parameters exist for the `$html->getCrumbs()` function to better manipulate how these links are rendered.

getCrumbs(separator[string], startText[string])

separator = '»': The text displayed in between crumbs when more than one crumb is found

startText = false: The first crumb in the breadcrumb trail; if set to false, the first crumb in the array will be displayed first

If you were to display the home page link that was added to the breadcrumb array in the previous example for the `$html->addCrumb()` function, you would use `$html->getCrumbs()` like so:

```
<?=$html->getCrumbs();?>
```

This will render the following when the Cake application is named `blog`:

```
<a href="/blog/">Home</a>
```

Of course, the link will change to match the specific server settings for the application.

Using the HTML Helper in the Default Layout

Currently, your blog application doesn't use much of the HTML helper in its default layout. To put some of these functions to good use, let's revamp the default layout to include more of them.

In `app/views/default.ctp`, replace its contents with Listing 9-1.

Listing 9-1. *Using the HTML Helper in the Default Layout*

```
<?=$html->docType('xhtml-strict');?>
<head>
    <title>The Extensive Blog</title>
    <?=$html->charset('UTF-8');?>
    <?=$html->meta('icon');?>
    <?=$html->css('cake.generic');?>
     <?=($this->params['controller'] == 'posts' && $this->params['action'] ==➥
 'add' ? $javascript->link(array('jquery.js')) : $javascript->link('prototype'));?>
</head>
```

```
<body>
 <?=$html->div(null,$session->flash().$html->div(null,$content_for_layout,array➡
('id'=>'content')),array('id'=>'container'));?>
</body>
</html>
```

Finding ways to use the HTML helper in the default layout has allowed you to replace much of the HTML with PHP. By using the $html->docType() and $html->charset() functions, you've been able to bypass all the standards-compliant declarations coding and still future-proof the layout against possible standards changes. Also, the $html->div() function allowed you to wrap the layout's contents in <div> tags that match the app/webroot/css/cake.generic.css style sheet and reduce this to one line.

In the individual views, you could repeat this process and look for ways to use the HTML helper to replace your hand-coded markup with PHP.

Working with the Form Helper

Just as the HTML helper is essential to streamlining your use of HTML markup in the view, the Form helper is indispensable for form processing. In fact, avoiding this helper would likely take more effort than learning its functions.

A couple of important points ought to be explained before examining the Form helper functions in detail. First, some functions are designed to display the results of a processed form. In a way, these functions act as a kind of receiver and are not immediately visible in the page. Other functions work to format and send data for the model to use. Both receiver and supplier functions must follow model naming conventions to work properly. For instance, Model.fieldname is used to tell the $form->input() function in which field and in which table in the database to store the user input data. Whenever the field parameter or an array of fields are called in the function, be sure to name the fields properly. To ensure that the helper is able to send the data to the correct model, include the camel-cased model's name, followed by a period and then followed by the field name:

```
<?=$form->error('Post.content');?>
```

When you're sure the controller will experience no conflicts with multiple models, you can usually specify only the field's name:

```
<?=$form->error('content');?>
```

■**Note** Earlier versions of Cake followed this convention for specifying models and fields using the HTML helper and with a slash instead of a period, such as Model/fieldname. If you do come across earlier Cake applications, be sure to replace the forward slash with a period to be consistent with Cake 1.2. Use the Form helper to render all form elements, not the HTML helper.

Second, most form elements will use the options or attributes parameters the same way. Because form elements can be more elaborate than other HTML elements with regard to

JavaScript, Ajax, and other interactive functions, they may need more specific options to be passed along. You can fully customize an HTML attribute to be passed in a form element by keying the `options` or `attributes` array correctly. Just make sure that the key matches the name of the attribute and its value contains the proper values. The following line:

```
<?=$form->submit('Submit',array('onSubmit'=>'return false;'));?>
```

will return a submit button containing the onSubmit attribute, like so:

```
<input type="submit" value="Submit" onSubmit="return false;" />
```

Any attribute can be passed through the `options` and `attributes` arrays.

■**Note** Because the `options` and `attributes` parameters are mostly consistent for most Form helper functions, I'll forego describing them for each function. Where a particular option or attribute affects the function's output, I'll highlight that option in the description.

With these points in mind, let's take a look at the main functions of the Form helper. Most of them will work properly only when contained inside a `<form>` element, usually created with the `$form->create()` function listed next.

create

Rendering `<form>` tags is simplified by the `$form->create()` function. This function also manages the `action` HTML attribute and points the form to the correct model.

create(model[string], options[array])

> `model = null`: The model to which the form data should be sent.

> `options`: Aside from HTML attributes, this array can contain some specific options—`type`, `action`, `url`, and `default`.

When creating a new form for the controller and model to process, this function makes sure that the `<form>` tag points to the correct URL and sends the data appropriately. For instance, you can choose either `post` or `get` methods for handling the user data by specifying the `type` option in the `options` array. Or, for creating forms that handle file uploading, the necessary `enctype` attribute is automatically formatted correctly by specifying the `type` option as `file`. The `model` parameter ensures that the form data is sent to the appropriate model without worrying about URLs or other application paths. Possible form types include `delete`, `file`, `get`, `post`, and `put`.

When you need to specify the action to be called when the form is submitted, simply set the `action` option to the Cake-relative path of the action. This action must be in the current controller to work properly.

For sending the form to an action outside the current controller, use the url option. This can be either an array specifying the controller and the action or a Cake-relative path pointing to the action.

To suppress the default behavior of the form, set the default option to false. When set to false, the default option tells the form not to submit. This can allow for Ajax processing or other customized behaviors with the form data. By default, the default option is set to true, meaning that the form will behave as a normal HTTP request.

If I were to add a form that would submit data to another model, I could set this up with the $form->create() function like so:

```
<?=$form->create('Post',array('url'=>'/tags/add'));?>
```

In this example, the submission of this form would be sent to the Add action of the Tags controller. Generally, forms include only the current model's name. One thing to keep in mind is that you can pass along HTML attributes through the options parameter:

```
<?=$form->create('Post',array('id'=>'add','class'=>'form'));?>
```

end

However, the $form->end() function can conveniently combine into one string the submit button, which is typically the last form element displayed and the closing </form> tag.

end(options[mixed])

options: When entered as a string, this parameter is rendered as the value of the submit button; as an array, it passes along HTML attributes to the submit element.

If you use the options array to pass along HTML attributes, use the label option to set the value of the submit button:

```
<?=$form->end(array('label'=>'Submit Form','id'=>'submit_btn'));?>
```

This line will return the following output:

```
<input type="submit" value="Submit Form" id="submit_btn" />
</form>
```

In conjunction with the $form->create() function, this function closes off forms; a form at its most basic is condensed into just two lines:

```
<?=$form->create('Post');?>
<?=$form->end('Submit');?>
```

secure

To prevent cross-site request forgery (CSRF) attacks, many developers use the hash insertion technique. In short, the $form->secure() function facilitates hash insertions by generating a hidden form field containing a hash based on other fields in the form.

secure(fields[array])

fields: The list of fields to use to generate the hash

The `fields` parameter is required for the function to work correctly. When formatting the array, be sure to arrange it by model and field names:

```
<?=$form->secure(array('Post'=>array('id','name'));?>
```

This will output the hidden input element with a server-side-generated hash:

```
<fieldset style="display:none;">
<input type="hidden" name="data[_Token][fields]" value="1932368593ef664fc975581e➥
92e2df1490401570" id="TokenFields1314770757" />
</fieldset>
```

The value of the hidden input element will certainly change depending on the `Security.salt` value set in the `app/config/core.php` file and the function's own randomization algorithm. This hash is accessible in the `$this->data` array under the `['_Token']['fields]` key.

label

This function renders a `<label>` element and wraps it around a specified input field. The `$form->input()` function automatically runs this function when rendering input fields (which can be suppressed in that function's options).

```
label( field[string], text[string], attributes[array] )
```

field: The field around which to wrap the `<label>` HTML element

text = null: The label's text

To change the label's class name or provide other HTML attributes settings, just enter these customizations in the `attributes` array:

```
<?=$form->input('Post.name','Title of Post',array('class'=>'post_label'));?>
```

input

```
input( field[string], options[array] )
```

Perhaps no other helper function is quite so versatile as the `$form->input()` function. This tool works both to receive and to send data; when receiving data, it will display its contents in a form element, and when sending it, it will handle all the form fields and naming conventions so that the controller and model can parse the user's data automatically. Each of the form input elements is rendered by this function as well. When data validation errors or messages are sent back to the view, this function also renders those messages and highlights the field, if desired. By sticking with this function, many of the typical form structures are reduced to less code (often just one line).

Automagic

For the field entered, the `$form->input()` function will interpret the field and automatically render a form element based on the kind of data it finds. Most of the time, especially with simple forms, only the field name is needed:

```
<?=$form->input('content');?>
```

In this example, the function would recognize that the matching field in the database table is a text field and would consequently render a `<textarea>` element with its necessary parameters to work with the model. Table 9-2 shows how the `$form->input()` function inspects the database field types and what it will return to the browser.

Table 9-2. *The* `$form->input()` *Function's Automagic Responses to Database Field Structures*

Field Type	Returns
Boolean	Check box input element
Date	Day, month, and year select menus
Datetime	Day, month, year, hour, minute, and meridian select menus
String (for example, varchar)	Text box input element
Text	Text area element
Time	Hour, minute, and meridian select menus
Timestamp	Day, month, year, hour, minute, and meridian select menus
Tinyint(1)	Check box
String or text fields named `password`, `passwd`, or `psword`	Password

By following Table 9-2, you can build the database structure to be automatically recognizable by the Form helper. Making a field the type tinyint and giving it a length of 1 will save you from having to tell the `$form->input()` function that the field is a Boolean value and that it should be rendered as a check box. Of course, if the special needs of the application demand otherwise, you can specify particulars as well. For instance, suppose you wanted to force the user to submit a string rather than paragraphs of text without changing the database structure. You would need to add some options to override the `$form->input()` function's automagic behavior.

The Type Option

The `type` option allows you to explicitly choose the type of form element. For example, you could show a text box instead of a `<textarea>`:

```
<?=$form->input('content',array('type'=>'text'));?>
```

To go back to the `<textarea>` element, you can enter that in the `type` option (or let the default behavior do it for you):

```
<?=$form->input('content',array('type'=>'textarea'));?>
```

Table 9-3 lists the options available to use with the `type` parameter. When these options alias another Form helper function, the same options for that function can be used in the `options` array in the `$form->input()` function and will produce the same effect.

Table 9-3. *Options Available for Use in the* `type` *Parameter in the* `options` *Array*

Option	Description
checkbox	Alias for the `$form->checkbox()` function
date	Renders select menus ordered as month, day, and year
datetime	Alias for the `$form->dateTime()` function
file	Alias for the `$form->file()` function
hidden	Alias for the `$form->hidden()` function
password	Alias for the `$form->password()` function
radio	Alias for the `$form->radio()` function
select	Alias for the `$form->select()` function
text	Alias for the `$form->text()` function
textarea	Alias for the `$form->textarea()` function
time	Renders select menus ordered as hour, minute, and meridian

Other Options

A plethora of other options allow for more customization and functionality. Many of these options can be used in the other form input element functions, depending on the context of the function. Table 9-4 lists these options as well as a general description of how they are used.

Table 9-4. *Options for Use in the* `options` *Parameter in Many Form Helper Functions*

Option	Description
before[string]	Markup to be injected into the output of the function; comes before the label element.
between[string]	Injected markup that comes between the label and field elements.
after[string]	Injected markup that appears after the field.
options[array]	Manually specified options for use in a select element or radio group; may be supplied as a simple array of values or also a key-value pair; keys are rendered in the value attribute and the value is displayed in the element.
multiple[mixed]	When set to `true`, select menus are displayed to allow multiple selections; when set to `checkbox`, a select type is rendered as check boxes and not a multiple-select menu.
maxLength[int]	Sets the HTML `maxLength` attribute.
div[bool] = true	When set to `false`, the wrapper `<div>` tag is disabled.
label[mixed]	As a string, results in the text to be displayed as the label; when set to `false`, disables the label element.

Continued

Table 9-4. *Continued*

Option	Description
id[string]	Sets the ID attribute to the value supplied.
error[string]	When set, the text here will be displayed in the event of a validation error; leave blank to allow the default message to appear.
selected[string]	The value of the item in a selection-based input element to be selected when the field is rendered.
rows[int]	The number of rows to size the <textarea> element.
cols[int]	The number of columns to size the <textarea> element.
empty[mixed]	When set to true, the field is forced to remain empty upon submission; when used with a select menu, a string may be supplied to be displayed as an empty option (for example, "Please Select One...").
timeFormat[string]	The format of select menus for time-related fields; the only options are 12, 24, none.
dateFormat[string]	Like the timeFormat option; the only possible values are DMY, MDY, YMD, and none.

If you mix and match the available options skillfully, you may find there is no scenario that the $form->input() function can't handle.

At times you may need to use a form element function directly instead of specifying the type in the $form->input() function. Or, perhaps you would just rather organize your views with functions specific to the types of fields being rendered. In either case, the Form helper comes with element-specific functions that behave exactly like the $form->input() function. Other Form helper functions help with other tasks, such as displaying an error or splitting apart the datetime elements into separate menus. Table 9-5 contains a list of these functions and their parameters.

Table 9-5. *Form Input Element Functions*

Function Name and Parameters

```
button( title[string], options[array] )
checkbox( field[string], options[array] )
file( field[string], options[array] )
hidden( field[string], options[array] )
password( field[string], options[array] )
radio( field[string], options[array], attributes[array] )
submit( caption[string], options[array] )
select( field[string], options[array], selected[mixed], attributes[array],➜
 showEmpty[mixed] )
text( field[string], options[array] )
textarea( field[string], options[array] )
dateTime( field[string], dateFormat[string], timeFormat[string], selected[string],➜
 attributes[array], showEmpty[mixed] )
```

Function Name and Parameters
day(field[string], selected[string], attributes[array], showEmpty[mixed])
month(field[string], selected[string], attributes[array], showEmpty[mixed])
year(field[string], minYear[int], maxYear[int], selected[string], attributes[array], ➡ showEmpty[mixed])
hour(field[string], format[bool], selected[string], attributes[array], ➡ showEmpty[mixed])
minute(field[string], selected[string], attributes[array], showEmpty[mixed])
meridian(field[string], selected[string], attributes[array], showEmpty[mixed])
error(field[string], message[string], options[array])

Using Other Built-in Helpers

Useful as they are, the HTML and Form helpers are not the only helpers that Cake has to offer. Cake 1.2 includes a handful of other helpers that extend the available functions that your application can use. For a list of each helper's current function set, refer to the Cake 1.2 API (http://api.cakephp.org). Here, I'll just explain each helper and give an overview of what it does.

The Ajax Helper

In Chapter 8, you worked with the Ajax helper to create a comments voting system. I explained that many of its functions require the Prototype JavaScript framework to behave properly in the view. Be sure that you have that installed correctly to make full use of this helper. Not only can the Ajax helper simplify using Prototype, but it can also make animation effects easier to use. (For a more in-depth explanation of the Ajax helper, see Chapter 8; to see a list of Ajax functions, refer to Table 8-1.)

The JavaScript Helper

This helper is used mainly to simplify coding JavaScript. A common function that you have already referenced is the $javascript->link() function that works as an automator for creating <script> tags in the view. Other uses of this helper include JavaScript object and event functions that provide some common JavaScript functions and code. Both this helper and the Ajax helper can simplify emerging Ajax technologies and implementing advanced JavaScript methods.

To include this helper in the application, use this:

```
var $helpers = array('Javascript');
```

The JavaScript helper comes with the functions listed in Table 9-6.

Table 9-6. *Functions in the JavaScript Helper*

Function	Description
$javascript->afterRender()	Callback for after rendering; writes cached events to the view or a temp file
$javascript->blockEnd()	Ends a block of JavaScript code
$javascript->cacheEvents()	Caches JavaScript events created with the event() function
$javascript->codeBlock()	Wraps JavaScript code with the <script> tag
$javascript->escapeScript()	Escapes carriage returns and single or double quotes for JavaScript code segments
$javascript->escapeString()	Escapes strings to be JavaScript compatible
$javascript->event()	Used with the Prototype framework to attach an event to an element
$javascript->getCache()	Gets the current JavaScript cache; also clears JavaScript caches
$javascript->includeScript()	Includes a script inside a single <script> tag
$javascript->link()	Links to JavaScript files for use in a web page
$javascript->object()	Creates a JSON object from an array
$javascript->writeEvents()	Writes cached JavaScript events

The Number Helper

This is a simple helper for dealing with number formats. From currency formatting to making memory file sizes readable, the Number helper condenses some common tasks into some handy helper functions. If your application must deal in multiple number formats or if it must display file sizes, then give some of the functions listed in Table 9-7 a try. To include this helper in the application, use this:

```
var $helpers = array('Number');
```

Table 9-7. *Number Helper Functions*

Function	Description
$number->currency()	Formats a floating-point integer into a currency format
$number->format()	Formats a floating-point integer according to provided settings
$number->precision()	Formats the number based on the specified precision value
$number->toPercentage()	Makes a number a percentage
$number->toReadableSize()	Returns a number of bytes into a readable size format (for example, KB or MB)

The Paginator Helper

This helper works together with the Pagination component to break up data into multiple pages or to sort data by specified parameters. The Paginator helper works in the view to manipulate the display of supplied data to fit the customized needs of the application. In other words, when the Pagination component is used in the controller (which is the case whenever you create standard actions for a controller in Bake), the data sent to the view is *paginated* data. To work through the pages of data, use the Paginator helper. Table 9-8 lists the functions that let you customize how to display paginated data in the view.

To include this helper in the application, use the following:

```
var $helpers = array('Paginator');
```

Table 9-8. *Paginator Helper Functions*

Function	Description
$paginator->counter()	Returns a counter string for the current paginated results set
$paginator->current()	Returns the current page of the paginated results set
$paginator->defaultModel()	Returns the default model of the paginated sets
$paginator->first()	Returns the first or set of numbers for the first pages of paginated results
$paginator->hasNext()	Returns true if the supplied result set is not the last page of paginated results
$paginator->hasPage()	Checks whether a given page number has a result set in paginated results
$paginator->hasPrev()	Returns true if the supplied result set is not the first page of paginated results
$paginator->last()	Returns the last or set of numbers for the last pages of paginated results
$paginator->link()	Creates a link with pagination parameters
$paginator->next()	Creates a link to the next set of paginated results
$paginator->numbers()	Returns a set of numbers on each side of the current page for more direct access to other results
$paginator->options()	Sets default options for all pagination links
$paginator->params()	Returns the current page of the results set for a given model
$paginator->prev()	Creates a link to the previous set of paginated results
$paginator->sort()	Creates a sorting link for a column in the results set
$paginator->sortDir()	Returns the direction by which the given results set is ordered
$paginator->sortKey()	Returns the key by which the given results set is ordered
$paginator->url()	Creates a pagination URL to access other pages of the results set

The RSS Helper

The RSS helper creates standards-compliant RSS feeds. See Table 9-9 for a list of RSS helper functions. To include this helper in the application, use the following:

```
var $helpers = array('Rss');
```

Table 9-9. *RSS Helper Functions*

Function	Description
$rss->channel()	Returns the <channel> element
$rss->document()	Returns an RSS document contained in <rss> tags
$rss->item()	Converts an array to an RSS element
$rss->items()	Converts an array of data using an optional callback; maps the array to a set of RSS tags
$rss->time()	Converts a specified time stamp in any format to an RSS time specification

The Session Helper

The Session helper displays session information as provided by its component and controller. It displays flash messages, errors, and reading session data with convenience functions listed in Table 9-10. To include this helper in the application, use this:

```
var $helpers = array('Session');
```

Table 9-10. *Session Helper Functions*

Function	Description
$session->activate()	Turns on session handling if the app/config/core.php file's Session.start attribute is set to false
$session->check()	Returns true if a session key is set
$session->error()	Returns the last error encountered in the session
$session->flash()	Renders messages set with the Session component setFlash() function
$session->id()	Returns the session ID
$session->read()	Returns all values stored in a given session key
$session->valid()	Returns whether a session key is available in the view
$session->write()	Overrides the Session component write() function; should not be used in a view but may be called in other helper functions

The Text Helper

When dealing with text, tasks such as truncating and highlighting can require complicated regular expressions or tedious PHP operations. The Text helper condenses some of these common web text methods into helper functions. See Table 9-11 for a list of Text helper functions. To include this helper in the application, use this:

```
var $helpers = array('Text');
```

Table 9-11. *Text Helper Functions*

Function	Description
$text->autoLink()	Converts all links and e-mail addresses into HTML links
$text->autoLinkEmails()	Provides an e-mail link for given text
$text->autoLinkUrls()	Finds text beginning with http:// or ftp:// and wraps a link tag around it
$text->excerpt()	Extracts an excerpt of text by a given phrase
$text->highlight()	Highlights a given string of text
$text->stripLinks()	Removes links from text
$text->toList()	Formats an array as a comma-separated, readable list
$text->trim()	Alias for truncate()
$text->truncate()	Truncates text to a given length

The Time Helper

Variations when working with date and time strings can be frustrating—60 seconds in a minute, 60 minutes in an hour, 24 hours in a day, 7 days in a week…. You get the idea. Date and time methods that compare times or automate date tasks can get confusing or complex quickly. Add storing dates in a database, and the level of difficulty increases as well. Thanks to the Time helper, some common date-time methods are easier to manage. From SQL query string handling to rendering nicely formatted dates, this helper is useful for any Cake application that relies on time elements. See Table 9-12 for a list of Time helper functions. To include this helper in the application, use this:

```
var $helpers = array('Time');
```

Table 9-12. *Time Helper Functions*

Function	Description
$time->dayAsSql()	Returns a partial SQL string to search for records between two times occurring on the same day
$time->daysAsSql()	Returns a partial SQL string to search for records between two dates
$time->format()	Returns a formatted date string; converts valid strtotime() strings or Unix timestamps
$time->fromString()	Returns a Unix timestamp from a given valid strtotime() string or integer
$time->gmt()	Converts a given Unix timestamp or valid strtotime() string to Greenwich mean time
$time->isThisMonth()	Returns true if given datetime string is within this month
$time->isThisWeek()	Returns true if given datetime string is within this week
$time->isThisYear()	Returns true if given datetime string is within this year

Continued

Table 9-12. *Continued*

Function	Description
$time->isToday()	Returns true if given datetime string is today
$time->isTomorrow()	Returns true if given datetime string is tomorrow
$time->nice()	Formats a datetime string into a readable string
$time->niceShort()	Like nice(), except it condenses the string to less words and digits
$time->relativeTime()	Alias for timeAgoInWords(); can also calculate future dates
$time->timeAgoInWords()	Compares the difference between a given datetime string and the current time; expresses the difference in past terms (for example, three days ago)
$time->toAtom()	Formats date strings to be used in Atom feeds
$time->toQuarter()	Returns the quarter for a given date
$time->toRSS()	Formats date strings to be used in RSS feeds
$time->toUnix()	Convenience wrapper for the strtotime() function
$time->wasWithinLast()	Returns true if the given date is within the given interval
$time->wasYesterday()	Returns true if given datetime string represents yesterday

The XML Helper

As a data storage file format, XML has gained significant popularity in recent years. Some developers favor it over database engines for its flexibility and ease of use. However you use XML, this helper can streamline some typical XML processes. See Table 9-13 for a list of XML helper functions. To include this helper in the application, use this:

```
var $helpers = array('Xml');
```

Table 9-13. XML Helper Functions

Function	Description
$xml->elem()	Creates an XML element
$xml->header()	Generates an XML document header
$xml->serialize()	Converts a model result set, or a Cake-formatted array, into XML

Creating Custom Helpers

An important key to creating the best web applications is making sure the front end of the program is crisp and well organized. In this regard, helpers are invaluable. The HTML and Form helpers slash the time required to produce effective forms or HTML displays.

Consider the possibilities of being able to craft your own customized helper functions. Not only does Cake allow for custom helpers, but it also makes creating them simple. Of course, the full power of a helper can be extended with more impressive code, and you can find a wide variety of third-party helpers designed by the most talented Cake developers.

This section will explore how to create custom helpers and how to use functions from other helpers. You'll build a helper for your blog application with some specific methods designed for the blog itself. First, let's build the App helper.

Using the App Helper

Like the controllers and models, the Helper object that Cake uses to process helpers can have an overall helper for the application. This is called the App helper, and it is stored in the application as app/app_helper.php. Create this file, and copy the contents of Listing 9-2 into it.

Listing 9-2. *The Contents of the* app/app_helper.php *File*

```
1    <?
2    class AppHelper extends Helper {
3
4    }
5    ?>
```

Notice that on line 2 of Listing 9-2 the App helper is an extension of the Helper object. Now, whatever functions you place in this helper can be accessed by any of the helpers you may create. For now, I've left the AppHelper class empty, but later I'll use it to build some functionality into all the helpers to fit your customizations.

Creating the Helper File

Custom or third-party helper files are stored in the app/views/helpers folder and are named like elements—just the name of the helper followed by the .php extension. Inside the file, the helper's class is specified with the name of the helper and the word *Helper* as one word, camel-cased:

```
class CustomHelper extends AppHelper {
```

This helper will extend the App helper object, so you include that extension as well. Any object variables you want to be available to all functions in the helper can be specified like any class object:

```
var $variable = true;
```

Individual functions are created like typical PHP functions:

```
function myHelperFunction() { }
```

The helper function will, most of the time, be called by the view. Therefore, you need to return a value to be used in the view with the return command:

```
return '<p>Test Helper Function</p>';
```

The helper will be installed like any other built-in helper I've already discussed. In the view, the helper will be called as an object following the name specified in the file name and the class object declaration:

```
$custom->myHelperFunction();
```

Using Outside Helper Functions

You may want to extend the capabilities of one of Cake's built-in helper functions, combine the processes of a few functions, or use a process already defined in a function in your own custom helper. To do this, just specify the helpers to be used as referenced in the controller by filling in the var $helpers array:

```
var $helpers = array('Html','Ajax');
```

Then, within the helper file, use the outside helper functions with $this->Helper, as needed:

```
$this->Html->link('Use an Outside Function','/');
```

Making a Helper for Your Blog

Let's build some customized functions for your blog. The first function will simplify the displaying of comments with their Ajax voting links. To build this, you'll first need to create the helper itself. Create a new file named app/views/helpers/blog.php. In it, create the new BlogHelper class like so:

```
<?
class BlogHelper extends AppHelper {

}
?>
```

Including the Ajax Helper

Recall that you already built the Ajax voting feature into the comments in the app/views/posts/view.ctp file. To reduce this comments section into one line in the view, you can bring them into the $blog->comments() function. Notice, though, that the Ajax helper is already being used for the voting links. To make this helper's functions available in the Blog helper, you'll need to include the Ajax helper before creating the $blog->comments() function. On line 3 of the app/views/helpers/blog.php file, insert the following line:

```
var $helpers = array('Ajax');
```

Writing the Comments Function

Now that the Blog helper file is sufficiently prepared, let's create the $blog->comments() function (see Listing 9-3). Copy and paste lines 9–23 of the app/views/posts/view.ctp file (the comments loop) into this function with a little bit of processing around it as a starting point; then, you'll add some parameters and functionality into this function to make it portable to other areas of the site, if need be.

Listing 9-3. *The* `$blog->comments()` *Function in the Blog Helper*

```
1    function comments($comments=null) {
2        if (!empty($comments)) {
3            $out = null;
4            foreach($comments as $comment) {
5                $out .= '<div class="comment">
6                    <div id="vote_'.$comment['Comment']['id'].'">
7                    <div class="cast_vote">
8                        <ul>';
9                $out .= $this->Ajax->link('<li>up</li>','/comments/vote/up/'.➥
 $comment['Comment']['id'],array('update'=>'vote_'.$comment['Comment']['id']),➥
null,false);
10                $out .= $this->Ajax->link('<li>down</li>','/comments/vote/➥
down/'.$comment['Comment']['id'],array('update'=>'vote_'.$comment➥
['Comment']['id']),null,false);
11                $out .= '</ul>
12                    </div>
13                    <div class="vote">'.$comment['Comment']['votes'].'</div>
14                </div>
15                <p><b>'.$comment['Comment']['name'].'</b></p>
16                <p>'.$comment['Comment']['content'].'</p>
17                </div>';
18            }
19            return $this->output($out);
20        } else {
21            trigger_error(sprintf('No comments found', get_class($this)),➥
 E_USER_NOTICE);
22        }
23    }
```

In Listing 9-3, I've essentially translated the loop from the Posts view to be returned by the helper function. Using the `$out` variable, I'm able to loop through the `$comments` variable and catch all the iterations into this one array. Then on line 19, the final output of `$out` gets returned to the view. Notice that on line 19 I've used the `output()` function. This is a basic return function for handling the final output; it can be overridden in other subclasses for post-processing. When unaffected by post-processing methods, it will return the passed variable as is.

Line 21 uses the `trigger_error()` function to pass an error if no comments are passed to the helper function. This line passes the class itself (as `$this`) to be used in a debugging message.

Now that you've made the `$blog->comments` function, let's use it in the view. In the App controller load the Blog helper in the `var $helpers` array:

```
var $helpers = array('Html','Form','Ajax','Javascript','Blog');
```

Next, in the `app/views/posts/view.ctp` file, replace the comments loop on lines 9–23 with one line:

```
<?=$blog->comments($comments);?>
```

Refresh the Posts view, and you should see nothing change; this is good since it means that the helper is working properly.

Comparing Helpers and Elements

The current `$blog->comments()` function is not much different than an element; it essentially takes a variable and creates some view markup around it, which can be used in multiple views if necessary. A fundamental difference between helpers and elements should be noted, however. As it is, the `$blog->comments()` function really should be placed in an element rather than a helper for a couple reasons:

- Elements provide display markup to be used across multiple views without much logic; helpers generally include more logic tests and methods.

- Helpers are usually adaptable for any type of application, whereas elements are more specific to its application.

- Elements should not include several options to manipulate the displays; this is more a function of helpers.

Despite these suggestions, it may be more effective to group a series of view functions together in one helper file than to split them apart into elements. Taking the current `$blog->comments()` function from an element to a helper would require expanding the function to take on more dynamic methods. Right now, `$blog->comments()` is rather static, so the next step is to expand it to include more logic and options. By so doing, you make the function accessible in more scenarios than one, which is probably the best reason for writing a helper function.

Extending the Comments Function

The aspect of passing options to a helper function allows you to extend the function to include more customized possibilities. With the `$blog->comments()` function in particular, there are a couple of features that could be made custom for use across the application. First, the voting link might need to change depending on how you may want to use the function. Second, the voting link itself may need to change with different content from one area to the next. Third, the update element may also need to be adjusted for different areas in the site. A look into the built-in helper functions reveals that parameters are often used to allow for these customizations. Let's then extend the `$blog->comments()` function to include more parameters. In a way, this is the work of building customized helpers—to allow for specific operations to be used across the application for various uses.

In the `$blog->comments()` function, you'll allow for an `options` array that will contain the following parameters:

link: The voting link to be used for both up and down votes; optional override for upLink and downLink parameters

upLink: The voting link for up votes only

downLink: The voting link for down votes only

text: The contents of the voting links; optional override for upText and downText parameters

upText = 'up': The contents for the up voting links only

downText = 'down': The contents of the down voting links only

update = 'vote_'+comment ID: The ID for the HTML element to receive the returned Ajax response

To build these options into the function, consult Listing 9-4.

Listing 9-4. *The* Options *Array in the* $blog->comments() *Function*

```
1    function comments($comments=null,$options=array()) {
2        if (!empty($comments)) {
3            $out = null;
4
5            if (isset($options['link'])) {
6                $up = $down = $options['link'];
7            }
8
9            if (isset($options['upLink'])) {
10                $up = $options['upLink'];
11            }
12
13            if (isset($options['downLink'])) {
14                $down = $options['downLink'];
15            }
16
17            if (isset($options['text'])) {
18                $upText = $downText = $options['text'];
19            } else {
20                $upText = 'up';
21                $downText = 'down';
22            }
23
24            if (isset($options['upText'])) {
25                $upText = $options['upText'];
26            }
27
```

```
28              if (isset($options['downText'])) {
29                  $downText = $options['downText'];
30              }
31
32              if (isset($options['update'])) {
33                  $update = $options['update'];
34              }
35
36              foreach($comments as $comment) {
37                  if (empty($update) || !isset($options['update'])) {
38                      $update = 'vote_'.$comment['Comment']['id'];
39                  }
40                  $out .= '<div class="comment">
41                      <div id="vote_'.$comment['Comment']['id'].'">
42                      <div class="cast_vote">
43                          <ul>';
44                  $out .= $this->voteUpLink($comment['Comment']['id'],array(➡
'upLink'=>$up,'text'=>$upText,'update'=>$update));
45                  $out .= $this->voteDownLink($comment['Comment']['id'],array(➡
'downLink'=>$down,'text'=>$downText,'update'=>$update));
46                  $out .= '</ul>
47                      </div>
48                      <div class="vote">'.$comment['Comment']['votes'].'</div>
49                  </div>
50                  <p><b>'.$comment['Comment']['name'].'</b></p>
51                  <p>'.$comment['Comment']['content'].'</p>
52                  </div>';
53              }
54          return $this->output($out);
55      } else {
56          trigger_error(sprintf('No comments found', get_class($this)), ➡
E_USER_NOTICE);
57      }
58  }
```

Lines 9–39 of Listing 9-4 are all logic tests to check the options array for values. If values are present, then these lines pass them into variables to be used when the comments are rendered. If those values are not present, then some important defaults are generated.

Notice that lines 44–45 refer to the $blog->voteUpLink() and $blog->voteDownLink() functions. I've constructed these to strip out of the $blog->comments() function the methods for generating the voting links. You don't know yet whether you'll use these methods elsewhere for other views or other helper functions. In any case, it might be a good idea later to have these operations outside the $blog->comments() function, so let's build those functions after this one. See Listings 9-5 and 9-6 for how to create these new functions.

Listing 9-5. *The* $blog->voteUpLink() *Function*

```
1    function voteUpLink($id=null,$options=array()) {
2        if (isset($options['text'])) {
3            $text = $options['text'];
4        } else {
5            $text = 'up';
6        }
7
8        if (isset($options['update'])) {
9            $update = $options['update'];
10        } else {
11            $update = 'vote_'.$id;
12        }
13
14        $up = $options['upLink'].$id;
15        return $this->output($this->Ajax->link($text,$up,array('update'=>➥
$update),null,false));
16    }
```

Listing 9-6. *The* $blog->voteDownLink()*Function*

```
1    function voteDownLink($id=null,$options=array()) {
2        if (isset($options['text'])) {
3            $text = $options['text'];
4        } else {
5            $text = 'down';
6        }
7
8        if (isset($options['update'])) {
9            $update = $options['update'];
10        } else {
11            $update = 'vote_'.$id;
12        }
13
14        $down = $options['downLink'].$id;
15        return $this->output($this->Ajax->link($text,$down,array('update'=>➥
$update),null,false));
16    }
```

Again, in these functions, lines 2–14 of Listings 9-4 and 9-5 manage the options array. Line 15 returns the Ajax link for voting up and down a comment. Because all three of your Blog helper functions allow for options, you can now use these functions anywhere you want to display comments and provide Ajax comments voting.

Now that you've built the options array into the helper functions, you must change the use of the function in the Posts view. To make the $blog->comments() function work with your application, you'll need to specify the upLink and downLink parameters. Replace line 9 of the app/views/posts/view.ctp file with the following:

```
<?=$blog->comments($comments,array('upText'=>'<li>up</li>','downText'=>'<li>down➥
</li>','upLink'=>'/comments/vote/up/','downLink'=>'/comments/vote/down/'));?>
```

Refresh the Posts view, and you should see the comments all the same—except now, they are all managed by your custom Blog helper functions (see Figure 9-1).

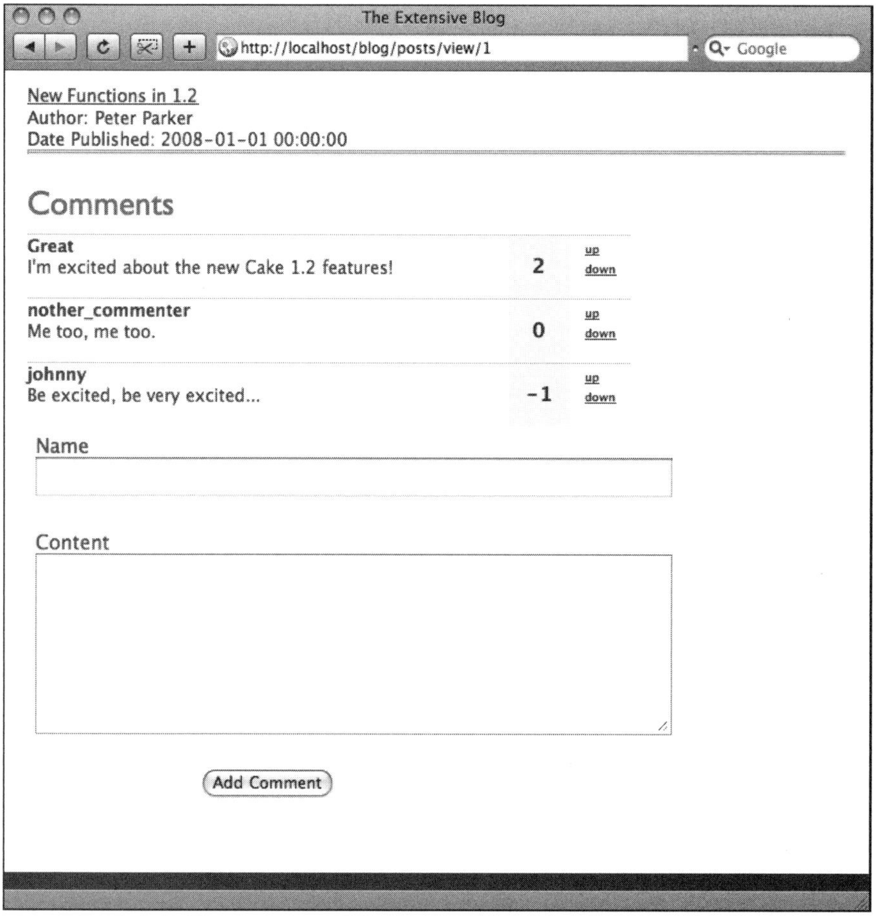

Figure 9-1. *The comments section now displayed by the* $blog->comments() *function*

Customizing Helper Variables

You've built a custom helper with functions to handle specific operations. But what about customizing the variables used by built-in helpers? Suppose you want to perform the same operation that is already written in the HTML helper but you want to change the display of the HTML helper's output. Rather than build a completely different helper to fit your customized output, you can simply alter the variables the HTML helper uses and then call the needed function.

Recall that you already created the App helper file in the app/ directory. There, you can intercept the global variables used by any helper and insert your own code. Open the cake/libs/view/helpers/html.php file to read the raw HTML helper code. Scroll down to line 47 and see the $tags array (as shown in Listing 9-7).

Listing 9-7. *The HTML Helper's* $tags *Array*

```
47    var $tags = array(
48–96        …
97        'error' => '<div%s>%s</div>'
98    );
```

I've deliberately skipped over lines 48–96 in Listing 9-7 because the same idea is repeated throughout the array. The HTML helper uses this array to construct the HTML tags that are returned with its functions. Changing one of these keys and values will change the output for the whole HTML helper. In other words, whenever the HTML helper, in any function, displays the error tag, you can replace its value on line 97 with your own, and all error tags will reflect the change.

The most direct way to alter the $tags array would be to create your own in the App helper. However, you would have to specify *all* tags used by the HTML helper, which would result in duplication between the App helper and the HTML helper. To trim the amount of data you supply to affect the $tags array, you can use the Helper object's loadConfig() function with the __construct() function.

In the App helper, insert the contents of Listing 9-8.

Listing 9-8. *The* __construct() *Function in the App Helper*

```
1    function __construct() {
2        parent::__construct();
3        $this->loadConfig();
4    }
```

This function will be called when any helper is included in a controller. Line 2 makes sure that all the default constructions of the Helper object are performed first. Then, on line 3 you've included the loadConfig() function. By default, this function will search for the tags.php file in the app/config folder and merge its contents with the $tags array. You can specify which file to merge by including its name in the function:

```
$this->loadConfig('blog');
```

In the previous example, the App helper will search for the app/config/blog.php file and merge its contents with the $tags array.

With the App helper as it is, you still need to create the app/config/tags.php file and write in the $tags array for the __construct() function to behave properly. Create this file, and insert Listing 9-9 into it.

Listing 9-9. *The* $tags *Array to Be Used in the App Helper*

```
<?
$tags = array(
    'button' => '<div class="button"><input type="%s" %s/></div>'
);
?>
```

Listing 9-9 wraps a <div> element around all input buttons used in the helper, which is not there by default. You can extend this array to include new tags that aren't already specified or to produce custom elements. In your $blog->comments() function, you do use some tags to produce the voting links, namely, <li> tags. In the custom tags.php file, you can insert a tag called vote with all the necessary markup to create a default tag for the helper to use without writing the markup in the helper file itself. Rewrite the $tags array in the app/config/tags.php file to include the contents of Listing 9-10.

Listing 9-10. *The* $tags *Array with the Vote Tag*

```
<?
$tags = array(
    'vote' => '<li>%s</li>'
);
?>
```

To use this tag in the Blog helper, go to the $blog->voteUpLink() function. On the last line of the function where the output is returned, replace the $text variable with the $tags['vote'] value. In keeping with how the $tags array is organized, you'll need to use PHP's sprintf() function to replace the %s character with the contents of $text (see Listing 9-11).

Listing 9-11. *Replacing the* $text *Parameter with the Vote Tag*

```
return $this->output($this->Ajax->link(sprintf($this->tags['vote'],$text) … );
```

Again, nothing should change in terms of the final output when you refresh the Posts view. But by building these options and variables into your Blog helper, you allow for more customization down the road. Now, instead of having to get into the code of the helper itself, you can edit a configuration file (tags.php) to adjust the displays. Keep this in mind when building customized helpers. You never know where these functions will end up, especially when you distribute them through the Internet or pull them into other Cake applications.

Making as many features of the helpers editable in other areas like a config file or customizable in the views through the use of parameters allows the helper to be more portable and, ultimately, useful.

The Vote Tag

Listing 9-11 showed how to replace the `$text` parameter in the `$blog->voteUpLink()` function with the vote tag from the `tags.php` file. In this exercise, do the same for the `$blog->voteDownLink()` function. You can also look for ways to generate other tags for use in the `$blog->comments()` function. Consult the PHP manual for help with the `sprintf()` function to extend the capabilities of your custom tags.

Summary

This chapter explored Cake's built-in helpers. The two used in most Cake applications are the HTML and Form helpers. Together, they simplify rendering HTML and processing forms. Thanks to the Form helper, passing along user form submissions is easy and provides the controller and model with a standardized method for handling data. Several other helpers are available in Cake. This chapter outlined what these helpers are and what functions they include. Many times you will want to create your own custom helper. I showed how to write one for your blog application that renders the comments for the view. By using this helper, you can reduce the amount of code in the view to a couple of strings. Customizing helper variables is one way to expand the functionality of the helper. This chapter also explained how to provide a set of output variables that make the helper more portable. In Chapter 10, you'll move to routing in Cake and examine how to customize URL structures for your applications.

CHAPTER 10

■■■

Routes

Out of the box, Cake intercepts all URLs and maps them to their appropriate controllers and actions. This is a wonderful aspect of the framework that improves the speed of developing applications. Rather than having long strings of passed variables in the URL or creating dozens of individual scripts to handle every function in the application, Cake's routing system manages all the requests, as you saw in previous chapters. But what about customizing the routing scheme? Or what if you want to generate non-HTML files such as PDFs, RSS feeds, or some kind of XML output? And what about search engine optimization? For these purposes, Cake's routing features will remove the headache of mapping URLs, handling dynamic requests, and customizing the paths and URL structure of the application.

Almost all the main routing action will take place in the `app/config/routes.php` file. All the routes and their configurations are stored in this file and use a specific syntax. A few default routes, which serve to handle the main URLs, are already written to the `routes.php` file. By default, Cake parses the passed values listed between slashes and derives a path to controllers and actions as well as passing parameters to those actions. By using magic variables, arguments, extensions, parameters, and other features, you can fully manipulate the routes to fit your application and still maintain the MVC structure.

Caution Remember that the `routes.php` page is cascading, meaning that the order of routes matters. If Cake resolves a URL with one route, it will immediate end there and not proceed to check other routes down the page. Although this generally doesn't affect the overall application, it can make a difference if you are working with more complex routes that occur in the same controller or action.

The Basic Route

As you can see in the default `routes.php` configuration file, the basic route is called as the `Router::connect()` function with a path as well as an array storing route parameters:

```
Router::connect('/', array('controller' => 'pages', 'action' => 'display', 'home'));
```

The previous line is the base route for the application. It connects URL elements to the Pages controller's Display action and sends the value home as a parameter to be used in the action. By specifying another controller and action, you can change the base route so that, by default, the home page is other than the Pages controller's Display action.

The first value in the `Router::connect()` function is the path that the routing engine has received. If it checks out, then the parameters array will be called, and the user will be taken to whatever is specified there. Another way of looking at this path is like an if-then statement; if the URL entered has no parameters but the base URL only, then pass the value home to the Display action in the Pages controller. You can specify the value by hand or use placeholders to accept all possible values for that URL parameter:

```
Router::connect('/articles/*', array('controller'=>'posts','action'=>'index'));
```

The previous line shows a new method for connecting with the Posts controller in your blog application. By using the asterisk in the path, you're essentially telling the router to accept and pass along anything it finds following the word *articles*. As in the base path example, the path will be tested like an if-then statement: if the supplied URL begins with the word *articles*, then pass along whatever else follows in the URL to the Posts controller. By default, the Index action will be called. You've more or less constructed an alias for the Posts controller. Now, if you wanted, you could enter all your links that point to the Posts controller as if they pointed to an Articles controller.

Arguments

Traditionally, assigning values to request variables is done in PHP by constructing a serialized string with arguments:

```
http://localhost/script.php?variable=value&another_var=another_val
```

In the previous code, the arguments in the string are `variable` and `another_var`. When a controller action interacts with a variety of arguments and combinations of possible arguments, then it may be necessary to construct the URL string differently than Cake's default route pattern.

Arguments in the router appear in the URL with a colon followed by a value:

```
http://localhost/blog/posts/view/id:5/set:2
```

In the previous code, the arguments are `id` and `set`, and their values are 5 and 2. Usually, this example would be better managed without the arguments in view, namely, with just the values. But when the action uses components such as the Paginator, arguments may need to be passed along for the component to work properly. For instance, in the case of the Paginator, normal Cake URLs are defaulted to the first page of the data set. But by adding arguments to the string, the Paginator is able to retrieve another page in the data set:

```
http://localhost/blog/posts/index/page:2/sort:id/direction:asc
```

Passed arguments are contained in the `passedArgs` array. The previous string would store the values like so:

```
$this->passedArgs = Array(
    'page'=>2,
    'sort'=>'id',
    'direction'=>'asc'
);
```

Arguments are passed to the controller as keys and values in this array unless it is bypassed in the `routes.php` configuration file.

One important use for arguments is as Cake's way of passing variables to the actions. Notice that because the router has found arguments in the URL string, it does not pass them as variables in the action:

```
http://localhost/blog/posts/view/5/comments:false
```

The previous URL would *not* result in the second parameter (`comments:false`) being passed in the action, like the first parameter:

```
function view($id=null) {
    $displayComments = $this->passedArgs['comments'];
…
```

This distinction between typical action parameters and passed arguments can make a difference when constructing methods in the controller. The action can still execute without any passed arguments, which can be an important option depending on the specific needs of the action.

Reverse Routing

Web applications have begun to prefer friendly URLs to convoluted URL strings. URLs like `www.site.com/cart/item/race_car` work better, for example, than `www.site.com/index.php?page=cart&item=race_car`. This is happening not just for search engine optimization purposes or to make the application more accessible for users but to facilitate simple changes to the overall routing of the application. Consider the difficulty, if a web application were built on GET variables, in revamping its entire routing structure. New problems would present themselves in maintaining legacy URLs and at the same time in implementing new ones. Much would depend on the application itself, but in general, it would take some added functions to reverse URLs.

Lookups

By default, URL lookups run through the router in one direction, meaning that when a link is clicked, the router performs a lookup and maps the appropriate controller, action, and parameters. Entering `/posts/view/17` will cause the router to look up where the Posts controller's View action is in the application and pass the parameter to it. But what about lookups going the other way? Suppose you wanted to write a link and have the router look up how to construct the link. This would be a *reverse lookup*, or a lookup in the reverse direction.

Rewriting URLs in the Router

In the blog application, suppose that at some future date you needed to stop using the Posts controller name in the URL. This would mean going through the entire application changing every instance of a link to the Posts controller to the new route. That would obviously slow down development and make it harder to change the structure of the site. Or, you could use Cake's reverse routing mechanism to rewrite all URLs pointing to the Posts controller.

Verbose Linking

To reverse a route, you first must use the verbose method for writing links. Instead of writing a path string in the $html->link() function, you include some URL parameters in an array like this:

```
$html->link('View Post',array('controller'=>'posts','action'=>'view',$post➡
['Post']['id']));
```

This array does not tell the function what the URL path is but rather gives it the necessary parameters to construct the path dynamically. Although this array does result in more characters being entered to put a link together, it allows you to use the router to intercept any links in the entire application in one place, the routes.php configuration file, and not have to go back and find links that needed changing.

To complete the reverse route, you need to enter only a new connection string in the routes.php configuration that changes the route:

```
Router::connect('/articles/*', array('controller'=>'posts','action'=>'view'));
```

Without using the verbose array in the $html->link() function, the router would still try to access the Posts controller and the word *posts* would still appear in the URL. However, now that you've specified that you want the word *articles* to link up with the Posts controller, the router will construct the paths in the application for you. Wherever links call for both the Posts controller and the View action, the router will substitute *articles* in the path. For example, the link that would normally point here:

```
/posts/view/25
```

will be dynamically changed by the router to point here:

```
/articles/25
```

Remember that for reverse routing to work across the whole application, you will need to use verbose linking consistently.

Admin Routing

Many applications require some kind of administrative area to manage web site functions with a user interface. Making entirely different controllers to manage these administrative features would contravene Cake's conventions. But how do you distinguish between front-end users and site administrators in building the application? The router can dynamically manage admin routing for you, which means you can make some actions available only to an administrator while the URLs still follow the Cake standard structure.

Rather than build your own controller to manage administrator actions, like so:

```
posts_admin_controller.php
```

you can point all links to the following to the Posts controller:

```
http://localhost/blog/admin/posts
```

First you must choose an admin prefix and then name your actions and view files accordingly.

Choosing an Admin Prefix

The admin prefix can be any one word you like. Most use `admin` (as in the previous example), but you could make it `webmaster` or `superuser` if you like. The admin routing must be turned on in the core configuration, and the prefix must also be provided there. Open the `app/config/core.php` file, and scroll down to the admin routing preference:

```
Configure::write('Routing.admin', 'admin');
```

Around line 69, you should see the preference, commented out; uncomment it to activate admin routing. Notice that by default, the prefix is set to `admin`. You can enter any string here that meets standard HTTP URL syntax as a prefix. The router will map this prefix to the appropriate admin actions.

Linking Admin Actions and Views

Once the prefix is defined in the core configuration, you can begin to create administrator actions. These actions may appear in any controller; they only need to be named with the prefix included. Suppose you wanted to change the Edit and Add actions in your Posts controller to be accessible via an admin route. You would need to rename the actions in the controller to `admin_edit` and `admin_add`, respectively.

The prefix is attached to the name of the action with an underscore. So, if the prefix were defined in the core configuration as `superuser`, then these Edit and Add actions would need to have the `superuser` prefix added to the name:

```
function superuser_edit($id=null) { …
```

When some actions are changed to be accessed through the admin route, these actions' views will need to be renamed as well. The view files need to be named to link with the corresponding actions. So, the `admin_edit` action will need its view file to be named `admin_edit.ctp`.

These admin actions are not called in the URL with the underscore. For example, the Admin Edit action is not executed by typing this:

```
http://localhost/blog/posts/admin_edit/16
```

but by using the admin prefix before the controller name:

```
http://localhost/blog/admin/posts/edit/16
```

To restrict these admin routes, an authentication system must be built to check users against the database and grant them privileges. At least with this routing mechanism you can create the necessary paths to differentiate between administrators and front-end users.

Baking Admin Routes

The Bake script automates the process of building admin routes. When creating controllers or views with Bake and using the "build interactively" feature, you can enter options to build the actions and views with admin routing. In other words, simply tell Bake when it asks if you want admin routing what the admin prefix is, and it will not only build the typical CRUD actions and views but will do so with the admin prefix added to action names and view files.

Route Parameters

You may need to specify which sections of the URL correspond to parameters in the controller. With route parameters, you can tell the router how to parse the URL. Consider the Posts controller. You may want a particular route to be called only when this controller is entered in the URL. But what about routes that are called for certain actions without using the controller name? In this scenario, you would need to specify a route parameter for the controller; in other words, the router will need to know that the first parameter in the path represents the controller and the other parameters represent other elements. For example, if you wanted to affect the View action for all controllers, you could enter a route along these lines:

```
Router::connect('/:controller/view',array('action'=>'read'));
```

Here, whenever a View action is called, it will point to the Read action instead. You've used the route parameter :controller to tell the router that the first part of the path represents the controller to map.

Route parameters may be anything as long as they are one word, are preceded by a colon, and are defined in the parameters array. They can be checked by magic variables or regular expressions for the route to be activated. Route parameters do not need to be separated by slashes. Symbols such as slashes, dashes, colons, and ampersands can be used to separate parameters since the router can detect the route parameter.

Magic Variables

What about passing variables through the routing engine? You can accomplish this in part with magic variables. These include common action names, date elements, and ID numbers. In other words, the router will automatically detect months and years in the URL if you want and will determine where to map those types of requests.

For instance, most blog applications manage their posts by date. To do this, you'd need to use magic variables in the Router::connect() function:

```
Router::connect('/:controller/:month-:day-:year', array('action'=>'view',array(➥
'month'=>$Month,'day'=>$Day,'year'=>$Year)));
```

You can see that in the path you've entered some placeholders—specifically a controller, month, day, and year placeholder between each set of slashes. These are "magic variables," and they always begin with a colon. In other words, you've defined the slots in the URL and have given them a name. The first one will contain the controller name, the second will contain a month value, and so forth. The router will check these slots against the magic variables used in the parameters array, and if they return true, it will pass them along to the specified controller's View action.

Values entered in the place of magic variable slots in the URL are passed to the action through the $this->params array. In the previous example, the given month would be available in the array as this:

```
$this->params['month']
```

and so forth. The $this->params array may be checked or called in the controller and the view.

The available magic *functions* include the following:

- $Action
- $Day
- $Month
- $Year
- $ID

Each will automatically determine whether the supplied value checks out. For example, the $Action magic variable checks for common action names such as View, Delete, Edit, and so on. The $Year magic variable checks for a typical year value, and $ID checks for a valid whole number.

Using this route in the blog application, the following URL:

```
http://localhost/blog/posts/12-24-2008
```

would format the $this->params array like so:

```
$this->params = Array(
    'month' => 12,
    'day' => 24,
    'year' => 2008,
…
);
```

Custom Expressions

Using regular expressions in conjunction with route parameters, custom logic tests can be performed before a route is mapped. These are specified in the same array where magic variables are used.

```
Router::connect('/:controller/:id/:month-:day-:year',array('action'=>'view'),➥
array('month'=>$Month,'day'=>$Day,'year'=>$Year,'id'=>'[\d]+'));
```

Here the ID is tested in the route by use of the :id route parameter and the regular expression definition in the parameters array. If the ID slot contains a value that passes the regular expression test [\d]+ (and the other slots pass as well), then the route will be mapped. If the ID slot does not contain a valid integer, then the route will be bypassed, and the router will move on to the next definition in the routes.php configuration file.

The Pass Key

So far, any values in the URL that are passed by a route that uses a nondefault method are placed in the $this->params array; arguments are placed in the $this->passedArgs array. But what about mapping values so that they are passed to the action as a typical parameter? The Pass key allows you to accomplish this. In the mapping array (which contains the controller and action definitions), add the Pass key with an assigned array. Then, provide values in the array that correspond to the route parameters you are using. For instance, the route with parameters title and id can have their values appear in the action like normal Cake parameters like so:

```
Router::connect('/posts/:title/:id',array('controller'=>'posts','action'=>'view',➥
'pass'=>array('title','id')));
```

The router will now pass the values contained in the :title and :id slots to the action in the function definition:

```
function view($title=null,$id=null) { …
```

This is beneficial because it can save time; you won't have to work through the $this->params array to work with passed values.

Parsing Files with Extensions Other Than .php

As of yet you have mapped only routes to controllers and actions in Cake. What about other file types such as RSS or XML files? Because of how Cake's .htaccess files are constructed, the server will supply files when they are directly referenced and available on the server. So, you can feasibly write static files such as RSS feeds, PDF files, or XML files and place these files in the app/webroot directory, and they can be accessed directly by entering the file name in the URL. But the router can also parse extensions, which makes it possible to use Cake to dynamically create and render non-HTML file types.

The Process

Understanding the process of how the router parses extensions is key to building the right route configurations and other Cake elements. First, you need to tell the router to look out for any URLs that point to a specific extension. Let's say you want to dynamically build an RSS feed for the blog application. Then you would need to use the Router::parseExtensions() function for the router to detect when the .rss extension is called in the URL:

```
Router::parseExtensions('rss');
```

Next, you need to tell Cake what kind of MIME type this extension is. Some extensions already get recognized by default, but others need to be defined. In the case of the RSS extension, Cake won't need the MIME type to be defined, but to see how this is done, open the App controller and add these lines:

```
var $components = array('RequestHandler');
function beforeFilter() {
    $this->RequestHandler->setContent('rss','application/rss+xml');
}
```

Now Cake can respond to the browser and the HTTP request with the correct MIME type definition. But the last step is to create the layout to wrap the standard file contents around the view. Once the layout is defined correctly, the controller can include actions that output RSS in the view rather than HTML, and the browser will recognize the route as a file even though Cake is dynamically creating it.

Creating the RSS Feed

Knowing the process for the router to parse the RSS extension, let's build an RSS feed into the blog. First, write the parse extensions function in the routes.php configuration file near the top:

```
Router::parseExtensions('rss');
```

Next, run the RequestHandler component in the App controller to filter HTTP requests through the controller.

Listing 10-1 contains all the contents of the App controller. Notice that this uses the beforeFilter() function to run the RequestHandler component's setContent() function before every controller action is called.

Listing 10-1. *The App Controller with the RequestHandler Component in Use*

```
1   <?
2   class AppController extends Controller {
3       var $helpers = array('Html','Form','Ajax','Javascript','Blog');
4       var $components = array('RequestHandler');
5
6       function beforeFilter() {
7           $this->RequestHandler->setContent('rss','application/rss+xml');
8       }
9   }
10  ?>
```

Now that the router and the App controller can handle the HTTP requests that contain RSS file extensions, you need only to create the necessary layouts and views to generate the feed.

Extension Layouts

For the RSS extension, the router will look to the app/layouts/rss directory to find the default RSS layout. Create the default.ctp layout file, and place it in this directory. Paste into this new file the contents of Listing 10-2.

Listing 10-2. *The File Contents of* app/layouts/rss/default.ctp

```
<?=$rss->document(null,$content_for_layout);?>
```

With the help of the built-in $rss->document() function, you don't have to worry about knowing the format of a standard RSS file. In the event that you use a file type not included in Cake's helpers, you would have to supply the proper headers yourself; of course, this will depend on the appropriate syntax and specifications of the file type in question.

The Controller Action

Now, all you have to do is create an action to act as the file name for the parsed extension. For the blog, you will have the RSS feed be accessible as follows:

```
http://localhost/blog/posts/feed.rss
```

So, let's create the Feed action in the Posts controller (see Listing 10-3). You should not append the extension in the function definition. This action will be like the Index action in that you want to provide only the most recent five posts for the feed.

Listing 10-3. *The Feed Action in the Posts Controller*

```
1    function feed() {
2        $this->set('posts',$this->Post->feed());
3    }
```

Notice that line 2 of Listing 10-3 references a model function named feed(). Since the RSS output will require an array formatted with keys and values matching a specific syntax, you ought to let the model handle the data. In the Post model, paste in the feed() function shown in Listing 10-4.

Listing 10-4. *The Feed Function in the Post Model*

```
1    function feed() {
2        $posts = $this->find('all',array('order'=>'date DESC','limit'=>5));
3        $out = array();
4        foreach ($posts as $post) {
5            foreach ($post as $key=>$val) {
6                if ($key == 'Post') {
7                    $out[$val['id']]['pubDate'] = date('D, d M Y H:i:s +0',➥
strtotime($val['date']));
8                    $out[$val['id']]['title'] = $val['name'];
9                    $out[$val['id']]['description'] = $val['content'];
10                    $out[$val['id']]['content'] = $val['content'];
11                }
12            }
13        }
14        return $out;
15    }
```

Line 2 of Listing 10-4 retrieves the five most recent posts and places them in the $posts array. The rest of the function cycles through this array and pulls out only the parts you want to appear in the feed. Notice how lines 7–10 name the key in the output array after the actual tag names that will appear in the RSS feed. This is because once you code the Feed view, you'll use the RSS helper to render the tags. The RSS helper will need the array to be formatted this way to fetch the right data for each tag.

Now that the data is handled correctly and the layout is working right, all you have left is the Feed view.

The Feed View

Finally, create the Feed view to match the action (see Listing 10-5). It will need to use the RSS helper to render the various tags, so be sure to include this helper in the Posts controller or App controller (see Chapter 9 for more information on including helpers in the controller). Notice that the Feed view file is stored in a folder in the Posts views folder named `rss`.

Listing 10-5. *The* `app/views/posts/rss/feed.ctp` *File Contents*

```
<?=$rss->channel(null,array('title'=>'Extensive Blog','description'=>'My Blog',➥
'language'=>'en-us'));?>
<? foreach($posts as $post): ?>
<?=$rss->item(null,$post);?>
<? endforeach;?>
</channel>
```

The RSS helper here takes care of building the channel and the item tags automatically. You've passed the `$post` array that has been formatted correctly in the `Post` model, and now the process is complete. Open the new feed in any news aggregator, or use your browser to subscribe to the feed. You should end up with a valid RSS feed instead of an HTML page thanks to the router parsing the extension and the controller handling the request properly.

Custom Routes Exercise

This chapter explored some of the methods for building custom routes in Cake. For this exercise, construct a route that will display blog posts by their date and ID. Providing the correct route configuration is only half the problem; be sure to rebuild the View action to run the lookup correctly. Also build the admin route to handle editing and adding blog posts. You have completed the exercise correctly if posts are editable by accessing `http://localhost/blog/admin/posts/edit/{id}` rather than with the standard path to edit and add.

Summary

Rewriting URLs for the application is made much easier by editing Cake's routing configuration file. Not only can you make URLs friendlier with the `app/config/routes.php` file, but you can even set up reverse routes, or routes that are dynamically mapped by the dispatcher; just use verbose linking syntax when creating links, and Cake will automatically change all URL strings for any controllers and actions you specify. The router also includes an admin routing feature with which you can attach a prefix to any action name and view file, and Cake will map URLs containing the prefix to these files. This is useful for distinguishing between CRUD actions that should be accessed only by an administrator and those that are available to a public user. For applications that create output as non-HTML files, the dispatcher can parse extensions. For instance, in this chapter I described how to use Cake to generate an RSS feed as an `.rss` file. When a URL containing the `.rss` extension is entered, the router detects this extension and maps the request accordingly. Now that you understand how to customize URLs and other paths in Cake, it's time to explore more of Cake's advanced features. In Chapter 11, I'll explain components and utilities, which can dramatically enhance your Cake application and cut down on several web-related tasks.

CHAPTER 11

■■■

Components and Utilities

Cake uses helpers to extend the functionality of views. By placing several view functions in helpers, not only do your views remain light but the application is better organized. There is no precise method for how to organize functions in a helper other than keeping order and maintaining consistency in the application. Helpers are to the view what components and utilities are to the controller. In a way, you could think of components as "controller helpers."

Why Use Components?

But you may ask, why have components when there's an App controller? Shouldn't the App controller hold all the functions used by multiple controllers? Yes and no. The App controller does hold more generalized actions, or actions that more than one controller will use. Rather than employ the requestAction() function to allow a controller to access a function in another controller, you could just place the function in the App controller and scale it to be brought across the application into multiple controllers.

Consider the actions in the App controller like you consider display elements in the layout; parts of the view that you want to be visible across all views. Multiple views should be placed in a layout, and in a similar way, actions that will be used across controllers should be placed in the App controller. However, there are still helpers for the views that are used for *specific* display output tasks. The $html->link() helper function, for example, can be used only in the view because it generates HTML output, but being repeated throughout multiple views, it makes sense to house this function in a helper file rather than in the layout or in the controller. Components serve a similar purpose in Cake applications in the sense that they house specific functions that the controller or multiple controllers can use.

For example, consider the built-in components in Cake. Some of these are the Auth, Session, and RequestHandler components. Their functions all serve to specifically help the controller perform actions relating to their specific method; actions in the authentication component all have to do with helping the controller manage user authentication processes, and so forth. In a sense, helpers are *portable view functions* in that they can be distributed and pulled into any Cake application and work in a specific way to enhance and simplify the processes the views may need. Similarly, components are *portable controller functions* that serve a specific purpose and can be distributed to any controller in any Cake application.

Using Components

All components are stored in the app/controllers/components directory and are pulled into the controller like helpers, with the $components array. Like other parameters, components must be camel-cased and separated in the array by commas. Built-in components as well as custom ones must be included in the $components array to work in the controller, and like helpers, the App controller can include components for use in any or all controllers. See Listing 11-1.

Listing 11-1. *Including Components in the Controller with the $components Array*

```
var $components = array('Session','RequestHandler');
```

Once a component is included in the controller, the controller references its functions by using the $this identifier. Remember to specify the component like you do with models: $this followed by the camel-cased name of the component and the function in use. Listing 11-2.

Listing 11-2. *Running a Component Function in the Controller*

```
$user = $this->Session->read('User');
```

Components are not intended to work directly with the database, so the component does not do much more than return a variable, a string, or an array for the controller to use. If database calls are necessary, the controller using the component ought to run these calls through the model and provide the component with the necessary data. This does not mean that the components are limited to logic tests or reformatting forwarded data; like the Session and Cookie components, functions here can write to outside files or process images, and so forth.

Besides allowing for custom components, Cake comes with several built-in components and utilities. Before building your own components, let's first examine what Cake has to offer and explore how these component functions might improve an application.

Using Built-in Components

Like the helpers, Cake has a wealth of component functions that make running processes in the controller much easier. In fact, some components are intended to work hand in hand with helpers like the Session component. Running some functions in the controller makes it easier to organize and format the data forwarded on to the view for use by the Session helper. Knowing what built-in components can do for your controllers will save you from "reinventing the wheel" and help you exploit some of the snazzy functions that make Cake such an attractive framework.

In each of the following descriptions, I'll give a basic overview of what the component offers and list some of its functions. In the future, more functions may be added to these components, and sometimes third-party components will extend them too. Cake's core components are stored in the cake/libs/controller/components folder; if you'd like to take a look at the code itself, refer to the component files there.

Authentication

The Auth component helps with managing user authentication of the application. Many times you may want an area of the site to be protected from ordinary users. Common processes such as logging in to view an area of the site are made easier by the Auth component. Like other components, it needs to be included in the $components array to be available in the controller:

```
var $components = array('Auth');
```

With the Auth component, you can require authentication for miscellaneous areas of the application such as models, controllers, or other objects. Auth also provides methods for automating logging in and automatically redirecting the user to accessible areas of the site. A database table containing stored user information is necessary for the Auth component to work correctly.

Setting Up the Users Table

By default, Auth will look for a table named users with fields named username and password. Of course, these default parameters can be changed by entering custom parameters into the component before runtime. Whatever the case, a table somewhere in the database will need to be present to store all the users and their passwords. The users table doesn't need to store only username and password fields; it can also include roles, privileges, e-mail, and more. You'll have to tell Auth how to use these types of metadata.

The users table is already built into your blog application. Because the Auth component hashes all passwords, you'll need to make sure the password field has enough space to store the hashes. Remember that Security.salt value in the core configuration? The Auth component will use this salt value to generate its hashes, so putting a more complicated string in this preference will improve the security of your passwords.

With the users table ready to store usernames and passwords, you can implement the Auth component in your blog application. First let's initialize some parameters in the Posts controller.

Initializing Variables

Several parameters need to be set for Auth to work correctly. You specify these parameters by setting variables in the beforeFilter() controller action for the controller that will require authorization before letting the user access it. In this case, you will want to block out certain editing and deleting actions in the blog except for logged-in users. In the Posts controller, you need to tell the Auth component which actions are allowed and where to redirect the user upon a successful login. Listing 11-3 contains the beforeFilter() action for the Posts controller.

Listing 11-3. *Some Auth Parameters in the beforeFilter() Action*

```
1    function beforeFilter() {
2        $this->Auth->loginAction = array('controller'=>'users','action'=>'login');
3        $this->Auth->allow('index','view');
4        $this->Auth->redirectLogin = array('controller'=>'posts','action'=>'add');
5    }
```

Notice in Listing 11-3 that each class variable is set like any typical PHP variable. On line 3, I used the `allow` function to tell the Auth component which actions don't require authentication to be accessed. You do not need to specify the login and logout actions; otherwise, this will trip up the Auth component; it automatically assumes these functions are accessible to everyone.

Now that the Auth component has been called in the controller and the `beforeFilter()` action sets some parameters for Auth to use; Auth will check each action against what you've specified. If a request is made for an action that is not allowed, Auth will require the user to log in for access, which is specified in line 2 of Listing 11-3. In this case, the user will be redirected to the Login action in the Users controller (which hasn't been created yet). Auth will not be run if the user requests the Index and View actions in the Posts controller.

The next step is to create the Login action in the Users controller. Because the Auth component does almost all the work, you will need only to create the view with the username and password fields.

HASHED PASSWORDS

Because the Auth component requires that stored passwords be hashed, setting up user passwords can be tricky. Using Auth's `password()` function, you can pass a string, and Auth will return the hash. This same hashing process will be applied to whatever the user submits as a password and will be compared to the database, so you will need to store the hashed version of the user passwords and not a plain-text version. I've included a password generator with the following line:

```
$this->set('password',$this->Auth->password($this->data['User']['password']));
```

Of course, in the view, I'll need to provide a form with an input field named `password` for this to work, as well as a view to display what `Auth->password()` returns. If a form view elsewhere in the site creates new user accounts, it must use the `Auth->password()` function when saving the password.

Logging In

As long as the view that renders the login form is named appropriately (in other words, its names correspond to the parameters set in the `beforeFilter()` function), the Auth component will automatically check the `$this->data` array for the username and password and check it using the `userModel` and `fields` settings. Listing 11-4 shows the view file for the Users Login action.

Listing 11-4. *The app/views/users/login.ctp File*

```
1    <h1>Log In</h1>
2    <? if ($session->check('Message.auth')) $session->flash('auth');?>
3    <?=$form->create('User',array('action'=>'login'));?>
4    <?=$form->input('username');?>
5    <?=$form->input('password',array('type'=>'password'));?>
6    <?=$form->end('Login');?>
```

Simple enough—the Login view contains a form to render input fields for the username and password and submits it to the Login action. If there are any errors, like an incorrect match, they will be displayed in line 2 with the flash function.

To complete the login process, you need only to prepare the Users controller. Listing 11-5 shows the contents of the Users controller with the login function.

Listing 11-5. *The Auth Component in the Users Controller*

```
1    <?
2    class UsersController extends AppController {
3        var $name = 'Users';
4        var $components = array('Auth');
5
6        function beforeFilter() {
7            $this->Auth->allow('*');
8        }
9
10        function login() {
11
12        }
```

You can see that the Login action is empty. This is because the Auth component takes care of everything for you; you only need to specify the action so that Cake appropriately renders the Login view. Line 7 shows the use of the asterisk in the Auth->allow() function. This tells the Auth component to allow all actions in the current controller.

With the Users controller working correctly with the Auth component and the Login action and view provided, Auth can now manage authentication for the Posts controller. Try editing a post, and you'll notice that the Auth component requires you to log in.

Logging Out

Logging a user out is even easier than logging one in. Simply add the Auth->logout() function to the Users controller, as shown in Listing 11-6.

Listing 11-6. *The Logout Action in the Users Controller*

```
14    function logout() {
15        $this->redirect($this->Auth->logout());
16    }
```

Now, whenever the user requests `http://localhost/blog/users/logout`, they will be logged out by the Auth component, and the session will be deleted. The user will need to log back in to access blocked actions.

Checking a User's Role

The Auth component can check for a user's role to see whether the user is an administrator. To do so, you will need to add one more field to the `users` table: `role`. See Listing 11-7.

Listing 11-7. *The SQL Query for Adding the Role Field in the* `users` *Table*

```
ALTER TABLE `users` ADD `role` varchar(50) DEFAULT 'www'
```

Because the Auth component does not check user roles by default, you will need to run your own login process instead. First, in the Posts controller, you must tell the Auth component not to perform its default logic:

```
$this->Auth->authorize = 'controller';
```

This line essentially tells Auth to look in the active controller for an action named `isAuthorized()`. In this function, you'll run your own authorization logic; if it returns `true`, then the user is authorized, and so forth. Now let's create the `isAuthorized()` function to check the user's role. See Listing 11-8.

Listing 11-8. *The* `isAuthorized()` *Function in the Posts Controller*

```
1    function isAuthorized() {
2        if ($this->Auth->user('role') == 'admin') {
3            return true;
4        } else {
5            return false;
6        }
7    }
```

Line 2 performs the test. Using the `Auth->user()` function and passing the value `role`, you're telling Auth to look for a field named `role` and see whether it contains `admin`. If the user is not given the admin role in the `users` table, then he will not be authorized to view anything other than the Index and View actions.

This same check can be accomplished in the model rather than the controller. Rather than set `Auth->authorize` to `controller`, set it to `model` instead. Then run the `isAuthorized()` function in the model rather than the controller. The function will need to include the `$user`, `$controller`, and `$action` parameters to work in the model (see Listing 11-9).

Listing 11-9. *The* `isAuthorized()` *Function in the* Post *Model*

```
1   function isAuthorized($user, $controller, $action) {
2       if ($user['User']['role'] == 'admin') {
3           return true;
4       } else {
5           return false;
6       }
7   }
```

The $user array will contain the Auth component's retrieval of the user record where the username and password match, so line 2 uses this array rather than the `Auth->user()` function. Both methods for checking a user's role will work; following the convention of having larger models than controllers will mean that most of the time you'll check user roles in the model.

Using Other Auth Parameters and Functions

The following is a list of other parameters that can be used with the Auth component. They are used to customize the way in which Auth manages user logins, sessions, and authentication.

`deny( actions )`

> `actions`: The actions, separated by commas, which should be denied access without authentication

`hashPasswords( data[array] )`

> `data`: Takes values assigned to keys named `password` in an array and returns their hashed equivalents

`$userModel = 'User';`

> Used to customize the table name where users are stored. By default this is set to `User`. Be sure to use the model name, not the table name (for example, the `bloggers` table would need to be set to `Blogger` here).

`$fields = array('username'=>'username','password'=>'password');`

> This array can be changed to reflect customized field names for the username and password.

`$loginAction = array('admin'=>false,'controller'=>'users','action'=>'login');`

> Setting the keys in this array to other controllers or actions tells Auth where to run the Login action. Admin routing (see Chapter 10) and subsequent actions can be used by setting `admin` to `true`.

`$loginRedirect = array('controller'=>'users','action'=>'index');`

> This parameter tells Auth where to redirect the user after a successful login.

`$loginError = 'Login failed. Invalid username or password.';`

The error message displayed in the event of a login error can be customized here.

```
$autoRedirect = true;
```

If you set this parameter to `false`, the Auth component will not automatically redirect the user after authenticating. Other checks can be run in the Login action after a successful authentication occurs, such as writing information to or checking the contents of a cookie or checking other session variables.

```
$ajaxLogin = null;
```

When doing Ajax-based logins, set this preference to the view the file that should be displayed in the event of an unsuccessful login.

Session

The Session component handles various methods for reading, writing, starting, and destroying sessions.

Some settings may be manipulated to change how Cake saves sessions in the core configuration. The `Session.save` parameter in the core configuration file contains one of three possibilities: `php`, `cake`, and `database`. By default, this value is set to `php`, which means that sessions will be saved depending on the current PHP settings on the host. Setting this to `cake` will tell Cake to write session information in temporary files in the `app/tmp` folder. The third option, `database`, requires that a table be present in the database that has corresponding fields where Cake can save session information. The necessary SQL statements to generate this table are found in the `app/config/sql/session.sql` file. Simply run this file through your database, and a default table named `cake_sessions` should appear with all the necessary fields to store session data. Other session settings that the Session component will use follow the `Session.save` preference and are fairly self-explanatory.

Reading and Writing Session Variables

Reading and writing variables in a session are easy with the Session component. In the controller, after instantiating the Session component, of course, you can create a new session by specifying a session name with the `create()` function:

```
$this->Session->create('User');
```

Now, anywhere in the application, this session can be read by using the `read()` function:

```
$user = $this->Session->read('User');
```

This function will produce an array that follows the typical Cake array structure, allowing you to pull anything you want to store in the session by calling the key:

```
$password = $user['password'];
```

Writing to the session is just as simple. With the `write()` function, supply the session name and the value:

```
$this->Session->write('User',$locale);
```

Deleting and Destroying Sessions

The `delete()` and `destroy()` functions allow you to stop storing session information or kill a session entirely. With `delete()`, supply the name of the session key you want to remove. This will not completely destroy the whole session—only the data associated with the provided key. The `destroy()` function, on the other hand, removes all sessions for the current user; it's the equivalent of PHP's `session_destroy()` function.

Cookie

When writing cookies, the Cookie component simplifies the process. Much like the Session component, the Cookie component creates new cookies on the user's system, checks for cookies, and reads and writes to those cookies as well. For the Cookie component to work correctly, be sure to provide the necessary parameters when setting up the component.

Setting Up the Cookie Component

Three variables are required for this component to run: `cookieName`, `cookieKey`, and `cookieDomain`. These tell the Cookie component, respectively:

- The name of the cookie

- The string used to encrypt information written to the cookie

- The domain with access to the cookie

Other Cookie component preferences include the following:

- `cookiePath`: The path where the cookie is stored on the server; the default is set to the entire domain

- `cookieSecure`: A boolean value set to `false` by default; tells the component whether to save cookies over a secure connection

- `cookieTime`: The number of seconds before the cookie will expire; the default value is 0, meaning that when the browser is closed, the cookie will expire

These settings are called in the controller as class properties, like so:

```
var $cookieName = 'super_duper_cookie';
var $cookieKey = '$%sdkj29KA9Ne@@uxlqW';
var $cookieDomain = 'www.domain_name.com';
var $cookieTime = 5400;
```

Writing to a Cookie

Storing information in the cookie is simple with the `write()` function and is similar to the `Session->write()` function. The first value in the function is the cookie's key, and the second contains the value to be written. Remember that this value will be encrypted using the `cookieKey` preference.

```
$this->Cookie->write('User',$user_agent);
```

Reading a Cookie

Just like the Session component, reading a cookie is done with the read() function:

```
$user = $this->Cookie->read('User');
```

As long as the cookie hasn't expired, the information should be available.

Deleting Cookies

Delete cookies using the del() function. Supply the name of the cookie to be deleted, and the component will eliminate the cookie for you:

```
$this->Cookie->del('User');
```

Email

One of the most common tasks of web sites is to send automated e-mails to users. Whether it is an e-commerce web site or a marketing tool for spreading the word, automated e-mail find wide use on the Web. But they can be frustrating to implement, especially when using HTTP headers in the PHP mail() function. The Email component provides a method for sending e-mails in your Cake application using layouts and views rather than coding long strings of e-mail text in the script or controller.

Setting Up the E-mail Layouts

The Email component distinguishes between HTML and plain-text e-mail. To create a layout for each, you must create the folders in the app/views/layouts/email directory. The HTML layouts are stored in a folder named html, and the plain-text layouts are stored in the text folder. In each folder, create a default.ctp file with the necessary layout markup surrounding the $content_for_layout variable. For example, the HTML layout might include the following:

```
<!DOCTYPE XHTML PUBLIC "-//W3C//DTD XHTML 1.0 strict//EN">
<html>
    <body>
        <?=$content_for_layout; ?>
    </body>
</html>
```

The plain-text layout will probably not need much more than the $content_for_layout variable itself.

Sending an E-mail

In the controller action that sends the e-mail, provide some settings for the Email component and then run the send() function to send the e-mail. Available settings include the following:

- $to
- $cc
- $bcc

- $replyTo

- $from

- $sendAs

- $subject

As you will notice, these parameters are self-explanatory and correspond to typical e-mail settings. The sendAs setting tells the Email component how to send the e-mail, either as html or text.

Say you have a basic message you would like to send in the email() action in one of your controllers. It may go something like this:

```
function email() {
    $this->Email->to = 'foo@bar.com';
    $this->Email->cc = 'another@email.com';
    $this->Email->replyTo = 'me@sender.com';
    $this->Email->from = 'do-not-reply@domain.com';
    $this->Email->subject = 'Basic Email Greeting';
    $this->Email->send('Glad to see you');
}
```

The text passed in the send() function is the body of the e-mail to be sent.

Using a Template for E-mail Messages

Creating e-mail templates and sending those rather than providing the content in the controller is simple. Make elements that are stored in keyed folders to create e-mail templates. For example, a basic plain-text template would be stored in the app/views/elements/email/text/hello.ctp file and could contain the following:

```
Hello! This message is from <?=$sender;?>.
```

Then, in the email() function, you could set the $sender variable if you want:

```
function email() {
    $this->Email->to = 'foo@bar.com';
    $this->Email->cc = 'another@email.com';
    $this->Email->replyTo = 'me@sender.com';
    $this->Email->from = 'do-not-reply@domain.com';
    $this->Email->subject = 'Basic Email Greeting';
    $this->set('sender','Me, Myself, and I');
    $this->Email->template = 'hello';
    $this->Email->send();
}
```

Notice that by using the set() function, you were able to pass a value to the $sender variable in the template file. You also told the Email component which template to use when sending the message; in this case, you'll need to name the template file hello.ctp.

HTML templates can behave just like other views in Cake and may draw upon images stored on the web site; remember to use absolute URLs for any graphics because the user's e-mail client won't be able to pull relative paths when opening the e-mail.

Other Components

Cake's built-in components certainly cut down on the amount of code needed to run common web application methods. Not only does it include the components discussed earlier, but it also includes others that are more advanced: the ACL (which stands for "access control list"), RequestHandler, and Security components.

ACL

One of the most complicated methods for building web applications is access control for multiple users. The Auth component takes care of simple authentication, but what if you wanted to have multiple layers for users and their access levels? Or, better yet, what about dynamically altering a user's privileges across the site? This more complex system for assigning areas for the user requires access control lists that outline a tree or matrix of who gets access to what areas in the site. The ACL component simplifies this type of user management with an assortment of functions and methods.

RequestHandler

This component helps with managing HTTP requests and obtaining more client-side information. Features such as SSL detection, reading the type of HTTP request, and responding with a unique MIME type give the RequestHandler a lot of power for making your web application accessible to more than one type of user. For instance, web services can be managed with the RequestHandler, which allows for other web sites to access information and talk to your application. The RequestHandler can also output information as a MIME type other than `text/html`, which allows your application to even work in nonbrowser client applications.

Security

The Security component provides ways for tightening up the security of the web application and avoiding vulnerabilities. Together with the Auth component, Security can provide extra mechanisms for checking user authentications and also display more complex error messages depending on how the user interacts with the application. You can require that certain actions run only under an SSL-secured request or hash strings with this component. By sticking to secure methods for building your applications and by running the Security component to protect the site, you more effectively prohibit unwanted intrusions or other attacks.

Utility Classes

As noted earlier, components serve a specific purpose or function that the controller may need depending on its own actions and processes. Other class functions that are used by the components themselves, or that are used throughout Cake's core libraries, perform more functions that can be used in a controller or a custom component. These functions are housed in utility classes and are accessible anywhere in the application through the `App::import()` function. Several built-in utility classes are available in Cake, but it is assumed that no third-party utilities will be distributed because these classes are contained deep inside the core libraries and as a rule should not be manipulated for applications. To create your own utilities, you would need to create third-party vendor files and bring them into your application using `App::import()` as well (see Chapter 12 for more information on what Cake's vendors are and how to install them in your Cake application). You would usually want to program your own utility class only if you're trying to incorporate third-party software into your application; otherwise, the solution will generally be found in building one of Cake's resource files like a helper or component.

Configure

The Configure utility is responsible for storing global variables. Such variables are generally stored in the core configuration file and are accessible throughout the whole Cake application.

Reading and Writing Global Variables

Just as you see in the core configuration file, constants or global variables are set using the `Configure::write()` function. The first parameter is the name of the variable, and the second is the assigned value.

```
Configure::write('Site.title','My Favorite Web Site');
```

To read these globals, simply use the `Configure::read()` function like so:

```
$title = Configure::read('Site.title');
```

The `Configure::read()` function can be called in the controller, model, or view.

File and Folder

The File and Folder utilities are especially helpful when writing and reading files on the server or listing the file names of a folder's contents. They can also be used to set folder and file permissions or delete files and folders. Unlike the Configure utility, the File and Folder utilities must be imported into the controller or model where they are used with the `App::import()` function by instantiating a new class object.

For the File and Folder utilities to work correctly, the path to the file or folder on the server must be supplied. As in Listing 11-10, you can perform several operations on this object, which represents the file. Some of these operations are listed in the following sections.

Listing 11-10. *Importing a Utility and Instantiating the Class Object*

```
App::import('Core','File');
$file =& new File('path/to/file');
```

Reading Files

The read() function extracts the contents of the file:

```
$contents = $file->read();
```

Creating New Files

If you instantiate a File object for a file that doesn't actually exist, you can use the create() function to create a new, blank file on the server:

```
$file->create();
```

Writing to Files

The write() function writes content to a file:

```
$file->write($filedata);
```

By default, the method the write() function uses is the PHP w type. The w type overwrites content previously in the file. Other methods used in PHP's fwrite() function can be provided as a second parameter. For example, the a parameter allows contents to be appended to the file:

```
$file->write($filedata,'a');
```

Changing File and Folder Permissions

Using the Folder utility, you can run chmod commands on files and folders. The Folder utility is instantiated like the File utility:

```
App::import('Core','Folder');
$folder =& new Folder();
```

The new $folder object can have its permissions changed with the chmod() function:

```
$folder->chmod('/path/to/folder',0777);
```

Other permissions values can be used as well. The chmod() function can also apply permissions recursively by using the recursive parameter. One last feature of this function is the exceptions parameter; if there are any files or folders that should not receive the permissions, they can be skipped by specifying their names in an array.

```
$folder->chmod('/path/to/folder',0777,true,array('nested_1','nested_3'));
```

Reading Folder Contents

When the Folder utility is instantiated, a path can be provided:

```
$folder =& new Folder('/path/to/folder');
```

This utility can return an array containing the contents of this folder by using the read() function:

```
$folder->read();
```

Reading Folder Trees

To get an array of nested directories or trees with the files in each directory, just use the `tree()` function like so:

```
$folder->tree();
```

Copying, Creating, and Deleting Folders

You can copy a folder's contents to another area on the server with the `Folder::copy()` function. Notice that this function requires an array with some parameters included:

```
$folder->copy(array('to'=>'/path/to/new/folder'));
```

Of course, the `$folder` object represents the current folder.

Creating new folders is done just like the File utility, with the `Folder::create()` function. The second parameter sets the permissions value for the new folder:

```
$folder->create('/path/for/new/folder',0755);
```

Deleting folders is also easy. Just run the `delete()` function, and Cake will remove the directory, if its permissions allow this:

```
$folder->delete('/folder/to/be/deleted');
```

Calculating the Folder Size

To find the current folder's file size in bytes, just run the `dirsize()` function:

```
$folder->dirsize();
```

Finding Files in a Folder

Searching for files by their file name can be tricky, but not with the Folder utility. To search in a folder, just provide the `find()` function with a regular expression, and it will return an array of all matching files in the current directory:

```
$results = $folder->find('title(.*).pdf');
```

HTTP Socket

When running HTTP requests or constructing headers, the HTTP Socket utility comes in handy. Like the other utilities (getting the hang of this?), it's imported in the controller or model with `App::import()`.

```
App::import('Core','HttpSocket');
$http =& new HttpSocket();
```

Making HTTP Requests

One of the most useful features of the HTTP Socket utility is its request handling. Not to be confused with the RequestHandler component, HTTP Socket can perform the nitty-gritty of HTTP requests such as GET and POST.

To run a POST with the HTTP Socket utility, first create an array that contains the post variables. The keys in the array correspond with the `name` attribute in HTML input elements, and the values match the `value` attribute.

```
$post = array('username'=>'cakeuser','password'=>'somehashedpassword');
```

Then, using the `HttpSocket::post()` function, pass the array to a specific URL:

```
$result = $http->post('http://domain.com/',$post);
```

A successful POST will return `true`; an unsuccessful one will return `false`.

GET methods are also run with the HTTP Socket utility. The serialized set of GET names and values is generally appended to the URL string, so with the `HttpSocket::get()` function you can provide a GET query as the second parameter. The contents of the GET response are returned to the variable, so if the server returns some HTML or an error message or HTTP headers, it will appear as the returned string.

```
$response = $http->get('http://domain.com/');
```

To run a page scrape of another web site or to perform other HTTP requests, use the `HttpSocket::request()` function. This function will perform an HTTP request and return the raw server response, be it a web page or some other text.

```
$response = $http->request('http://domain.com/web_page.html');
```

Using Other HTTP Socket Functions

Other functions in the HTTP Socket utility include `buildHeader()`, `buildRequestLine()`, `buildUri()`, `decodeBody()`, `delete()`, `parseHeader()`, `parseUri()`, `put()`, and more. When considering how to perform HTTP requests or socket methods for your site, consult this utility, and it will likely contain useful functions to minimize the amount of coding you will have to write.

Localization and Internationalization

For web sites that will have an international audience, translating site content can be difficult. In recent years some important localization (L10n) and internationalization (I18n) standards have been implemented for the Web and other software systems. Cake makes use of L10n and I18n standards and methods with their respective utilities.

Note The "10" and "18" in L10n and I18n represent the number of letters between the first and last in the words *localization* and *internationalization*. (Developers use these terms so often that spelling them out was taking too long.) Cake's utility classes are named using these abbreviated versions, not the full titles, so the `Localization` utility class is named in the core `L10n`, not `Localization`.

Working with Locale Files

To localize a web site, or in other words, to make the site content fit the language, number system, currency, and other standards of visitors, use the L10n utility. For example, if a user in Spain were to need the application, you might want to translate some important titles, buttons, links, and other strings into Spanish. To do so, you must first set up Spanish locales or locale files for L10n to use in translation.

Locale files are stored in the app/locale directory and are arranged in subfolders named for the language or locale. The names and strings that L10n uses conform to the ISO 639–2 standard (for more information, consult the Library of Congress, which is the official registration authority for the standard: http://www.loc.gov/standards/iso639-2/). Locale files use the .po file extension and are arranged by locale.

By default, Cake includes the English locale folder, app/locale/eng. In it you'll see another subfolder, which contains locale files for translating strings and messages, LC_MESSAGES.

For each language you'd like to localize, create a default.po file and store this in its locale folder. For Spanish, for example, you would need to create not only the default.po file for the app/locale/eng/LC_MESSAGES directory but also one for the app/locale/spa/LC_MESSAGES folder. The next step is to write in these locale files the string you want to be translated.

Translating Strings

Translating strings is made easy by using two keys: msgid and msgstr. In the default.po locale file, for each line provide one of these keys with an associated value. For example, in the English locale file, you could include the contents of Listing 11-11.

Listing 11-11. *An Example of Content in the English Locale File*

```
msgid    "home"
msgstr    "Welcome to Our Site"
msgid    "contact"
msgstr    "Contact Us"
msgid    "login"
msgstr    "Log In"
msgid    "logout"
msgstr    "Log Out"
```

As long as the other locales contain the same msgid values, the L10n utility can fetch the msgstr values depending on the locale. The default locale is set in the core configuration under Config.language. This value is set by default to English but may be changed to any locale. When L10n looks up msgid keys, it will first visit the locale specified in the Config.language setting.

A corresponding Spanish locale would look something like this:

```
msgid    "home"
msgstr    "Bienvenidos a Nuestro Sitio"
msgid    "contact"
msgstr    "Contactarnos"
```

```
msgid    "login"
msgstr    "Ingresar"
msgid    "logout"
msgstr    "Salir"
```

Localizing Content

Once the locale files are in place, localizing content is simple. First, instantiate the L10n utility class like other utilities:

```
App::import('Core','L10n');
$l10n =& new L10n();
```

Then, run the L10n::get() function to tell the controller which locale to use for localizing. Now, everything contained in the convenience function, __(), will be looked up in the locales.

```
$l10n->get('spa');
__('home');
```

The previous lines will output the msgstr following the msgid with home as its value. If you want returned localized strings to be passed along as raw data and not echoed, set the escape parameter to true:

```
$form->error('Post.title',__('postTitleError',true));
```

Sanitize

The Sanitize utility contains functions designed for cleaning up data and text. Stripping white-space, HTML tags, and references to scripts and style sheets, as well as escaping text for SQL, can be accomplished with the Sanitize utility.

Remember to instantiate the Sanitize utility first with App::import() and assign the utility as a class object for use in the controller or model:

```
App::import('Core','Sanitize');
$sanitize =& new Sanitize();
```

Sanitize can strip out HTML tags from a block of text by using the stripTags() function:

```
$this->set('output',$sanitize->stripTags($output,array('<p>','<em>','<div>')));
```

Other functions include clean(), escape(), html(), stripImages(), stripScripts(), and stripWhitespace(). If you need to clean data, text, or SQL queries, consult the Sanitize utility.

Third-Party Components

Cake's built-in components and utilities are extremely helpful in extending the functionality of the controller and model. Even more components are available online through Cake's open source service CakeForge (www.cakeforge.org) and the Bakery (http://bakery.cakephp.org). These third-party components cover all sorts of functions that can reduce the amount of code you need to write. When running components, remember to follow the instructions supplied by the developer, which usually assume you know how to install a component (which was covered in "Using Components" earlier). Third-party components available at the Bakery include Twitter, Image Resizer, LastRSS, SMS Text, Authorize.net AIM Integration, and Yahoo! Weather. Searching for components first before trying to write a long controller process yourself can yield excellent results.

Creating Custom Components

Creating your own custom components is simple and follows the pattern shown in earlier chapters. All components are stored in the app/controllers/components directory and follow Cake's naming scheme. If you want to install your own utilities, you will need to install them as vendor files, since utilities are stored in the Cake core.

The basic component file has a file name that matches its class name. Like controller classes, these are camel-cased and have the .php extension. See Listing 11-12.

Listing 11-12. *The Basic Component File, Named blog.php, Stored in the components Directory*

```
<?
class BlogComponent extends Object {
}
?>
```

The component contains functions like the controller. Because these functions are called by noncomponents, or in other words, a controller, they will run the return() function to send back its output. These functions can also have parameters.

Using the Initialize and Startup Functions

To run logic before the controller's functions are called (like the beforeFilter() function in the controller), use the initialize() function. This function can contain any logic to be run before the component's functions are processed.

Sometimes a component function will need access to its parent controller, meaning the controller that is currently calling it. Properties like $this->data and $this->params, as well as any other properties currently in use by the controller can be pulled, into the component. By using the startup() function, you can provide the component with the controller object and thus give any component function access to its parent controller. See Listing 11-13.

Listing 11-13. *The startup() Function in the Component*

```
function startup(&$controller) {
    $this->data = $controller->data;
}
```

Anything in the controller that appears under the $this object is made available to the component as $controller, as shown in Listing 11-13. You can set a component class variable to contain the controller object:

```
var $controller = null;
```

and then use the startup() function to instantiate the controller object. Then all functions in the controller can use $this->controller to access anything in the parent controller.

```
function startup(&$controller) {
    $this->controller = $controller;
}
```

Now in a placeholder function, you can pull the parameters from the parent controller and use them in the component:

```
function test() {
    $params = $this->controller->params;
    $data = $params['data'];
    return $data;
}
```

Writing Vendor Files Instead of Components

Remember that the idea behind components is to share code for cross-controller functions that are portable. In theory, you should be able to distribute any component, and it should work for any Cake application regardless of how the application is designed. If the code does not fit in the CakePHP framework, or an MVC model, then you ought to create vendor files and not components. By adhering to this standard, you ensure that other Cake developers can benefit from your work, and vice versa.

Like helpers, components are designed to cut down on superfluous code in the controller. When the controller begins to look more bloated than the model, you will generally want to find ways to move more code to the model. When code is shared across multiple controllers, you may want to consider placing that logic in a component and scaling the code to be more portable than in one specific controller or Cake application. In the long run, your site will be better organized, cleaner, and lighter—always good reasons for taking the extra step.

Summary

Components extend the controller like helpers extend the view. They provide a set of functions and methods that are specific to a certain overall scheme to the controller and are designed with portability in mind. In other words, if you've built your components right, you should be able to distribute them for use in any Cake application. In this chapter, I discussed how to include a component class in the controller and how to put its functions to work. You wrote some user authentication methods into your blog application using the Auth component to better secure areas of the site and limit access to the general user. This chapter also explained how to work Cake's utility classes into your application. Many of these classes condense the time and code involved to perform some typical web-related tasks such as reading and writing files and folders. I outlined some other utility classes, and I discussed some important differences between vendor files, utilities, and components. In Chapter 12, I'll go into more detail about vendors and how to use them in your Cake project.

CHAPTER 12

■■■

Vendors

One of the benefits of using Cake is that it is built on PHP, one of the most popular languages in web development. Thousands of developers from across the globe actively contribute to the available body of PHP classes and scripts, which makes using PHP advantageous. However, a major concern of PHP developers choosing a framework is how to port over existing projects or use those long hours of developing their own classes in the framework.

PHP uses the `include()` and `require()` functions to reference external scripts or multiple files. Why not just run one of these to implement an outside script? Again, Cake's "convention over configuration" mantra applies. Cake is concerned not just with providing shortcuts and automating typical web functions but also with ways of naming and arranging the various application resources. Rather than arbitrary includes, Cake suggests that any third-party script or non-Cake objects be organized as vendors.

Using Vendors

Simply put, a *vendor* is a non-Cake script of some kind. For example, let's say you want to include a snazzy PHP class script you found on the Internet that simplifies generating CAPTCHA[1] images. You can assume that the developer was not thinking of CakePHP specifically when building the script, so its functions and classes won't be structured to work in Cake. No problem—you just have to bring the script into the application as a vendor.

The first step is to place the PHP script into the `app/vendors` folder. By doing so, you make the script available to the Cake application while keeping all the vendors in one place. You won't need to rename the file to fit Cake's conventions.

Next, you include the file's contents in the controller, model, or view where you'd like to use the script. You do this by using the `App::import()` function (see Listing 12-1).

Listing 12-1. *Including a Vendor*

```php
<?php
App::import('Vendor','some_captcha_script.php');
```

---

1. "Completely Automated Public Turing test to tell Computers and Humans Apart"; in other words, by supplying images that are difficult for a computer to decipher but easy for a human to read, the web site can differentiate between automated requests and legitimate user form submissions.

Notice that in Listing 12-1 the first parameter is Vendor; this tells Cake to import a vendor file. Also, I've included the standard PHP opening line, <?php, to emphasize where this function is called: before any class declarations. So if Listing 12-1 occurred in the Posts controller, the App::import() function would appear before the class declarations:

```php
<?php
App::import('Vendor','some_captcha_script.php');
class PostsController extends AppController { …
```

Finally, you can use the vendor's contents in the controller or view by simply calling its functions or classes as if it were brought in with the include() function (see Listing 12-2).

Listing 12-2. *An Example Vendor Function Being Used in the Controller*

```php
1    <?php
2    App::import('Vendor','some_captcha_script.php');
3    class PostsController extends AppController {
4        function index() {
5            $captcha = new someCaptchaClass();
6            $captcha_image = $captcha->generateImage();
7            $this->set(compact('captcha','captcha_image'));
8        }
9    }
10   ?>
```

Remember that Listing 12-2 is a basic example that would require more work to be done in the view to work properly. But you can see how the vendor is imported on line 2 and how its class object is brought into the controller on lines 5–6.

Using vendor functions without class objects is just as simple. Let's assume the contents of some_captcha_script.php include just one function:

```php
function cleanAmpersands($text=null) {
    return str_replace('&','&amp;',$text);
}
```

Then, in the action, simply use the function as in a normal PHP script:

```php
function view($id=null) {
    $post = $this->Post->read(null,$id);
    $text = cleanAmpersands($post['Post']['contents']);
    $this->set(compact('post','text'));
}
```

Referencing outside scripts through the vendor system can be extremely useful, especially when you want to use available scripts that are not constructed as Cake functions. Using the App::import() function makes this a simple task, keeps vendors organized, and manages the paths to the vendor files.

Dealing with File Names

The `App::import()` function is used for more than just including vendors. Other Cake core class objects can be brought into a controller or view with this function as well. Because of this, `App::import()` performs some default methods that affect how you specify a vendor file for inclusion in the application. Cake will automatically include vendor files based on the name as long as the specified name is all lowercase and matches the file name exactly. This means you must specify the vendor by using all lowercase letters. If a file name is uppercased, title-cased, camel-cased, or anything other than all lowercase, the vendor will not be automatically included, and more parameters will need to be provided.

```
App::import('Vendor','Title'); //will not bring in the file Title.php
```

If the vendor file is in a folder or has any uppercase letters, then you must manually specify the file name using a parameters array. To bring `Title.php` into the controller, you would have to pass along the file name in the parameters array or rename the file itself:

```
App::import('Vendor','title',array('file'=>'Title.php'));
```

Dealing with Nested Folders

Suppose the vendor you're importing into the application has an internal folder structure that needs to be preserved if it is to work properly. The `App::import()` function can also take care of vendors in these folders so long as the path supplied is correctly formatted. Remember that all paths will be relative to the `app/vendors` directory.

```
App::import('Vendor','title',array('file'=>'my_vendors/title.php'));
```

The previous line will include the `app/vendors/my_vendors/title.php` file for use in the application.

Making No Assumptions for Third-Party Scripts

An important point about vendors must be made: Cake makes *no assumptions* about vendors. Doing so would contradict the whole purpose of having a vendor in a Cake application in the first place. In other words, the main reason you might use a vendor in a Cake application is to take advantage of a feature, method, or task that Cake cannot already handle by itself. So if you pull a third-party script into Cake that performs methods Cake doesn't understand, then you must accept that Cake cannot help if anything goes wrong.

Simply put, including vendors is a mechanism to give you the flexibility to pull outside resources into your application without being limited by the framework; but Cake, as a framework, cannot assume to manage the limitations of the vendor. Therefore, the number of functions and methods provided by Cake to support vendors really goes only so far as including them in the application. From there, getting the vendor to work will require understanding the specific construction of the vendor itself and how it will react with Cake.

Furthermore, naming conventions, patterns, and the MVC structure cannot be expected to extend into vendors. If you needed to perform controller logic, you ought to write the code in a controller or component, not in a vendor. I once spoke with a beginning

Cake developer who tried to get around learning Cake's functions and structure by writing everything as vendor files and pulling in only one or two Cake resources. This not only defeated the purpose of using Cake in the first place but also resulted in more time being wasted debugging vendor files.

Should you want to distribute a resource you built in Cake, you'll probably want to keep it the way it is and not release it as a vendor. In other words, if what you have written is a helper class, then make it available to other developers as such; they will better understand what you have in mind with the script, and more important, they will know how to use it in their applications. Vendor includes are best for libraries or other scripts that were developed independently of CakePHP for use in a wide variety of applications.

Unidirectional Scripting

Another important point about vendors is that Cake supports them unidirectionally. The vendor file itself cannot use Cake helper functions, class objects, or other resources. Trying to pull, say, the Ajax helper into a vendor would be more problematic and would require a lot of retooling to pull it off. The problems associated with this are apparent; forcing the vendor to change its behavior cancels out the utility of using Cake. A lot can be said for vendors, simply because so often beginners to Cake think in terms of include files and not the other way around. So, remember—Cake can use the functionality of a vendor, but the vendor cannot use the functionality of Cake. Vendor data flows in one direction, not back and forth.

Installing a Third-Party Script

Now that I've covered the basics of installing a vendor, let's use a third-party script in your blog application. Rather than build a wiki engine from scratch, let's choose one of the many open source text-parsing engines: Textile.

First, obtain a copy of Textile, which is available at http://textile.thresholdstate.com. In this tutorial, I'll be using version 2.0. Once you have downloaded the file and decompressed it, you'll find the main engine file named classTextile.php. Place this file in the app/vendors folder for the blog application.

Including Textile

Make the classTextile.php file contents available to the Posts controller by using the App::import() function for including vendors (see Listing 12-3). Be sure to place this line before the Posts controller class instantiation line. Since the file name is not all lowercase, you must specify the file name in the parameters array.

Listing 12-3. *Including Textile As a Vendor*

```
<?
App::import('Vendor','textile',array('file'=>'classTextile.php'));
class PostsController extends AppController { …
```

Now that Textile is included in the Posts controller, the view can use its functions to parse the post content. Vendors included in the controller will be available in the view, so you need to add nothing else in the controller. Now, because everything will depend on the vendor itself and because Cake cannot provide conventions for third-party scripts, this process may need to change depending on what vendor is being used. Textile itself comes into play when any kind of text needs to be rendered in the browser following a wiki-style parser. Thus, this vendor in practice would be executed in the view as the view renders the contents provided by the database.

Instantiating and Running Textile

In the `app/views/posts/view.ctp` file, start a new instance of the `Textile` class by inserting Listing 12-4 into line 1.

Listing 12-4. *Starting a New Textile Class*

```
<? $textile = new Textile();?>
```

Thanks to the Posts controller and Listing 12-4, the class object functions in `classTextile.php` are now available for use in the view. Textile has the `TextileThis()` function to filter the final text through its engine and parse out its own unique wiki-style commands. Line 6 now contains the post's article content as passed in the `$post['Post']['content']` variable. Let's run this variable through Textile's `TextileThis()` function by substituting the following line for line 6:

```
<?=$textile->TextileThis($post['Post']['content']);?>
```

Writing Posts with Textile

Now that Textile is running in your application, you can use its syntax when writing blog posts to easily add some text-formatting touches. Since Textile works on final output, you don't have to rework anything in the other Add or Edit actions; simply adhere to the syntax when entering text, and all should appear correctly.

To test your implementation of Textile, try adding some content in a blog post using some of Textile's wiki commands. For example, placing underscores around a word will result in the `<em>` tag being wrapped around the word, and so forth.

Using Other Frameworks with CakePHP

Perhaps one of the most complicated aspects of using a PHP framework is working it into a large enterprise-level application that runs on multiple frameworks. You may be familiar with some of the other web frameworks out there; you may even have experimented with a few of them before trying Cake. The question of how to implement another framework with Cake is sometimes the most important concern of all.

Because you can't assume that these frameworks are entirely compatible with Cake, conventions for using them have not been arranged or included in the core. To bring them into the application, you must tackle the project on an individual basis; each framework will have very different methods of working by itself and will certainly require a unique set of parameters and methods to work with Cake.

Zend Framework

One of the most popular PHP frameworks is Zend Framework (`http://framework.zend.com`). You may need to take advantage of its functions for your web applications. To do so, you must use Zend Framework (Zend, or ZF for short) as a vendor in the Cake application.

ZEND OR ZF?

There are some nuances when referring to Zend Framework. The *company* that created the framework is called Zend, and the official title of the *framework* is Zend Framework. On its site and elsewhere, the framework is often referred to as ZF to avoid confusion with the company name. In this section, however, I prefer to avoid the acronym, so I'll stick with Zend to refer both to the company and to the framework. Be advised that when reading up on Zend Framework on the Web, you may need to be more specific than just using the company name.

Fortunately for Cake developers, Zend is less of an MVC framework than a set of libraries (or as they are often referred by Zend developers, *components*). Each of its components can be brought into a stand-alone PHP application through includes. As already noted, using these components as vendors allows you to integrate Zend with your Cake application. Each component will have its own specific installation procedures for which you will need to consult Zend's support web site and documentation. But the general steps when installing a Zend component in Cake are explained in the following sections. First, let's see whether you can use anything that Zend has to offer in your blog application.

Blocking Spam in the Comments Add Action

One of the competitive features of Zend is its web service library. As of version 1.5, Zend comes with these web services components:

- Akismet
- Amazon
- Audioscrobbler (Last.fm)
- Del.icio.us
- Flickr
- Nirvanix
- Simpy
- SlideShare

- StrikeIron

- Technorati

- Yahoo!

You could take your blog in any number of directions, from doing automatic title checking in Amazon to fetching images from Flickr. However, the most immediate and probably the most important basic feature of the blog is spam checking. Since the blog provides an arena where users can enter their own comments, you have opened up the possibility of your blog being spammed, especially if the blog becomes well known. Thanks to Zend, the Akismet web service component is already available, and all the hard work has already been done for you. The trick is just getting it to work in your Cake application.

After doing some homework on what Zend is offering with its Akismet component, you will find that you will need an API key (common for using any type of web service), which is provided by Akismet (`www.akismet.com`). Be sure to obtain this API key; otherwise, the Akismet component will not run properly. (More information on the Akismet component is available at `http://framework.zend.com/manual/en/zend.service.akismet.html`.)

Download the Zend Framework library, and extract its contents. You should find a folder named `Zend` that contains all the components for the framework. If you already are running Zend on your server, then take note of the path relative to the `app/vendors` folder. Otherwise, place the `Zend` folder in the `app/vendors` directory. As with the Textile installation, write the `App::import()` function in the Comments Add action to include the Zend Akismet component (Listing 12-5).

Listing 12-5. *Importing the Akismet Component in the* `app/controllers/comments_controller.php` *File*

```
5    function add() {
6        App::import('Vendor','akismet',array('file'=>'Zend/Service/Akismet.php'));
```

At this point, you will need to deviate from the typical Cake protocol because you are now dealing with Zend. In line 6 of Listing 12-5, you brought in the Akismet component by referencing the `Zend/Service/Akismet.php` file. But there is one problem with this script when it is called in the Comments controller: it runs its own includes relative to the Zend directory. This will need to change to keep it from conflicting with Cake's paths. Open the `Zend/Service/Akismet.php` file, and insert a new `include_path` definition before any include functions to fix this:

```
22    ini_set('include_path', dirname(dirname(dirname(__FILE__))));
```

Now you can begin using the Akismet component in the controller. Next, instantiate a new object by calling the `Zend_Service_Akismet` class in the Comments Add action:

```
7    $akismet = new Zend_Service_Akismet('************','http://localhost/blog');
```

Notice that to begin a new Akismet object, you must supply the API key in the first parameter and the URI to the blog in the second. The key, which you should have obtained from Akismet, is usually a 12-digit alphanumeric string.

Because you changed the INI settings to make the include_path parameter work for Zend, you will need to go back and override this exception. After line 7, insert the original include_path definition (which is stored in the app/webroot/index.php file):

```
8    ini_set('include_path',CAKE_CORE_INCLUDE_PATH.PATH_SEPARATOR.ROOT.DS.↦
APP_DIR.DS.PATH_SEPARATOR.ini_get('include_path'));
```

For Akismet to run a spam check, it will need a few important variables:

- The user's IP address

- The user agent

- The type of comment (for example, blog or contact)

- The comment's author name

- The comment's content

Other variables may be passed along as well, including the author's e-mail, the author's web site URL, the permalink location, and so forth. The more variables you can pass to Akismet, the more effective it will be at filtering spam. Let's specify these variables by assigning them to the $this->data array (see Listing 12-6). Then, run the Akismet component's isSpam() function to perform the spam check.

Listing 12-6. *The Rest of the Akismet Component in the Comments Add Action*

```
9    if (!empty($this->data)) {
10          $this->data['akismet'] = array(
11              'user_ip' => $_SERVER['REMOTE_ADDR'],
12              'user_agent' => $_SERVER['HTTP_USER_AGENT'],
13              'comment_type' => 'blog',
14              'comment_author' => $this->data['Comment']['name'],
15              'comment_content' => $this->data['Comment']['content']
16          );
17
18          if ($akismet->isSpam($this->data['akismet'])) {
19              $this->render('add_spam','ajax');
20              exit();
21          }
```

Lines 10–16 contain the keys and values to properly format the array to be sent to the Akismet component for processing. Notice that the keys adhere to the documented parameters listed on Zend's Akismet web page. Then, on line 18, you pass the whole $this->data['akismet'] array to the $akismet->isSpam() function and check for a true return value. Line 19, which is called if Akismet determines that the submission is spam, renders a new view in the comments folder (app/views/posts/add_spam.ctp). Line 20 exits the controller.

That's all! Now you can test the spam check by pasting in some obvious spam messages, and it should return the add_spam.ctp view. Rather than building your own Akismet component for Cake, you can take advantage of Zend's Akismet library, which combines the best of both worlds: Cake's MVC and mature framework structure and Zend's powerful web services components.

▓Tip Depending on your server setup, you may encounter some problems with getting the Zend component to instantiate the class properly. A common error is the "cannot access protected property" error, which is often because of a PHP caching engine or accelerator being turned on. Be sure to check the details of your setup before turning off the caching engine or PHP accelerator, but a good way to test this problem is by toggling this setting from on to off. Other issues could be because of conflicts with Zend; check Zend's recommendations to resolve the bug.

Outputting Posts as PDF Files

Zend also comes with a powerful PDF component that would be useful for your blog application. Let's create an action that will output the contents of the post as a PDF.

In the Posts controller, insert the action shown in Listing 12-7.

Listing 12-7. *The PDF Action in the Posts Controller*

```
1    function pdf($id = null) {
2        if (!$id) {
3            $this->redirect(array('action'=>'index'),null,true);
4        }
5
6        $text = $this->Post->read(null,$id);
7
8        App::import('Vendor','pdf',array('file'=>'Zend/Pdf.php'));
9        $pdf =& new Zend_Pdf();
10       ini_set('include_path', CAKE_CORE_INCLUDE_PATH.PATH_SEPARATOR.ROOT.DS.➥
APP_DIR.DS.PATH_SEPARATOR.ini_get('include_path'));
11
12       $page = $pdf->newPage(Zend_Pdf_Page::SIZE_LETTER);
13       $pdf->pages[] = $page;
14       $page->setFont(Zend_Pdf_Font::fontWithName(Zend_Pdf_Font::FONT_➥
HELVETICA), 12);
15       $text = wordwrap($text['Post']['content'], 80, "\n", false);
16       $token = strtok($text, "\n");
17       $y = 740;
18       while ($token != false) {
19           if ($y < 60) {
20               $pdf->pages[] = ($page = $pdf->newPage(Zend_Pdf_Page::SIZE_➥
LETTER));
21               $y = 740;
22           } else {
23               $page->drawText($token, 40, $y);
```

```
24                    $y-=15;
25                }
26                $token = strtok("\n");
27            }
28
29        $data = $pdf->render();
30        header("Content-Disposition: inline; file name=blog_post.pdf");
31        header("Content-type: application/x-pdf");
32        echo $data;
33        exit();
34    }
```

Notice how Listing 12-7 uses the PDF component. On line 8, the component is imported as a vendor, and then line 9 instantiates a new PDF class object. Line 10 reverts the include path setting back to the default Cake path (since we will soon change the include path to work in Zend). Lines 12–33 follow the generic pattern for creating PDF files with the PDF component.

For more detailed help on using the PDF component, consult the online documentation (http://framework.zend.com/manual/en/zend.pdf.html). In short, you create a new PDF file and write new pages to the file. Since lines of text are "drawn" rather than "typed" in a PDF file, you must manually wrap the lines. This is accomplished on lines 15–27. Lines 29–32 send the formatted data to the browser with PDF-specific HTTP headings, and then line 33 exits to prevent Cake from rendering any views.

The script cannot work yet unless (as with the Akismet component) you alter the include_path setting for Zend to work correctly. Open the app/vendors/Zend/Pdf.php file, and place the following line near the top and before any includes:

```
ini_set('include_path', dirname(dirname(__FILE__)));
```

You're all set. Launch the PDF action, and a basic PDF file should automatically render. You may want to add a link in the Posts view to output as a PDF file:

```
<?=$html->link('Save as PDF','/posts/pdf/'.$post['Post']['id']);?>
```

Other Zend Components

Many other powerful components are included in the Zend Framework. Aside from some components that make Zend work in an MVC environment, you ought to be able to bring various components into a Cake application. In this exercise, try your hand with a couple of unique components that aren't already available in Cake, such as Lucene, Translate, or Validate, by bringing them into a Cake application as vendors. Remember to fix the include paths for Zend to work properly and test the components thoroughly since they are third-party elements.

Summary

When you must use third-party scripts in your Cake application, it's best to include them as vendors using the `App::import()` method. Once the script is available, its functions and objects can be directly called in the application. Of course, because vendors work in Cake unidirectionally, how you further implement the vendor will depend on the vendor's own methods. In this chapter, we discussed using components from Zend Framework to perform Akismet spam checks and PDF file rendering. Other web service components can be used in Cake using similar methods. In Chapter 13, we'll examine plugins—resources that allow you to create a mini-application of sorts that can be distributed across multiple Cake applications.

CHAPTER 13

■■■

Plugins

In some situations, developers may want to use a Cake application in several other applications. Sometimes another Cake application may be useful in your project but may be difficult to fit in because of its independent structure; controllers, models, and such may conflict with the current project's namespaces. Plugins are elements that function as mini-applications inside the main Cake application. They include their own models, views, and controllers, and they make it possible to reuse an entire application within other applications.

Cake comes with no built-in plugins. Thus, only third-party applications can be used inside an existing Cake application. Of course, you may build your own plugins to fit your needs, but be aware that plugins are available online at various locations. The Bakery (`http://bakery.cakephp.org`) and CakeForge (`www.cakeforge.org`) host plugins along with other Cake applications, components, helpers, and more. The Bakery also hosts articles explaining how developers wrote their plugins—which can be useful in learning advanced CakePHP methods.

Third-party plugins save time. Because they follow the MVC structure, they can do much more than a component or helper alone. A plugin may contain its own models and therefore work with the database in ways that a component or helper doesn't. Often, running a complex method for an application is as simple as dropping a plugin in the `app/plugins` directory and tweaking some settings in the application to get it running.

Installing a Third-Party Plugin

Plugins are fairly simple to install because of their design. Simply put, they are self-contained folders that can be dropped in the `app/plugins` directory and referenced in the model, view, or controller. They should be written so that they require little configuration. Sometimes a plugin may require a database table to be set up to work correctly, or it may need you to specify some global variables or settings in the core configuration. Whatever the case, the plugin will generally come with its own installation notes that should be fairly simple to follow. I'll show how to install an Ajax chat room plugin by Pseudocoder in your blog application to show how it's done.

First, you must obtain the plugin code. Pseudocoder's Ajax Chat plugin is available at `http://sandbox2.pseudocoder.com/demo/chat`. You should end up with a compressed file that contains a folder with some model, view, and controller files inside.

You should notice that this plugin calls for the Prototype JavaScript library to be running in the application. I have already gone through installing Prototype in the default layout, so you shouldn't have to change anything in the layout for this plugin to work. However, you may still want to double-check that Prototype is running correctly in the application. Open the app/views/layouts/default.ctp file, and look for the Prototype include line:

```
<?=$javascript->link('prototype.js');?>
```

Also make sure the prototype.js file is located in the app/webroot/js folder. With these two settings in place, the Ajax Chat plugin is ready to be installed.

Place the contents of the downloaded file in the app/plugins folder. The Ajax Chat plugin also uses its own database table, so you will need to run the SQL query to generate the appropriate table and fields. Pseudocoder makes this SQL available on its web page, which you already may have noticed when downloading the plugin. To save you time, Listing 13-1 contains the necessary SQL to build the table. Be sure to create the chats table in MySQL before running the plugin in the application; otherwise, errors will occur.

Listing 13-1. *The* chats *Table to Be Used by the Ajax Chat Plugin*

```
CREATE TABLE `chats` (
  `id` int(10) unsigned NOT NULL auto_increment,
  `key` varchar(45) NOT NULL default '',
  `handle` varchar(20) NOT NULL default '',
  `text` text NOT NULL,
  `ip_address` varchar(12) NOT NULL default '',
  `created` datetime NOT NULL default '0000-00-00 00:00:00',
  PRIMARY KEY (`id`),
  KEY `KEY_IDX` (`key`)
);
```

The plugin is now installed for use in your Cake application. To use it, you will need to call its actions and such in your own controllers or models, depending on the plugin's methods. This particular plugin is run in the view by calling its helper functions. Because the plugin needs more than just the helper to work, the necessary controllers and models are included as well, but you won't even notice those because of the way the plugin was designed.

Let's build a chat action in your application. In the Posts controller, create the chat() action, and get its view working (app/views/posts/chat.ctp). When accessing this action, the view should turn up a blank page with maybe a title at the top, so no more is necessary in the action itself.

The Ajax Chat plugin requires its own helper that must be made available to the controller like any other helper, so include this in the helpers array along with the Ajax helper:

```
var $helpers = array('Ajax','chat/AjaxChat');
```

The last step is to call out the Ajax Chat helper in the view with a simple command:

```
$ajaxChat->generate('chatroom');
```

Now when you fire up the Chat action in the Posts controller, the Ajax Chat plugin should automatically launch an Ajax chat room on the page. Literally, with only a couple lines of code and a SQL query you were able to launch a mini-application inside your own blog.

Creating Custom Plugins

Whether you use Cake plugins as add-ons to your projects or you want to contribute to the Cake community by distributing your own mini-applications, you will need to customize the plugin beyond what I've already explained. To begin writing a custom plugin, create a folder named after the plugin in lowercase letters. All the controllers, models, and views will be stored inside this folder. All plugins will need to have two additional files: the {plugin}_app_controller.php and {plugin}_app_model.php files where {plugin} is the name of the plugin in lowercase letters. These files will contain the class names and extensions that allow Cake to utilize the rest of the plugin's resources, so naming these files correctly is important for the plugin to function correctly.

The basic plugin will contain an App controller; an App model; and folders for controllers, models, and views. The organization mimics the overall Cake application structure, so any plugin helpers will be stored in the plugin's views/helpers directory, and so forth (see Listing 13-2). Be sure to replace {plugin} with the name of the plugin.

Listing 13-2. *The Basic Plugin File Structure*

```
{plugin root}/
    {plugin}_app_controller.php
    {plugin}_app_model.php
    controllers/
        {controller name}_controller.php
    models/
    views/
```

Naming Convention for Plugin Elements

Listing 13-2 shows the basic file structure inside the plugin's root directory. The naming convention for plugin elements is slightly different from the standard convention for naming other Cake resources. Table 13-1 shows how to name plugin elements.

Table 13-1. *Naming Conventions for Plugin Elements*

Type	File Name	Class	Extends	Example
App controller	{plugin}_app_controller.php	PluginAppController	AppController	CalendarApp Controller extends AppController
App model	{plugin}_app_model.php	PluginAppModel	AppModel	CalendarAppModel extends AppModel
Controller	Same as application	Same as application	PluginApp Controller	EventsController extends CalendarApp Controller
Model	Same as application	Same as application	PluginAppModel	Event extends CalendarAppModel

Continued

Table 13-1. *Naming Conventions for Plugin Elements*

Type	File Name	Class	Extends	Example
Helper	Same as application	Same as application	`Helper`	`CalendarHelper` `extends Helper`

Component	Same as application	Same as application	`Object`	`Calendar`
				`Component`
				`extends Object`

Behavior	Same as application	Same as application	`ModelBehavior`	`MonthBehavior`
				`extends`
				`ModelBehavior`

DataSource	Same as application	Same as application	`DataSource`	`CalSource`
				`extends`
				`DataSource`

Individual view files do not change naming conventions in plugins. In other words, they are named just like standard Cake view files. The Events views, for example, would be stored in the `app/plugins/calendar/views/events` folder. Individual plugin views are then named after the action: `index.ctp`, and so forth.

Not only do some file names for plugins need to be adjusted to work properly; so do the class names in the files. For the plugin not to conflict with the surrounding Cake application file names and class names, the naming conventions and syntax must be slightly adjusted. Instead of naming the class `AppController`, for instance, the class name will need to be prepended with the name of the plugin. A plugin named Calendar would need to have its class names named after the plugin. For example, the App controller would be named `CalendarAppController`, and the App model would be named `CalendarAppModel`. Other elements used by the plugin should have their class names adjusted depending on what type of element they are.

Controllers and models extend the plugin's App controller and App model, respectively (see Listing 13-3). Thus, the class name must reflect this extension when the plugin classes are instantiated.

Listing 13-3. *An Example of a Plugin Controller Extending the App Controller*

```
1   <?
2   class EventsController extends CalendarAppController {
3       var $name = 'Events';
4       var $uses = array('Event');
5   }
6   ?>
```

Notice that line 4 of Listing 13-3 shows the plugin controller using the $uses class attribute to specify the corresponding model. Though Cake should automatically pick up the appropriate models and views, consistently setting the $uses array will allow the plugin to be more portable and reduces the risk of the plugin controller conflicting with the surrounding application's namespaces.

Like the plugin controller, the plugin model extends the App model and has its naming syntax adjusted to work as a plugin (see Listing 13-4).

Listing 13-4. *An Example of a Plugin Model Extending the App Model*

```
<?
class EventModel extends CalendarAppModel {
    var $name = 'Event';
}
?>
```

Helpers, components, behaviors, and DataSources may also be used as part of a plugin. Their naming conventions generally remain the same as when used as elements of a Cake application and not as plugin elements. Refer to Table 13-1 for information on how to name other plugin classes and what objects they extend.

Running Plugin Actions

Once a plugin is installed in your Cake application, you may access its actions by adding the plugin name plus the action and parameters to the URL. The Events controller used in Listing 13-3 could be called in the blog application with the following URL:

```
http://localhost/blog/calendar/events
```

Of course, the action and parameters also follow:

```
http://localhost/blog/calendar/events/view/01/2009
```

Controllers in the surrounding Cake application can run a plugin's controller actions using the requestAction() function:

```
$events = $this->requestAction(array('controller'=>'CalendarEvents','action'=>➥
'getEvents'));
```

Using Plugin Layouts

By default, the plugin will use the default layout in the surrounding application's app/views/ layouts directory. Specifying a layout stored in the plugin is simple: just use the $layout class variable in either the action or the controller. Be sure to add the plugin name to the layout setting. Listing 13-5 gives an example of how to do this.

Listing 13-5. *Using a Plugin Layout in the Plugin Controller*

```
<?
class EventsController extends CalendarAppController {
    var $name = 'Events';
    var $layout = 'Calendar.default';
}
?>
```

The Calendar Plugin

Now that I've explained plugins and how to create one, let's build a plugin for the blog application. This Calendar plugin will be very simple: the author of the blog will store different events in the database, and the user will be able to visit a page showing a month with links to each event. For this plugin to be portable, I will approach writing it from a general standpoint. In other words, I won't necessarily be thinking of the blog application when writing the plugin, though ultimately the plugin will be implemented in the blog.

Setting Up the Files and Folders

Remember that the Calendar plugin will need the controllers, models, and views folders as well as the App controller and App model for it to work properly. In each of these files, the syntax will have to be adjusted so that they all work as a plugin and not as a Cake application element.

Create the plugin root folder, and name it `calendar` after the name of the plugin. In this folder, create all the basic files and folders:

```
calendar/
    calendar_app_controller.php
    calendar_app_model.php
    controllers/
        events_controller.php
    models/
        calendar_event.php
    views/
        events/
```

In the `calendar_app_controller.php` file, be sure to include the appropriate class names:

```
<?
class CalendarAppController extends AppController {
}
?>
```

The App model will also need to be named correctly:

```
<?
class CalendarAppModel extends AppModel {
}
?>
```

Without the App controller and App model, Cake will not be able to connect to the plugin's controllers, models, and views. By naming the classes in the plugin's App controller and App model files, I've made sure Cake knows how to use the plugin and by what name the various elements of the plugin will be called.

The rest of the plugin will be written as though it were a basic Cake application. Of course, you must remember to name the customized controllers, models, and views according to the plugin syntax.

Create the Events Table

The Calendar plugin will need to store data, so let's build an events table in the database. Listing 13-6 contains the SQL needed to create this table.

Listing 13-6. *The* events *Table for the Calendar Plugin*

```
CREATE TABLE `calendar_events` (
  `id` int(11) unsigned NOT NULL auto_increment,
  `name` varchar(255) NULL,
  `date` datetime NULL,
  `details` text NULL,
  PRIMARY KEY (`id`)
);
```

Notice that the table stores only the event's date and time with some details. The name field will contain the text the user will click to read more details about the event. To keep the records from being duplicated, the table includes an ID field that is set to auto_increment. Next, connect the plugin to this table by creating a plugin model.

Create the Event Model

The calendar_events table will need a model with which to connect. Because the table is named with an underscore, the model name will need to be camel-cased. Create a file named calendar_event.php, and store it in the app/plugins/calendar/models directory. Then paste into this file the contents of Listing 13-7.

Listing 13-7. *The* CalendarEvent *Model*

```
1    <?
2    class CalendarEvent extends CalendarAppModel {
3        var $name = 'CalendarEvent';
4        var $uses = array('CalendarEvents');
5    }
6    ?>
```

Notice that on line 2 this model extends the plugin's App model, *not* the surrounding application's App model. Line 3 assigns the model a name, and line 4 sets the $uses array to CalendarEvents, which ensures that the model will connect to the calendar_events table correctly. Lastly, create the controller that will run the plugin.

Create the Events Controller

The Events controller will contain all the actions for the Calendar plugin since the plugin itself is going to be fairly basic. To get this controller working inside the plugin, you must extend the Calendar App controller and provide actions to perform the plugin's logic. Listing 13-8 contains the initial content of the Events controller. Write this code to a new file called app/plugins/calendar/controllers/events_controller.php.

Listing 13-8. *The Initial Contents of the Calendar Events Controller*

```
<?
class EventsController extends CalendarAppController {
    var $name = 'Events';
    var $uses = array('CalendarEvent');
}
?>
```

To launch this new plugin controller, enter the following URL:

```
http://localhost/blog/calendar/events
```

and you should see an error screen asking you to create some actions in the controller. At this point, you should give some consideration to exactly how the plugin should work. The Index action, which is the default action, will show the user the current month's events in a calendar. The Add action will allow the administrator of the web site to write events to the database, and the Edit action will provide access to previously saved events. The View action will have a month and year rather than an ID number, so this action will need to run some more complex find queries through the model. Each of these actions will require views for displaying the results.

Building the Add and Edit Actions

To get started with the Events controller, let's build the actions that allow for adding and editing events to the database. These actions will follow the standard method used by the Bake script. Listing 13-9 demonstrates what to add to the Events controller for these actions to work.

Listing 13-9. *The Add and Edit Actions in the Events Controller*

```
1    function add() {
2        if (!empty($this->data)) {
3            $this->CalendarEvent->create();
4            if ($this->CalendarEvent->save($this->data)) {
5                $this->Session->setFlash(__('The Calendar Event has been saved'➥
, true));
6                $this->redirect(array('action'=>'index'));
7            } else {
8                $this->Session->setFlash(__('The Calendar Event could not be ➥
saved. Please, try again.', true));
9            }
10       }
11   }
12
13   function edit($id=null) {
14       if (!$id && empty($this->data)) {
15           $this->Session->setFlash(__('Invalid Calendar Event', true));
16           $this->redirect(array('action'=>'index'));
17       }
```

```
18          if (!empty($this->data)) {
19              if ($this->CalendarEvent->save($this->data)) {
20                  $this->Session->setFlash(__('The Calendar Event has been saved➦
', true));
21                  $this->redirect(array('action'=>'index'));
22              } else {
23                  $this->Session->setFlash(__('The Calendar Event could not be➦
saved. Please, try again.', true));
24              }
25          }
26          if (empty($this->data)) {
27              $this->data = $this->CalendarEvent->read(null, $id);
28          }
29      }
```

Of course, these actions require accompanying views for them to run properly. These views, too, will follow the standard method used by Bake. Listing 13-10 shows the code for the Add action, and Listing 13-11 provides the same for the Edit action. Save these views in the app/plugins/calendar/views/events directory as add.ctp and edit.ctp.

Listing 13-10. *The Contents of* app/plugins/calendar/views/events/add.ctp

```
<div class="calendar_events form">
<?=$form->create('CalendarEvent',array('url'=>'/calendar/events/add'));?>
    <fieldset>
        <legend>Add Calendar Event</legend>
        <?=$form->input('name');?>
        <?=$form->input('date');?>
        <?=$form->input('details');?>
    </fieldset>
<?=$form->end('Submit');?>
</div>
```

Listing 13-11. *The Contents of* app/plugins/calendar/views/events/edit.ctp

```
<div class="calendar_events form">
<?=$form->create('CalendarEvent',array('url'=>'/calendar/events/edit'));?>
    <fieldset>
        <legend>Edit Calendar Event</legend>
        <?=$form->input('id',array('type'=>'hidden'));?>
        <?=$form->input('name');?>
        <?=$form->input('date');?>
        <?=$form->input('details');?>
    </fieldset>
<?=$form->end('Submit');?>
</div>
```

Notice that in Listings 13-9 and 13-10 the Form helper is used with the URL option set to the path of the Calendar plugin's Events controller. This not only makes the plugin work correctly but also allows the plugin to be more portable. By specifying the path when creating the form, the plugin will point to itself and not accidentally search for a controller or model in the surrounding Cake application with which to save the form data.

Launch both the Add and Edit actions to make sure they run correctly. Also, add some test events to the database for use when building the Index and View actions. You should see a screen similar to Figure 13-1.

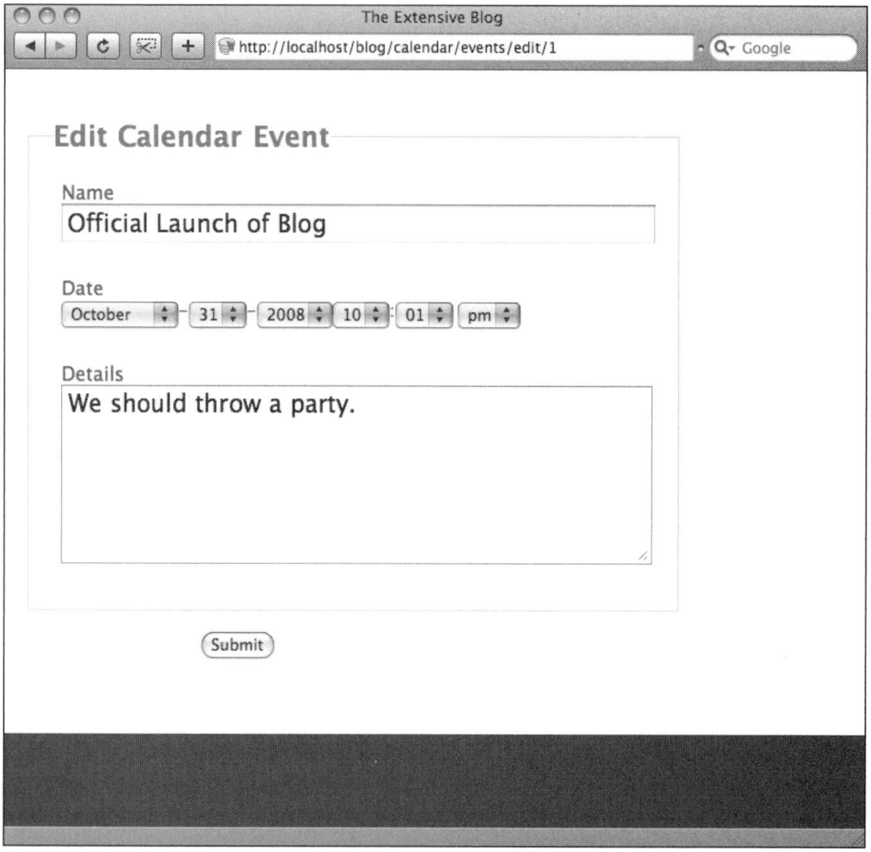

Figure 13-1. *Editing an already saved event. Notice that the default layout in the blog application is applied here, not a layout in the Calendar plugin.*

Building the Index Action

Normally the Index action is the easiest to build because it generally displays a list of records in the database. This plugin, however, is one that will require displaying a calendar of some sort. Thanks to inconsistencies in the calendar year, generating a calendar will take more work than simply running through a list of records. The Index action will have to create a table with rows for each week of the month and then display each day of the week; at the same time, the action must search out any events for the given day and insert those into the cell. Not only the Index action but also the View action will generate a calendar. This sounds like a perfect situation for building a helper function because of all the calculations required *in the view*.

The Calendar Helper

In the app/plugins/calendar/views directory, create a new folder named helpers, and insert a new file named calendar.php there. This file will contain a couple of custom helper functions that primarily render a month's view based on the parameters passed to it. In the Index and View actions, we'll set these parameters and then pass them along to this helper rather than render a calendar in each view file. Because I intend to perform logic in the view, I had better organize the Calendar plugin by using a helper instead of an element. Remember that helpers serve to perform logic in the view, whereas elements make basic displays, or *view templates*, for use across multiple views.

Rendering the month will be a two-step process. First, the helper function will cycle through the weeks of the month, and second, it will cycle through each week. Depending on the month and the year, the first day of the month will vary, so the helper must create some variables to figure out on what day of the week the first day of the month lands and then also figure out the weekends. In the Calendar helper, let's begin by inserting the lines shown in Listing 13-12.

Listing 13-12. *Initializing Some Variables to Be Used by the* app/plugins/calendar/views/helpers/calendar.php *Helper*

```
1     <?
2     class CalendarHelper extends Helper {
3         var $helpers = array('Html');
4
5         function render($events=array(), $month=null, $year=null) {
6             //Initialize variables for this function =>
7             $firstdate = mktime(0, 0, 0, $month, 1, $year);
8             $lastdate = mktime(0, 0, 0, $month+1, 0, $year);
9             $firstday = strftime("%a", $firstdate);
10             $day = 1;
11             $days_array = array(
12                 1=>'Sun', 2=>'Mon', 3=>'Tue', 4=>'Wed', 5=>'Thu', 6=>'Fri', 7➡
=>'Sat',
13                 8=>'Sun', 9=>'Mon',10=>'Tue',11=>'Wed',12=>'Thu',13=>'Fri',14➡
=>'Sat',
14                 15=>'Sun',16=>'Mon',17=>'Tue',18=>'Wed',19=>'Thu',20=>'Fri',21➡
=>'Sat',
15                 22=>'Sun',23=>'Mon',24=>'Tue',25=>'Wed',26=>'Thu',27=>'Fri',28➡
=>'Sat',
16                 29=>'Sun',30=>'Mon',31=>'Tue',32=>'Wed',33=>'Thu',34=>'Fri',35➡
=>'Sat',
17                 36=>'Sun',37=>'Mon',38=>'Tue',39=>'Wed',40=>'Thu',41=>'Fri',42➡
=>'Sat'
18             );
```

Line 7 in Listing 13-12 uses the mktime() function to assign a Unix timestamp to the variable $firstdate. Notice that variables named $month and $year are used to pass the timestamp as month and year values. The first day of the month is used here as well. The last date of the month is also set as a timestamp and assigned to $lastdate. This one is a little bit more complicated: essentially, mktime() is told to provide the timestamp for the following month's day zero, which is the same as the current month's last day. Because each month has a different number of days, this is much handier than trying to specify each month (for example, the last day of February is the 28th except on leap years, the last day of March is the 30th, but the last day of April is the 31st, and so on). Now with timestamps for the first day of a given month and the last day figured out, the helper can iterate through the difference in days and create a table cell for each one.

The layout of the days of the week will not change; in other words, the cells for Sunday will always be the first ones of their respective rows, and each row will represent a week. The trick is to get the dates of the month, which do change from month to month and year to year, to appear in the correct day of the week. Lines 11–18 are the $days_array array, which is a static set of days of the week as they will appear in the calendar. This array will be used to make sure that the helper's iteration of the days in the month breaks on the weekend at the same time the table cells do.

Line 10 contains the $day variable, which here is set to 1. This value represents the current day in the iteration. Each time a table cell is rendered for a day of the month, the $day variable will be called to display the date; then the value will increase by 1 for the next day, and so on.

Line 9 is key to getting the iteration started on the right day of the week. It uses the strftime() function to get a three-letter representation of the day of the week the timestamp $firstdate lands on. Later, this value will be compared with the $days_array values to make sure the first date is placed in the correct cell.

Rendering the First Week of the Month

Let's begin the iteration by placing Listing 13-13 into the Calendar helper.

Listing 13-13. *Starting the Month Table and Iterating Through the First Week of the Month*

```
19    $out = '<table class="calendar" cellspacing="0">';
20    $out .= $this->Html->tableHeaders(array('Sun','Mon','Tue','Wed','Thu',➥
'Fri','Sat'));

21        /*** WEEK ONE ***/
22        $out .= '<tr>';
23        for ($i=1; $i<=7; $i++) {
24            if ($day<=1 && $firstday != $days_array[$i]) {
25                $out .= '<td> </td>';
26            } else {
```

```
27                    $out .= '<td>'.$day.'<br/>';
28                    $out .= $this->events($month,$day,$year,$events);
29                    $out .= '</td>';
30                    $day++;
31                }
32            }
33        $out .= '</tr>';
```

Throughout the rest of this function, the $out variable will be assigned all the output data to be rendered in the view. Notice that line 19 in Listing 13-13 instantiates this variable, and every other time $out is used, new values are appended to its existing contents. Line 19 starts a new table, and line 20 uses the HTML helper to write the table's header cells. Notice that these header cells contain text telling the user which column represents which day of the week.

Lines 22–33 are the first iteration through week one. Notice that this iteration starts with a table row element (<tr>) and ends with the closing tag to finish the row. Line 23 starts a loop for each cell in this row, 1 representing the first cell, or Sun, and 7 representing the last, or Sat. Line 24 checks for where the first day of the month falls. If $day is less than or equal to 1 (in other words, if at this point in the iteration $day is set to the first date of the month) *and* the $firstday timestamp doesn't equal the current day (as specified in $days_array), then the element will display a blank cell. Otherwise, it will create a table cell with the $day value displayed along with any events stored in the database for that day. Such a cell is created with lines 27–30. When a day is displayed, the next day will become the new value for $day, so line 30 increases $day by 1.

Notice that line 28 uses a helper function, $calendar->events(), which has not yet been created. This function will cycle through the $events array, which will be the results from the Events controller. These results come from running a find request in the database for associated events and passed to the helper in line 5 of Listing 13-12. For each event in this array that matches the current day, month, and year in the iteration of week one in Listing 13-13, the $calendar->events() function will return to be displayed in the current day's cell. Since this operation of cycling through the $events array will be repeated for other weeks, it's best to write it as another helper function rather than write the same operation over again. We'll build the $calendar->events() function later. For now, the $out variable is set to pass a new table to the view with one row representing the first week of the month and any events found in the database for this week.

Rendering Weeks Two and Three

Like rendering the first week of the month, let's now add weeks two and three to the helper with Listing 13-14.

Listing 13-14. *Weeks Two and Three in the Calendar Helper*

```
35      /*** WEEK TWO ***/
36      $out .= '<tr>';
37      for ($i=8; $i<=14; $i++) {
38          $out .= '<td>'.$day.'<br/>';
39          $out .= $this->events($month,$day,$year,$events);
40          $out .= '</td>';
41          $day++;
42      }
43      $out .= '</tr>';
44
45      /*** WEEK THREE ***/
46      $out .= '<tr>';
47      for ($i=15; $i<=21; $i++) {
48          $out .= '<td>'.$day.'<br/>';
49          $out .= $this->events($month,$day,$year,$events);
50          $out .= '</td>';
51          $day++;
52      }
53      $out .= '</tr>';
```

Because each cell of weeks two and three must contain a date (in other words, there are no months where these weeks have a starting date or an ending date for the month), checking for the current value of $day is not necessary. The value of $i was last set by week one's loop, so week two begins its loop with values between 8 and 14. The rest of weeks two and three closely resemble what is happening in the loop for week one.

Rendering Week Four

Depending on the year, some months may end on their fourth week. So, for week four, checking for an ending date is necessary. See Listing 13-15 for week four's loop, and paste it into the helper.

Listing 13-15. *Week Four*

```
55      /*** WEEK FOUR ***/
56      $out .= '<tr>';
57      for ($i=22; $i<=28; $i++) {
58          if (strftime("%d",$lastdate) < $day) {
59              $out .= '<td> </td>';
60          } else {
61              $out .= '<td>'.$day.'<br/>';
62              $out .= $this->events($month,$day,$year,$events);
63              $out .= '</td>';
64              $day++;
65          }
66      }
67      $out .= '</tr>';
```

Week four is similar to the other weeks except for lines 58–59 of Listing 13-15. Line 58 checks to see whether the timestamp saved in $lastdate is less than the value for $day. If so, it will output a blank cell (line 59).

Rendering Weeks Five and Six

Not all months will have a fifth week, but some will. In some exceptional cases, there will be months that have a sixth row, so the helper will at least have to accommodate such occurrences. Notice that Listing 13-16 contains loops for weeks five and six and that these are almost the same as previous loops. Where they differ is in checking whether the current month has a fifth or sixth week. If not, the loop won't be performed.

Listing 13-16. *Weeks Five and Six*

```
69      /*** WEEK FIVE ***/
70      if ($day < strftime("%d",$lastdate)) { /* check if there is a fifth row */
71          $out .= '<tr>';
72          for ($i=29; $i<=35; $i++) {
73              if (strftime("%d",$lastdate) < $day) {
74                  $out .= '<td> </td>';
75              } else {
76                  $out .= '<td>'.$day.'<br/>';
77                  $out .= $this->events($month,$day,$year,$events);
78                  $out .= '</td>';
79                  $day++;
80              }
81          }
82          $out .= '</tr>';
83      }
84
85      /*** WEEK SIX ***/
86      if ($day < strftime("%d",$lastdate)) { /* check if there is a sixth row */
87          $out .= '<tr>';
88          for ($i=22; $i<=28; $i++) {
89              if (strftime("%d",$lastdate) < $day) {
90                  $out .= '<td> </td>';
91              } else {
92                  $out .= '<td>'.$day.'<br/>';
93                  $out .= $this->events($month,$day,$year,$events);
94                  $out .= '</td>';
95                  $day++;
96              }
97          }
98          $out .= '</tr>';
99      }
```

Rendering Event Details

Notice that Listing 13-6, which contains the SQL for creating the Calendar Events table, calls for a field named details. This is so that when an event appears in the calendar, the user can click it, and more details will be provided. So far, the $calendar->render() function has taken care of rendering the calendar and displaying events matching each day of a given month. However, the details saved for each event must be provided by the helper, which has not been written yet. Next, close out the month table now that the iterations through each week have been written in the function; then output the contents of the details field for each event using Listing 13-17.

Listing 13-17. *Rendering Event Details*

```
101        $out .= '</table>';
102
103        /*** RENDER EVENT DETAILS ***/
104        if (isset($this->Details)) {
105            foreach ($this->Details as $id=>$detail) {
106                $out .= '<div id="event_details_'.$id.'" style="display: none➥
;" class="_cal_event_detail">';
107                $out .= '<b>'.$detail['name'].'</b>';
108                $out .= '<p>'.date('g:i a',strtotime($detail['date'])).'</p>';
109                $out .= '<p>'.$detail['details'].'</p>';
110                $out .= '</div>';
111            }
112        }
```

Listing 13-17 uses a class attribute that hasn't been specified yet called $this->Details. This is because the $calendar->events() function, which was used to fetch matching events in the $events array earlier, will also pull the contents of details for any matching records and place them into the $this->Details array. Listing 13-17 then loops through the details array and outputs a <div> element for each set after the calendar. Notice that line 106 assigns the unique $id value to the <div> element's ID and uses the style attribute to hide the whole element. In the link provided for each event in the calendar, later you'll use this $id value to display the matching hidden <div>, thus displaying the details for the event when clicked.

The rest of this loop prepares the contents of the details array to be readable in the view. All that's left for the $calendar->render() function is to output the contents of the $out variable. See Listing 13-18 for how to close out this function.

Listing 13-18. *Closing Out the* $calendar->render() *Function*

```
113        return $this->output($out);
114    }
```

Before setting up the $calendar->events() function, the class variable $Details must be defined in the helper class. Scroll up toward the top, and insert the following line after the $helpers array definition:

```
var $Details = array();
```

Now when the $calendar->events() function is used by the $calendar->render() function, it will propagate the $Details array with each event's contents of the details field. The last step for the Calendar helper is to build the $calendar->events() function.

Building the Events Function

As the $calendar->render() function loops through the various weeks for a given month, it uses another function to fetch any matching events from the $events array. Listing 13-19 shows this function; paste it into the Calendar helper after the $calendar->render() function.

Listing 13-19. *The* $calendar->events() *Function*

```
116    function events($month=null, $day=null, $year=null, $events=array()) {
117        $stamp = mktime(0,0,0,$month,$day,$year);
118        $out = '<ul>';
119        foreach($events as $event) {
120            $event_stamp = strtotime($event['date']);
121            $event_stamp = mktime(0,0,0,date('m',$event_stamp),date('d',➥
$event_stamp),date('Y',$event_stamp));
122            if ($event_stamp == $stamp) {
123                $out .= '<a href="#" onClick="$(\'event_details_'.$event➥
['id'].'\').style.display = \'inline\';">';
124                $out .= '<li>'.$event['name'].'</li></a>';
125                $this->Details[$event['id']] = $event;
126            }
127        }
128        $out .= '</ul>';
129        return $this->output($out);
130    }
```

This function takes a preformatted $events array and detects any of its values that match the provided $month, $day, and $year. When the function finds a matching event, it copies the contents of the event's details field to the class array $Details, thus making the details available for any function in the Calendar helper. These details are displayed in the view in lines 104–112 of Listing 13-17. The function also generates an HTML list element and returns the list to its parent function (which so far is only the $calendar->render() function). Because it is currently used by the $calendar->render() function, this list of events will appear within the day cell in the month's table as the View and Index views render the month.

Notice that two timestamps are created to detect matching events: $stamp and $event_stamp. The $event_stamp represents each event's date value; if this value matches the timestamp of the given $month, $day, and $year values, then the function will add the event to the list and its details to the $Details array. The actual loop through the $events array happens on lines 119–127. Remember how the $calendar->render() function generated the hidden <div> elements for displaying event details? Well, line 123 contains the necessary JavaScript for the event's link to display the corresponding hidden <div> element. You could change this to include an animation effect such as scrolling down, depending on your own taste, but at least line 123 shows how the helper provides the user with the requested details. All that is left now is to complete the Index action and view.

Finishing the Index Action

With the Calendar helper able to render a calendar with events, links, and details, the Index action is now ready to request events from the database and pass them through the Calendar helper in the view. Listing 13-20 shows the Index action for the app/plugins/calendar/controllers/events_controller.php file.

Listing 13-20. *The Index Action in the Events Controller*

```
1    function index() {
2         $events = Set::extract($this->CalendarEvent->find('all',array(➡
'conditions'=>array('MONTH(CalendarEvent.date)'=>date('m'),'YEAR(CalendarEvent.➡
date)'=>date('Y')))),'{n}.CalendarEvent');
3         $this->set(compact('events'));
4    }
```

Line 2 of Listing 13-20 may look a little confusing, but actually it is just a typical find request for the model. It uses the Set::extract() function to clean up the array for the helper. I've opted to use this to demonstrate one method for cleaning up arrays. Recall that Cake automatically formats model results into arrays that follow a specific structure. To simplify the code in the $calendar->events() function, you can use Set::extract to take the results from the find() function and remove the CalendarEvent key from the array. For example, if the find returned two events, the result array would by default be formatted something like this:

```
$events = Array(
    [0] => Array(
        [CalendarEvent]=> Array(
            [id] => 1
            [name] => Test Event 1
            [date] => 2008-12-25 01:00:01
            [details] => Merry Christmas
            )
        ),
    [1] => Array(
        [CalendarEvent] => Array(
            [id] => 2
            [name] => Test Event 2
            [date] => 2009-01-01 01:00:00
            [details] => And a happy new year
            )
        )
    );
```

If you passed this same result set through Set::extract() with the following command:

```
$events = Set::extract($events,'{n}.CalendarEvent');
```

then the resulting array would be formatted like this:

```
$events = Array(
    [0] => Array(
        [id] => 1
        [name] => Test Event 1
        [date] => 2008-12-25 01:01:00
        [details] => Merry Christmas
    ),
    [1] => Array(
        [id] => 2
        [name] => Test Event 2
        [date] => 2009-01-01 01:00:00
        [details] => Happy New Year
    )
);
```

Simply put, Set::extract() cleans arrays by reformatting the array. Here in the Calendar plugin, this method of invoking Set::extract() makes looping through the $events array a little easier. More than anything, be advised that Set::extract() is available in your Cake applications or plugins and can help clean up nested arrays. Alternatively, in many cases, you would have to produce your own loops to sift through nested arrays.

Line 2 also uses some SQL syntax to search the date field. Notice that the query searches for events that match the current month and year. By wrapping MONTH() around the field name, Cake knows to run the right SQL query for datetime fields. In other words, by providing an integer representing the current month, the model will search the database for a matching month in the date field without needing a full datetime string. Wrapping YEAR() also works to find the correct year in the date field. The result set will be limited to just those events that occur this month and year.

Line 3 sends the results as the $events array in the view. In the app/plugins/calendar/views/events/index.ctp file, you can now use the $calendar->render() function to take this array and place its contents in the calendar with one string of code. First, make sure the Events controller has access to the Calendar plugin by including it in the $helpers class array near the top of the controller:

```
var $helpers = array('Calendar');
```

Next, create the app/plugins/calendar/views/events/index.ctp file, and paste Listing 13-21.

Listing 13-21. *Contents of the Index View*

```
<h2><?=date('M').' '.date('Y');?></h2>
<?=$calendar->render($events,date('m'),date('Y'));?>
```

Launch the event's Index action in the browser, and you should see a calendar rendered with any test events you may have saved for that month (see Figure 13-2). Remember that this calendar is displayed in the *surrounding application's* layout, not its own layout. Therefore, if you want to change the styles for the calendar, you will need to edit the application's styles, not the plugin's styles. Of course, you could build into the plugin a layout with its own styles, but this could get in the way of another application's views should you distribute the plugin. It's better to stick to the surrounding application's layouts and style sheets than to force the plugin to look a certain way regardless of its parent application.

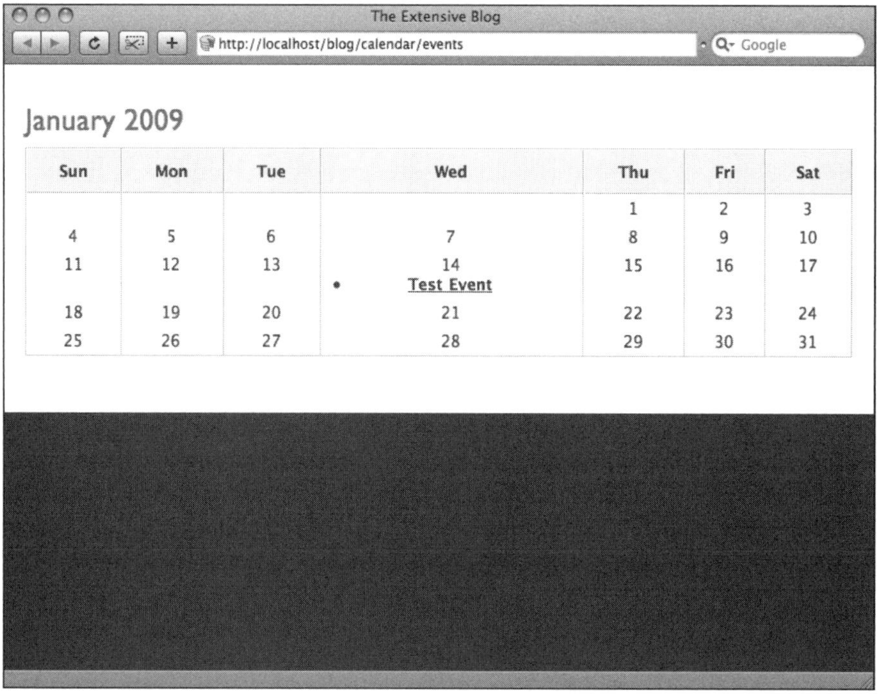

Figure 13-2. *The* `$calendar->render()` *function at work with the Index action view*

Building the View Action

Most of the work for the View action was done while building the Index action. Where this action differs from the Index action is that it bases its calendar on passed month and year values. The same process of formatting the calendar around the result set from the Calendar Events database occurs in the View action as well, so the `$calendar->render()` function is referenced all the same. Listing 13-22 contains the View action to be added to the `app/plugins/calendar/controllers/events_controller.php` file.

Listing 13-22. *The View Action for the Events Controller*

```
1     function view($month=null,$year=null) {
2         if (!$month || !$year || !is_numeric($month) || !is_numeric($year)) {
3             $month = date('m');
4             $year = date('Y');
5         }
6         if ($month > 12 || $month < 1) {
7             $month = date('m');
8         }
9         $events = Set::extract($this->CalendarEvent->find('all',array(➥
'conditions'=>array('MONTH(CalendarEvent.date)'=>$month,'YEAR(CalendarEvent.➥
date)'=>$year))),'{n}.CalendarEvent');
10        $this->set(compact('events','month','year'));
11    }
```

Notice that line 1 includes passed parameters that will come from the URL representing a month and year. Lines 2–5 check to make sure these values exist; if not, it defaults to the current month and year. Line 6 makes sure that the provided month value is between 1 and 12; if not, it sets $month to the current month. Line 9 is identical to Listing 13-20's line 2 except that it uses $month and $year instead of the current month and year. Line 7 also differs from Listing 13-20's line 3 in that it passes along $month and $year to the view.

The corresponding view will also be similar to the Index view. Create the app/plugins/calendar/views/events/view.ctp file, and paste Listing 13-23. This will complete the plugin and allow the parent application to provide calendar views by requesting plugin actions or pointing links to the plugin.

Listing 13-23. *The View Action's View*

```
<h2><?=date('M',mktime(0,0,0,$month,1,$year)).' '.$year;?></h2>
<?=$calendar->render($events,$month,$year);?>
```

Launch the View action by providing a month and a year as parameters, and check for test events to appear in the correct dates. You should be able to enter any integer for the month and year, and the plugin will render a calendar for those values (see Figure 13-3).

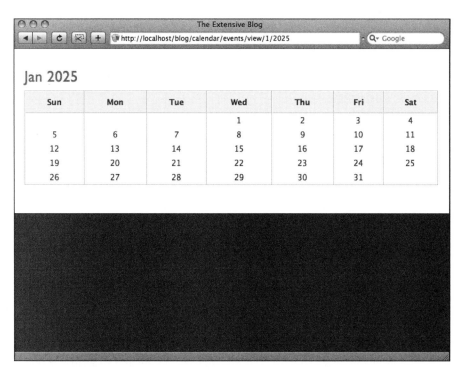

Figure 13-3. *The Calendar plugin using the View action to render a calendar for January, 2025*

Summary

Plugins are like mini-Cake applications that you can bring into any other Cake application. They are useful as third-party resources like Pseudocoder's Ajax Chat plugin but can also help with in-house applications that may need to use the same processes in several Cake projects. I explained how to build a custom plugin by writing the Calendar plugin, which renders calendars for any Cake application based on an events database table. This plugin uses controllers, models, views, and helpers to create a simple calendar view and can extend other Cake applications to handle calendar processes. The next chapter will discuss how to extend one of the most challenging but also efficient aspects of web application development: data handling. Using behaviors and DataSources, you will be able to connect your Cake applications to new data sources and work with data more efficiently.

CHAPTER 14

■ ■ ■

DataSources and Behaviors

Cake's core set of resources strictly adhere to the MVC paradigm, meaning that all output is configured by the view, all data handling is managed by the model, and all business logic is handled by the controller. At this point, however, you're aware of how much the model, view, and controller work together to run as an application. The view doesn't act alone without the controller providing needed variables, the controller doesn't process its logic without the help of the model, and so on. The degree to which these resources work together depends on the unique processes employed by the application. Because the MVC elements work together (more or less simultaneously), you could possibly manipulate one element to perform the work of another. For instance, the model could create output strings to be passed to the view, like HTML tags and form fields. This might work in the short run, but if you were to distribute this application later, it would prove difficult for other Cake developers to work with. Keeping Cake applications portable requires sticking to the MVC structure as much as possible.

But having only model, view, and controller files presents one potential problem: these files could get overdone, meaning that the more complex the application becomes, the more disorganized these resources could appear. True, all data handling is restricted to the model, but what if you want to work with multiple sources of data, such as an XML file here and two different database systems there? In this situation, the model would need to include a large number of connection functions, not to mention find, read, delete, and other necessary data-handling methods. Before long, the MVC structure would begin to lose one of its key advantages: lightweight organization, especially in cases where the application is more elaborate.

Rather than accept the need for very large model, view, and controller files, the Cake developers built into the framework resources that *extend* the MVC structure. I've already discussed a couple of these extensions, such as helpers and components, in previous chapters. By extending the MVC structure, model operations are kept to the model, and view and controller operations are kept to their respective places—but the model, view, and controller files don't get overloaded with functions and data that are repeated throughout the program. Just as basic application procedures (such as working with data and supplying output to the user) get separated by using models, views, and controllers, more complicated procedures (such as producing dynamic views) get separated from their respective resources. In other words, helpers and components provide a *second layer* to working with views and controllers, respectively. Table 14-1 illustrates resources in Cake that extend the MVC layout.

Table 14-1. *Cake Resources That Extend the MVC Layout*

Main Layer Resource	Background Layer Resource(s)
Model	Behavior; DataSource
View	Helper
Controller	Component

By using helpers, you keep the individual views from getting too bloated, and you make detailed output procedures available to other views across the application. Helper functions are processed in the background layer, or while the view is being rendered. Components provide a similar service to the controller by separating out a suite of functions that perform detailed operations. Figure 14-1 shows how the helper extends the view.

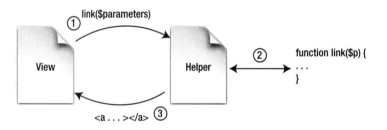

Figure 14-1. *The helper extends the view by housing more elaborate functions that would otherwise clutter the view.*

This is the process:

1. The view calls the $html->link() function to render a link and provides variable parameters for the helper.

2. The link() function processes the passed parameters and pieces together the final output to be used in the view.

3. The HTML helper sends the final <a> element with all the text and attributes back to the view.

The example in Figure 14-1 shows how the view is trimmed down by placing the repetitive task of generating links into the helper. In other words, rather than place the $html->link() function's procedure into the view, Cake keeps it in one place, thus making it accessible to the whole application and at the same time minimizing the amount of code in the view file. This chapter explains how to use two resources that extend the model in the background layer just as helpers and components extend the view and controller.

Extending the Model with DataSources and Behaviors

The first of these resources are *DataSources*.[1] These are resources that connect to extra data-sources in the background and provide data to the model. By using DataSources, you allow the model to work normally, without filling it up with connection, find, read, and other data-handling operations. The model can reference DataSource functions rather than perform the extra connecting itself.

The second resources that extend the model are *behaviors*. These are classes that allow the data used by the model to "behave" differently. In short, some data-processing methods go beyond table associations and simple callbacks; they may perform multiple tasks *with the data* as the data is saved, for instance. Behaviors are invoked when several updates need to be performed simultaneously across the database. Later, I'll describe how to use some of Cake's built-in behaviors to apply a tree structure to the blog application's tags.

Because extending the model is generally the most complicated of resources, this chapter will probably include some of the most difficult concepts to master when learning Cake. Just remember what the overall goal of the resource is and why it's available in Cake in the first place. Your application may not call for an added behavior for your model or a data-source beyond the typical MySQL setup, but knowing what these resources can do and how they work in Cake will almost certainly come in handy at some point.

Working with DataSources

So far in this book we've used only MySQL to work with data, but there certainly are other ways to store data for the application. PostgreSQL, Sybase, Oracle, and Microsoft SQL Server, to name a few, are some of the most popular database systems, and getting Cake to work with them may be important if the project requires it. Fortunately, Cake comes with some built-in DataSources that allow the application to connect to these other systems.

DataSources not only help with other database engines, but they also can be customized to work with other data formats. Reading XML, CSV, or other formats may be accomplished with DataSources. The application can also use other server systems such as LDAP or IMAP through DataSources. Many web applications use some kind of web service API to work with client-side programs that do not use HTML. Combining the power of a Cake application and client-side software can be done with DataSources as well.

The main goal of DataSources is to handle all the connection methods for the model and to provide the model with convenience functions to keep the amount of code in the model as low as possible. These convenience functions, though, do relate to talking with the datasource and not just any model-type procedure. In other words, you want the model to be able to stick

---

1. Defining DataSources can be tricky in Cake. In general, a *datasource* (lowercase) is any source for supplying or saving data. So, MySQL is a datasource, as is an XML file or pulling data from an LDAP server. Cake's method for connecting to these datasources is through a resource file called a *DataSource*, which is not the same as the source of data. To provide consistency in this chapter, I'll stick with DataSource, the camel-cased word, to refer to Cake's resource file and the lowercase word, *datasource*, to refer to the actual source of data. Simply put, in Cake you use DataSources to connect to datasources such as MySQL, XML files, and LDAP servers.

to the read() function rather than have to perform the step-by-step process of reading a record in whatever unique way the current datasource may require. As much as possible, the model shouldn't have to change its current methods to accommodate a particular datasource. For example, Figure 14-2 shows how the MySQL DataSource extends the model so that the model doesn't have to figure out the necessary SQL query strings and perform the connection methods for the database.

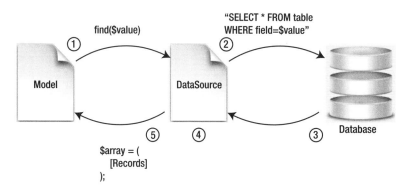

Figure 14-2. *The MySQL DataSource pieces together the connection strings and database queries for the model.*

Here's the process:

1. The model runs one of its functions, which gets sent to the DataSource; in this case, find() is invoked, and the contents of $value are sent.

2. The DataSource pieces together a query string based on the language of the source, connects to the source, and runs the query; in this case, the MySQL DataSource runs a query like "SELECT * FROM table WHERE field=$value".

3. The datasource returns a result set; here, the MySQL DataSource performs some mysql_fetch_array() functions and loops through the result set from the database to get the final results.

4. Once the final results are obtained, the DataSource formats the set for use in the model. This will usually be an array of some kind.

5. The formatted array or result set is sent back to the model. The model then uses the data for its own purposes.

Using Built-in DataSources

Cake's built-in DataSources include support only for relational database systems. Because they act as a layer between the model and the database, no additional DataSource functions are invoked in the model. To change from one DataSource to another, simply adjust the database configuration file.

The first step in changing the main DataSource for the application is to set the driver parameter in app/config/database.php. Open this file, and you'll find the DATABASE_CONFIG class; it should contain the original settings you used when first setting up the blog application (see Listing 14-1).

Listing 14-1. *The* `DATABASE_CONFIG` *Class in* `app/config/database.php`

```
1   class DATABASE_CONFIG {
2       var $default = array(
3           'driver' => 'mysql',
4           'persistent' => false,
5           'host' => 'localhost',
6           'port' => '',
7           'login' => 'root',
8           'password' => 'root',
9           'database' => 'blog',
10          'schema' => '',
11          'prefix' => '',
12          'encoding' => ''
13      );
14  }
```

Lines 2–13 of Listing 14-1 contain the `$default` variable that tells Cake where to connect to the default datasource. The blog application currently connects to MySQL through the built-in MySQL DataSource. This is set in line 3 with the `driver` parameter. By changing this to another driver, Cake will use the new corresponding DataSource instead of MySQL. Table 14-2 shows a list of available driver options that you can use depending on the DataSource you want to connect with.

Table 14-2. *Driver Options Available for the* `DATABASE_CONFIG` *Class*

Driver Parameter	DataSource	Minimum PHP Version Requirement
db2	IBM DB2, Cloudscape, and Apache Derby	PHP 4
mssql	Microsoft SQL Server 2000 and higher	PHP 4
mysql	MySQL 4 and 5	PHP 4
mysqli	MySQL 4 and 5 improved interface	PHP 5
oracle	Oracle 8 and higher	PHP 4
postgres	PostgreSQL 7 and higher	PHP 4
sqlite	SQLite	PHP 5
adodb-[drivername]	ADOdb interface wrapper	PHP 4
pear-[drivername]	PEAR::DB wrapper	PHP 4

To get an idea of how these DataSources work with their respective systems, you can open the files themselves. The `cake/libs/model/datasources/dbo` folder stores the DataSource files that Cake uses when you change the `driver` parameter to one of those listed in Table 14-2. Should you set `driver` to something other than what is stored in this directory, you would need to manually provide the DataSource code for Cake to work. When building a custom

DataSource, which I'll describe in this chapter, consulting these built-in DataSources can sometimes be helpful. In them are great examples of how to preserve the model layer; all the models behave the same regardless of the DataSource being used.

Building a Custom DataSource

Writing a custom DataSource requires a little more than writing other resources in Cake. You may be used to the usual routine of creating Cake files—first, create a new file with the appropriate file name and in the appropriate location; second, type the correct class name in the file; last, add to the file your customizations and methods. With DataSources, however, a couple of additional tasks are required to get them working in your application. You'll need to define the DataSource in the application's database configuration file: app/config/database.php. Then you'll need to define the DataSource in the model that calls it.

To walk you through writing a custom DataSource, let's build an XML DataSource for the blog application. This DataSource will open an XML file that is formatted to include stories for the blog and will prepare the file's contents for inclusion in the database. In a more ambitious (theoretical) project, this process could be amplified to include saving all the blog's information; you could bypass using a database altogether in favor of writing everything as XML to a file. Here, though, the DataSource will remain simpler and allow for simple updates. For instance, you may want to write your blog posts in an external editor and not directly to the database through a web browser. In your word processor you could export the posts as XML files and then import them to the blog with the XML DataSource in this chapter. Whatever the case, building the XML DataSource will at least demonstrate how to extend the capabilities of the model and how to customize a DataSource in the first place.

Creating the DataSource File

DataSources are stored in the app/models/datasources folder and are named in lowercase with _source.php appended to the end. To give the DataSource a title with more than one word, be sure to use the underscore character as a separator in the file name.

Create the XML DataSource file, and open it for editing: app/models/datasources/xml_source.php. The DataSource must be set up as a class object extending the DataSource object. Copy the contents of Listing 14-2 to the new app/models/datasources/xml_source.php file.

Listing 14-2. *The XML DataSource Class*

```
1    <?
2    class XmlSource extends DataSource {
3        var $description = 'XML DataSource';
4    }
5    ?>
```

Line 3 of Listing 14-2 contains the $description variable. Use this variable to provide a one-line description of the DataSource.

Starting with a Minimum Skeleton

DataSources differ from other resources in that they require several functions to be present, even if those functions do not contain any logic. Without this "skeleton" of basic functions, the model class will encounter errors. After line 3 of the xml_source.php file, paste Listing 14-3, which contains the necessary DataSource functions.

Listing 14-3. *The Main Skeleton for DataSource Files*

```
5     function __construct($config=null) {
6         parent::__construct($config);
7         $this->connected = $this->connect();
8         return $config;
9     }
10
11    function __destruct() {
12        $this->connected = $this->close();
13        parent::__destruct();
14    }
15
16    function connect() { }
17
18    function close() { }
19
20    function read() { }
21
22    function query() { }
23
24    function describe() { }
25
26    function column() { }
27
28    function isConnected() { }
29
30    function showLog() { }
```

Each of these functions may be called by the model as both the DataSource and the model work together. Even though the functions listed on lines 16–30 of Listing 14-3 don't yet contain any logic or parameters, their being entered in the DataSource keeps the model from calling a function that doesn't exist. True, when the model calls read() or query(), for instance, it will receive a null response, but this at least won't potentially result in a Warning: Function does not exist error. Later, you'll extend these skeleton functions as needed.

Two functions, however, not only are present as part of the skeleton but are key for the DataSource to work at all: __construct() and __destruct(). These functions are written in Listing 14-3 as lines 5–14. More could be included in them, but for the moment they contain the very basics for the DataSource to work. When the DataSource object is instantiated, Cake needs to pass along parameters from app/config/database.php to the object. In a sense, Cake "binds" the DataSource through the __construct() function and the $config variable. If __construct() isn't working with $config, Cake will not establish the binding correctly, and consequently the model won't be able to "talk" to the DataSource. In a minute you'll configure the $config variable in database.php, but for now the __construct() function has to include the basic code to handle the DataSource configuration Cake will use later.

Lines 6 and 13 of Listing 14-3 call out the parent object as part of this binding process. Notice that the parent object's constructor and destructor functions pass along the $config variable. By using these functions in this way, you keep settings in Cake's core configuration from conflicting with any existing DataSource parameters. In other words, Cake will link the right settings with the right DataSource.

Both __construct() and __destruct() use other functions—connect() and close(), respectively—which as yet don't do any connecting or disconnecting. This is only the case here because the actual method of connecting to the datasource is specific to the source itself. In this example, connect() will later open the XML file and will return a true or false result depending on how effective it is at finding and opening the file. This could change if, for example, this DataSource connected to a database—the method of connecting would be entirely different and therefore would require a different set of instructions for connect() to be able to establish a connection and return a response.

The object variable $connected in line 7 is referenced by the model to determine the status of the DataSource. When true, $connected tells the model that the DataSource is working correctly. Later, the destructor will set $connected to false, which will be the last method called for the DataSource. Together, __construct(), __destruct(), and the $connect object variable establish a connection with the datasource, indicate the status of the connection, and terminate the connection.

Setting Up the Database Configuration to Include the DataSource

As mentioned earlier, just creating the DataSource file and including the minimum skeleton of functions doesn't automatically include the DataSource in the application. Like the helper, the DataSource must be included with some code elsewhere in the application to work correctly. Though including helpers is done in the controller, DataSources differ in that they are included in the DATABASE_CONFIG class in app/config/database.php.

Paste the array in Listing 14-4 into app/config/database.php after the $default array to provide the necessary DataSource configuration.

Listing 14-4. *The* $xml *Configuration Array*

```
1    var $xml = array(
2        'datasource' => 'Xml',
3        'file' => 'data.xml'
4    );
```

Line 1 of Listing 14-4 instantiates a new object variable named $xml. This could be named whatever you like, but remember to link the datasource parameter in line 2 to the name of the DataSource. I've named the XML DataSource class XmlSource (see line 2 of Listing 14-2), so Xml is the necessary value to be set in the datasource parameter. The rest of the $xml array contains any keys and values you want to pass to the DataSource. Lines 5 and 6 in Listing 14-3 use the $config variable; this will be the same as the matching array from database.php, which in this case is the $xml array. This DataSource will need to connect to the XML file data.xml.

Later, you'll provide this file as app/webroot/files/data.xml. By specifying this parameter in the database configuration file, I've adhered to the consistency in the Cake application; all the datasource connections are defined in one place, the database.php file. Now that the database.php file includes the configuration settings for the XML DataSource, the model can work with the DataSource.

Using the DataSource in the Model

A couple of key setup routines have to be accomplished before the DataSource and model can begin working together:

1. The DataSource file must be appropriately named and placed in the app/models/datasources folder.

2. The DataSource class must be appropriately named and set to extend the DataSource object.

3. The DataSource file must include at least a minimum set of functions outlined in Listing 14-3.

4. The database configuration file must define the DataSource in an object array.

5. This same object array must be referenced by the setDataSource() function in the model.

6. The DataSource object must be instantiated in the model with the getDataSource() function.

At this point, you've completed steps 1–4 in setting up the DataSource. Notice that steps 5 and 6 are accomplished in the model. Let's open the app/models/post.php file and get the XML DataSource working there.

Listing 14-5 contains the xmlFindAll() function to be placed in the post.php file. This function uses the XML DataSource to return an array of values in the data.xml file.

Listing 14-5. *The* xmlFindAll() *Function in the* Post *Model*

```
1    function xmlFindAll() {
2        $this->setDataSource('xml');
3        $xml = $this->getDataSource();
4        return $xml->findAll();
5    }
```

Notice that lines 2–3 of Listing 14-5 accomplish the last steps of the DataSource setup routine. Line 2 uses the setDataSource() function to link the $xml array in app/config/database.php to the model. When this line is called, the XML DataSource __construct() function is automatically run, and the $xml array is passed to this function as the $config array. The setDataSource() function not only links up the model to the DataSource but also makes it the main driver for the model. In other words, the MySQL driver/DataSource is no longer being run in the model while the XML DataSource is being used. Whenever the controller calls on the model to connect to the default DataSource, this instance of the XML DataSource object is destroyed, and the __destruct() method is automatically invoked.

Line 3 assigns the XML DataSource object to the variable $xml. From now on in the model, any function in the DataSource file may be run by referencing the new $xml object, which is done in line 4; the $xml->findAll() function will be the same as the findAll() function you'll later insert into the DataSource.

When the controller calls the xmlFindAll() function, the model will return a set of values to be used in the controller and view. Notice that this model function doesn't have all the connection code that will soon appear in the DataSource. This will keep the model trim and able to deal with the data rather than managing all the connections to the datasource.

Reading the XML File

Now that the setup routine is complete and the model is ready to begin using DataSource functions, you're ready to put the DataSource to work. Right now the findAll() function does nothing. Before it can do any reading, the connect() function on line 16 in Listing 14-3 must connect to the XML file and fetch its contents for use in the DataSource. Replace connect() with Listing 14-6 to provide the DataSource with the necessary connection method.

Listing 14-6. *The Improved* connect() *Function in the XML DataSource*

```
16    function connect() {
17        App::import('Core','File');
18        $this->FileUtil =& new File(WWW_ROOT.'files/'.$this->config['file']);
19        $this->File = $file->read();
20        if (!$this->File) {
21            return false;
22        } else {
23            return true;
24        }
25    }
```

Throughout the DataSource file, the configuration array defined in app/config/database.php will be available as the object variable $config. Don't confuse this variable with the $config variable used by the __construct() function from Listing 14-3. In fact, the *result* of the constructor method—or, in other words, the returned value in the __construct() function—is assigned to the standard object variable $config for the DataSource. This means that anywhere in the rest of the DataSource (except the __construct() function), the configuration values returned by the constructor are available as $this->config. It just so happens that __construct() performs the necessary method to fetch the $xml array from app/config/database.php and return it as $this->config for the DataSource to use. The connect() function in Listing 14-6 uses $this->config to retrieve the datasource's file name. Notice that line 18 calls for this file name in the File utility. Using the WWW_ROOT global variable, line 18 also contains the path to the file relative to Cake. In this case, the file will need to be stored in the Cake file system as app/webroot/files/data.xml. Of course, $this->config['file'] corresponds to $xml['file'] defined on line 3 of Listing 14-4.

Thanks to the File utility class, reading the contents of app/webroot/files/data.xml is a snap. Line 18 grabs the file itself and assigns it as part of the File utility's class object. Then, on line 19, the File utility's read() function is used to read the contents of the file and assign them to a class variable named $File. You may have noticed that this variable hasn't yet been defined; do that by inserting the following string under the $description class variable shown in line 3 of Listing 14-2 (or in line 3 of the current XML DataSource file):

```
var $File = null;
```

Assigning the contents of the file to an object variable as opposed to a standard variable is important for making sure that all the other functions in the DataSource have access to this file. For this same reason, the resulting File utility object ought to be made available to the rest of the DataSource as well. This is done in line 18 by assigning the new File object to the instance variable $FileUtil. This, too, needs to be defined in the class to work correctly. Insert this definition near the $File definition:

```
var $FileUtil = null;
```

Later, the __destruct() and close() functions will close the data.xml file to keep the application's load on the server to a minimum. These functions will need the File utility object, which is accessible outside the connect() function because I've assigned it to the $FileUtil instance variable.

The connect() function has essentially performed a connection method by providing the file contents of data.xml to the rest of the DataSource. All that's left for this function is to return a true or false result to the constructor. Lines 20–24 check for any content in the $File variable and return this result. Now that the data.xml file has been opened and its contents made available to the rest of the DataSource, you're ready to move on to the findAll() function called by the model.

Disconnecting from the XML File

For good measure, the DataSource should include a method for disconnecting from the source. The __destruct() function defined in Listing 14-3 already does this, except that the close() function it calls has nothing in it yet. Replace the close() function (which should now appear on line 29 of the app/models/datasources/xml_source.php file) with the contents of Listing 14-7.

Listing 14-7. *The Improved* close() *Function*

```
29    function close() {
30        if ($this->FileUtil->close()) {
31            return false;
32        } else {
33            return true;
34        }
35    }
```

The result of this function may seem backward only because a false result usually means that the method failed. In this case, returning false sets the $connected class variable to the proper value; it tells the model that the connection status is disconnected, or zero.

Line 30 of Listing 14-7 uses the File utility class function close() to close the data.xml file. Simply put, if this is accomplished, then all close() has left to do is report false to the destructor, which is done on line 31.

Parsing the XML File

Before the DataSource parses the XML file, let's give it something with which to work. Paste something like the contents of Listing 14-8 into the `app/webroot/files/data.xml` file. Notice that Listing 14-8 is formatted as XML 1.0 standard tags named after fields in the current `posts` table in the database.

Listing 14-8. *Contents to be Added to the* `data.xml` *File*

```
<?xml version="1.0" encoding="UTF-8"?>
<blog>
    <post>
        <id></id>
        <name>Writing Posts in XML is a Snap</name>
        <date>2008-11-08 12:00:01</date>
        <content>Using the XML utility class in Cake with the Set::reverse()➥
 function makes parsing XML easy.</content>
        <user_id>1</user_id>
    </post>
    <post>
        <id></id>
        <name>More XML Posts, Not so Bad</name>
        <date>2008-11-08 12:00:02</date>
        <content>Using the XML utility class in Cake with the Set::extract()➥
 function makes parsing XML easy.</content>
        <user_id>1</user_id>
    </post>
</blog>
```

Aside from the XML specification string on line 1 of Listing 14-8, the tags used here are structured hierarchically like the `posts` table: the `<blog>` tag is named after the name of the database; `<post>` is used for each row in the `posts` table; `<id>` corresponds to the ID field, and so on, through `<user_id>`. Once these tags are parsed by the `findAll()` function, an array will be passed to the model just like when the default MySQL DataSource passes a result set from the database.

Currently, this same content in Listing 14-8 is assigned to `$File` upon connecting to the `data.xml` file. All the `read()` function has to do is parse through these XML tags and format the array for the model accordingly. Listing 14-9 contains the `findAll()` function that parses the XML. Paste this into the XML DataSource file.

Listing 14-9. *The* `findAll()` *Function*

```
37    function findAll() {
38        App::import('Core','Xml');
39        $xml = Set::reverse(new Xml($this->File));
40        return Set::extract($xml,'Post');
41    }
```

Thanks to the XML utility class (which is imported into the function on line 38 of Listing 14-9), parsing through all those XML tags is made much easier. Line 39, for instance, creates a new XML utility class object from the contents of `$File`, which currently contains the contents of the `data.xml` file. With this object, XML utility functions are available to the DataSource such as counting the number of child nodes for a particular tag, pulling names and values from the XML data, and so forth. A handy method for cutting down on the number of loops through all those tags and nodes is to use the Set utility class, which is done on lines 39 and 40.

The Set utility contains several functions for working with result sets of data. Cake's core libraries use this utility when constructing the arrays that make `$this->data` and `$this->params`, which has proven useful in earlier chapters when we explored the Form helper and managing form submissions. Using Set not only cuts down on the number of operations needed to construct Cake-friendly data arrays but can be used with the XML utility to piece together an array of data from the XML file that matches the standard arrays used in the model.

On line 39, `Set::reverse()` is used together with a new instantiation of the XML utility class object to create a Cake-friendly array out of the XML tags. The `Set::reverse()` function is used here because it converts objects into arrays.

This array would vary in its structure depending on the hierarchy in the XML file and can even be inconsistent depending on how many `<post>` tags appear in `$this->File`. To guarantee that the same structure is applied to the array, the `Set::extract()` function is used on line 40. In short, `Set::extract()` takes the `$xml` array formatted by `Set::reverse()` on line 39 and looks for array keys named `Post`. It then extracts each of those nested arrays and constructs a new array out of the results. This array is then forwarded to the model with the `return` command.

If you wanted to get more elaborate with this XML file, you could explore the XML utility in more depth and use more of its functions. Assigning attributes to tags, for example, could extend the XML file to include more types of data, not to mention more associations within the file with the use of other tags (like `<user>` or `<tag>` to match the `users` and `tags` tables in the current database). For the moment, the XML DataSource parses the `data.xml` file for use in the controller and view. All that's left is to display the data and make it accessible for the user.

Viewing the Data

The XML DataSource and the model are now working correctly. Viewing the XML data in `data.xml` is now as simple in the controller and view as fetching data from the database. In the Posts Index action in `app/controllers/posts_controller.php`, use the `xmlFindAll()` function from the `Post` model to run a "find all" query of the new datasource by inserting the following line:

```
$this->set('xml',$this->Post->xmlFindAll());
```

The parsed XML is now available in the Index view as `$xml`. Use the `debug()` function to view its contents. You should get the following results:

```
Array
(
    [0] => Array
        (
            [Post] => Array
                (
                    [name] => Writing Posts in XML is a Snap
                    [date] => 2008-11-08 12:00:01
                    [content] => Using the XML utility class in Cake with the ➥
Set::reverse() function makes parsing XML easy.
                    [user_id] => 1
                )
        )

    [1] => Array
        (
            [Post] => Array
                (
                    [name] => More XML Posts, Not so Bad
                    [date] => 2008-11-08 12:00:02
                    [content] => Using the XML utility class in Cake with the ➥
Set::extract() function makes parsing XML easy.
                    [user_id] => 1
                )
        )
)
```

This array looks just like those you're used to in Cake. In the Index view, you can add these results to the list by running a loop just like the current loop for the $posts variable. Of course, in the app/webroot/files/data.xml file, I left the <id> tags blank; you'll have to set those manually or build an auto_increment method into the DataSource to provide a unique ID for each post in the XML file.

Not only can DataSources connect with external files, but they can also be used for pulling data from just about anywhere, such as a web service, e-mail, or some legacy system. This tutorial explored using XML as an external datasource and demonstrated how extending the model in this way actually improves the code and maintains better order throughout the framework. Third-party DataSources by other developers are already available online; you might want to try installing one as practice for using DataSources in your Cake applications.

Working with Behaviors

Another way to extend the model is with behaviors. Behaviors provide "rules" for models, like the rules you may set on your mail program to apply to your incoming mail. For example, you may want the model, when updating a record in the database, to perform multiple calculations of the data on the fly and not only update one record or a couple of associated records but perform a series of updates across the database. Using a behavior, rather than building into the model all the necessary functions to manage this kind of updating, keeps repetitive tasks in a separate resource file and makes the model more versatile by allowing multiple models to access more complicated processes without bogging them down. Cake comes with four built-in behaviors: ACL, Containable, Translate, and Tree. In this chapter, I'll explain how to use the Tree behavior to improve how the blog categorizes posts. Creating custom behaviors is actually simpler than making your own DataSources; understanding how the built-in behaviors work will make crafting your own behaviors much easier.

Using the Tree Behavior to Categorize Blog Posts

The blog application uses the `tags` table to manage multiple tags to be applied to a post. What if you wanted to create a hierarchy of tags, or a "tree" of data of some kind? One tag could then become a "parent" of another tag, and a series of tags could be assigned as "children" to one tag. Then, once a tag is assigned to a post, by clicking the parent tag, all the associated posts for that parent tag and its child tags would be listed for the user. This method for working with hierarchical data is more effective than building several relational databases to manage the hierarchy. Fortunately, Cake comes with the Tree behavior that maintains a tree of data dynamically.

Inserting Required Fields into the Tags Table

Using the Tree behavior requires that the database table associated with the behavior be organized a certain way. In this case, the `tags` table will need to include a couple of extra fields for the Tree behavior to save its own parameters. Wherever you use the Tree behavior, remember to provide these three fields:

- `parent_id`
- `lft`
- `rght`

The left and right fields, or `lft` and `rght`, are used by the Tree behavior to organize the position of the node in the tree. The `parent_id` field links with the ID of the record in the table that behaves as the parent node of the current record. Currently, the `tags` table doesn't include these fields. To prepare the blog to use the Tree behavior, replace the `tags` table following the specifications in Listing 14-10.

Listing 14-10. *The Tags Table with Required Fields for the Tree Behavior*

```
CREATE TABLE `tags` (
    `id` int(11) unsigned NOT NULL auto_increment,
    `parent_id` int(11) unsigned default NULL,
    `left` int(11) unsigned default NULL,
    `right` int(11) unsigned default NULL,
    `name` varchar(255) default NULL,
    PRIMARY KEY('id')
);
```

Notice that Listing 14-10 doesn't call the left and right fields by their default values lft and rght; these may be set to whatever name you choose, and here I've opted for left and right. Later, when calling the Tree behavior in the model, I'll specify these field names.

Baking a New Tags Controller and Views

Now that the tags table includes the required fields for the Tree behavior to function correctly, the Tags controller and views will need to be regenerated. Use Bake to create a new controller—make sure *not* to use admin routing, scaffolding, additional components, or additional helpers; *do* make sure to use sessions and to create the basic view methods (index, edit, add, view). The new Tags controller should have the code shown in Listing 14-11, or something very similar.

Listing 14-11. *The Baked Tags Controller*

```php
1    <?php
2    class TagsController extends AppController {
3
4        var $name = 'Tags';
5        var $helpers = array('Html', 'Form');
6
7        function index() {
8            $this->Tag->recursive = 0;
9            $this->set('tags', $this->paginate());
10       }
11
12       function view($id = null) {
13           if (!$id) {
14               $this->Session->setFlash(__('Invalid Tag.', true));
15               $this->redirect(array('action'=>'index'));
16           }
17           $this->set('tag',$this->Tag->read(null,$id));
18       }
19
20       function add() {
21           if (!empty($this->data)) {
22               $this->Tag->create();
23               if ($this->Tag->save($this->data)) {
24                   $this->Session->setFlash(__('The Tag has been saved', true));
25                   $this->redirect(array('action'=>'index'));
26               } else {
27                   $this->Session->setFlash(__('The Tag could not be saved.➥
 Please, try again.', true));
28               }
29           }
30           $posts = $this->Tag->Post->find('list');
31           $this->set(compact('posts'));
32       }
33
```

```
34        function edit($id = null) {
35            if (!$id && empty($this->data)) {
36                $this->Session->setFlash(__('Invalid Tag', true));
37                $this->redirect(array('action'=>'index'));
38            }
39            if (!empty($this->data)) {
40                if ($this->Tag->save($this->data)) {
41                    $this->Session->setFlash(__('The Tag has been saved', true));
42                    $this->redirect(array('action'=>'index'));
43                } else {
44                    $this->Session->setFlash(__('The Tag could not be saved. ➥
Please, try again.', true));
45                }
46            }
47            if (empty($this->data)) {
48                $this->data = $this->Tag->read(null, $id);
49            }
50            $posts = $this->Tag->Post->find('list');
51            $this->set(compact('posts'));
52        }
53
54        function delete($id = null) {
55            if (!$id) {
56                $this->Session->setFlash(__('Invalid id for Tag', true));
57                $this->redirect(array('action'=>'index'));
58            }
59            if ($this->Tag->del($id)) {
60                $this->Session->setFlash(__('Tag deleted', true));
61                $this->redirect(array('action'=>'index'));
62            }
63        }
64    }
65    ?>
```

Next, use Bake to create the Action views for the Tags controller. You should end up with the app/views/tags folder with add.ctp, edit.ctp, index.ctp, and view.ctp files inside. With the Tags controller and views working properly, the blog now has a basic interface for adding, editing, and deleting tags. The Tag model already has the "has and belongs to many" relationship built into it, so tags can also be associated with specific blog posts. Here is where the Tree behavior will come in—rather than build into the application a mechanism whereby the user can click a tag and retrieve a list of related posts, the Tree behavior will be used as well. Thus, when clicking a tag, the user will not only get a list of associated posts but also a list of associated tags' posts.

Using the Tree Behavior in the Model

With the database ready to handle the Tree behavior and a baked controller with views, the model is ready to call out the behavior. This is done using the $actsAs property in the model.

Open app/models/tag.php, and insert the $actsAs property near the $hasAndBelongsToMany property. The value set in $actsAs corresponds to the behavior being used; in this case, $actsAs is set to Tree. Once you have entered the $actsAs property, your Tag model should appear like Listing 14-12.

Listing 14-12. *The* Tag *Model with the Tree Behavior Included*

```
1    <?
2    class Tag extends AppModel {
3        var $name = 'Tag';
4        var $actsAs = array('Tree'=>array(
5            'left'=>'left',
6            'right'=>'right'
7        ));
8        var $hasAndBelongsToMany = array('Post');
9    }
10   ?>
```

Lines 5 and 6 in Listing 14-12 show how I've specified the left and right field names. Since I didn't use the default names lft and rght, I've had to assign an array to Tree on line 4 and include the left and right parameters shown in lines 5–6. The values assigned to these parameters correspond to the field names of the left and right fields in the tags table, which in this case is left and right, respectively.

To attach multiple behaviors to the model, simply continue the $actsAs array. For example, if I wanted to attach a custom behavior as well as the Tree behavior to the Tag model, I would enter something like this:

```
var $actsAs = array('Tree','MyBehavior');
```

Each behavior name in the array can also include a set of parameters like those shown in Listing 14-12; just assign an array as a value to each behavior name:

```
var $actsAs = array(
    'Tree'=>array(
        'left'=>'left',
        'right'=>'right'
    ),
    'MyBehavior'=>array(
        'recursive'=>1
    )
);
```

Now that the $actsAs property is set to Tree, and the appropriate field names for the left and right fields are set in the parameters array, nothing else needs to be done in the model. All the Tree behavior's functions are accessible in the controller or model, which is the next task for getting the tags organized hierarchically.

Adjusting Views

When the Tags views were generated by Bake, they included behavior fields (parent_id, left, and right). These might conflict with the Tree behavior if they stay as part of a form submission, so it's important they be removed from the views. Find the Form helper functions in each of the baked views that call one of the behavior's fields, and remove them from the file. You should be left with the name field only and, in some instances, the id field.

Next, to give a tag a parent node, the Add and Edit views must have a way of selecting a parent ID. To do this, place a select menu containing a list of Tags in the Add and Edit views. For this menu to work, you will first have to generate a Tags list in the controller and then use the Form helper to render the select menu in the view. Open app/controllers/tags_controller.php, and add the following line to the Add and Edit actions:

```
$tags = $this->Tag->find('list');
```

Now that a list of tags is available as the $tags array, pass the variable to the view by rewriting the set() function to include both $posts and $tags:

```
$this->set(compact('posts','tags'));
```

In the Add and Edit views, use the Form helper to provide the select menu. Remember that it will need some added parameters to work correctly with the controller. Listing 14-13 includes the $form->input() function that renders the select menu. Add Listing 14-13 to app/views/tags/add.ctp and app/views/tags/edit.ctp in place of where Bake wrote the parent_id form input field.

Listing 14-13. *The* parent_id *Select Menu in the Add and Edit Views*

```
1    echo $form->input('parent_id',array(
2        'label'=>'Parent Tag',
3        'type'=>'select',
4        'options'=>$tags,
5        'empty'=>'- No Parent Tag -'
6    ));
```

Notice that on line 1 of Listing 14-13, the field name passed to the Form helper is parent_id, which corresponds with the parent ID field in the tags table. The rest of Listing 14-13 contains parameters that tell the Form helper to render a select menu (on line 3 with the type parameter), to use the $tags array passed by the controller as the options in the menu (on line 4 with the options parameter), to make the first and NULL option of the menu - No Parent Tag - (on line 5 with the empty parameter), and to give the menu the label Parent Tag instead of the default label (on line 2 with the label parameter).

To test the Tags Add and Edit views, let's add some categories to the tags table. For your information, I've included the following names with their respective IDs in Table 14-3; of course, you can enter whatever values you like.

Table 14-3. *Some Sample Tags to Test the Controllers, Views, and Eventually the Tree Behavior*

ID	Name
1	CakePHP
2	PHP
3	Programming
4	Web
5	Frameworks

Table 14-3 shows tags that can be easily ordered into a data tree. For example, "CakePHP" relates to "PHP" as a child node; "PHP" is a child of "Programming," as are "Web" and "Frameworks." The Tree behavior will allow you to assign the parent tags to each tag accordingly. Before it can do this, however, you'll have to make sure that the $this->data array contains the right parent ID name and value for the model to pass along the results of the select menu correctly. If $this->data['parent_id'] isn't set in the first place, no tags will have parents, and the Tree behavior won't be able to manage the data as you want. So, in the Edit action, use the debug() function to display the contents of $this->data, like so:

```
<? debug($this->data);?>
```

Next, open a tag record in the Edit view by entering a URL that matches one of the tags, something like http://localhost/blog/tags/edit/1. You should see the debug() function display $this->data, as shown in Listing 14-14.

Listing 14-14. *The Contents of* $this->data *After the* parent_id *Field and Select Menu Has Been Added*

```
1    Array
2    (
3        [Tag] => Array
4        (
5            [id] => 1
6            [parent_id] => 2
7            [left] =>
8            [right] =>
9            [name] => CakePHP
10       )
11       [Post] => Array
12       (
13           [0] => Array
14           (
15               [id] => 1
16               [name] => New Cake 1.2 Functions
17               [date] => 2008-01-01 01:01:01
18               [content] => Some snazzy new functions are now available in ➥
1.2 that you should check out!
19               [user_id] => 1
```

```
20                    [PostsTag] => Array
21                    (
22                        [id] =>
23                        [post_id] => 1
24                        [tag_id] => 1
25                    )
26                )
27            )
28    )
```

Notice that the associated post shows up in the $this->data['Post'] array (lines 11–27 of Listing 14-14) because of the hasAndBelongsToMany association already set up in the Post and Tag models. This array would be much larger if more posts were associated with the current tag, but Listing 14-14 at least shows how $this->data will contain these associated records. What I'm looking for in this array, however, is not the associated posts but the parent_id field. So, since I already selected a parent node from the Parent Tag select menu and saved the tag, $this->data shows that the value was saved properly; line 6 of Listing 14-14 shows that the ID value of 2 is now saved in the parent_id field for this current record.

Now that the Parent Tag select menu is working in the Edit view and saving the selected value in the parent_id field, paste the same line of Form helper code into the Add view file:

```
echo $form->input('parent_id',array('label'=>'Parent Tag','type'=>'select',➡
'options'=>$tags,'empty'=>'- No Parent Tag -'));
```

Fetching All Related Posts When a Tag Is Viewed

The Add and Edit views now support assigning parent tags, which the model saves in the parent_id field. Because the model is behaving like a data tree (see Listing 14-12), the Tree behavior automatically analyzes the tags table and each tag's parent node ID value and then assigns a left value and a right value. When creating and editing tags, you can now choose each tag's parent from a list of existing tags, and the Tree behavior does all the rest of the work. The only remaining task is to use the Tree helper to retrieve associated posts when a tag is called by the user.

Use the children() function to perform a find request of the provided tag ID and all of its associated tags. Depending on what parameters we provide, children() can also retrieve not just a list of these tags but all of their related posts as well. Replace the current View action in app/controllers/tags_controller.php with Listing 14-15.

Listing 14-15. *The View Action with the* children() *Function Included*

```
1    function view($id = null) {
2        if (!$id) {
3            $this->Session->setFlash(__('Invalid Tag.', true));
4            $this->redirect(array('action'=>'index'));
5        }
6        $children = $this->Tag->children($id,null,null,null,null,null,1);
7        $tag = $this->Tag->read(null,$id);
8        $this->set(compact('children','tag','list'));
9    }
```

Notice on line 6 of Listing 14-15 how the Tree behavior function children() is being used like any other model function. If the $actsAs property were not set to Tree in the Tag model, then this line would break; or, at least, the model would search for a custom function in app/models/tag.php named children(). But because the Tree behavior has been applied to the current Tag model, all of its functions are accessible in the controller by referencing the model, as in line 6 of Listing 14-15.

Let me explain the children() function. This function is how the Tree behavior performs the find request described earlier to return child nodes for a given record.

```
children( &$model, id[mixed], direct[bool], fields[mixed], order[string], ⟼
limit[int], page[int], recursive[int] )
```

id: The ID of the parent node record.

direct = false: Whether to return only the direct, or all, children. When set to true, returns only the direct child nodes, not child nodes of children also; when set to false, will return any and all child nodes of current parent.

fields = null: Either a single string of a field name or an array of field names; used to limit the returned fields from the find query.

order = null: SQL order conditions, for example, name DESC; defaults to the order in the tree.

limit = null: Used for calculating the number of items per page of data; entered as an SQL LIMIT clause.

page = 1: The page number; used for accessing paged data.

recursive = -1: When fetching associated records, used to specify the number of levels deep to be returned; corresponds to the recursive parameter used in model functions like find() and read().

On line 6 of Listing 14-15, the children() function is invoked using the id and recursive parameters. By entering null values for the other parameters in between, I've told the Tree behavior to stick with its defaults otherwise. Without changing the recursive parameter, the function would have provided the controller only with an array of child tags, not an array of those tags *and* their associated posts. So, you can see that line 6 sets the recursive value to 1 rather than the default value of -1.

The Tags controller now provides the view with an array of related tags and their associated posts. Let's loop through this array in the app/views/tags/view.ctp file to display the posts. Somewhere in this file (around line 16), insert Listing 14-16, which contains this loop and displays an HTML link for each associated post.

Listing 14-16. *Displaying Each Related Post As a Link in the View*

```
1    <? if (isset($children)): ?>
2    <? foreach($children as $child): ?>
3    <? foreach($child['Post'] as $post): ?>
4        <?=$html->link($post['name'],array('controller'=>'posts','action'=>➡
'view','id'=>$post['id']));?>
5    <? endforeach;?>
6    <? endforeach;?>
7    <? endif;?>
```

You can see that Listing 14-16 is a loop through the $children array passed by the controller (as shown in Listing 14-15). Because I'm interested only in displaying all related posts to the supplied tag, I've looped through each post contained in each tag record, so both lines 2 and 3 contain a foreach() function. Lines 1 and 7 are a way for testing whether anything is present in the $children variable to begin with. Using the HTML helper on line 4 let me render a link for each post that is reverse-routed and contains the post's name. To adjust how each post is displayed, just retool line 4 to meet your own styles; the full contents of the post record are available as $post at this point in the process.

That's it! Thanks to the Tree behavior and its children() function, all related posts, including those of related child tags, are displayed in this view. By applying this same process to other areas of the blog, the user could more quickly access categorized posts. And since the Tree behavior is managing the hierarchy, the work for the administrator is reduced by having only to set the parent ID value in the Tags Add and Edit views. The Tree behavior also let me bypass writing my own set of functions to find the child nodes and their associated posts.

Using Other Tree Behavior Functions

Like the children() function, other Tree behavior functions may be called in the model or controller by referencing the model. This is done in the controller by entering the model name and calling out the Tree behavior function desired, *not* by entering the name of the behavior:

```
$this->Model->children($id); // this will work
$this->Model->Tree->children($id); // this will not work
```

In the model, the model name is left out, as with referencing other model functions, like so:

```
$this->children($id); // this will work
$this->Tree->children($id); // this will not work
$this->Model->children($id); // neither will this
```

childCount

The childCount() function returns the number of child nodes for a given parent ID.

childCount(&$model, id[mixed], direct[bool])

When id is set to false, all top-level nodes will be read; otherwise, it will read only the supplied ID node as the parent; when direct is set to true, only direct children are counted.

generateTreeList

This function is a convenience method for returning a hierarchical array to be used in making HTML select boxes or breadcrumbs.

```
generateTreeList( &$model, conditions[mixed], keyPath[string], ➠
valuePath[string], spacer[string], recursive[int] )
```

> `conditions = null`: SQL conditions as a string or as an array (similar to conditions used in the `find()` model function)
>
> `keyPath = null`: A string path to the key, for example, `{n}.Tag.name`
>
> `valuePath = null`: A string path to the value; similar to `keyPath`
>
> `spacer = '_'`: For each level that a node falls under the parent, this character will be placed before the returned list item; for example, the grandchild of the parent node would be returned with two spacers in front of the name
>
> `recursive = -1`: The recursive value for the returned data

moveUp and moveDown

To reorder a given node without changing its parent, use the `moveUp()` and `moveDown()` functions.

```
moveUp( &$model, id[int], number[mixed] )
moveDown( &$model, id[int], number[mixed] )
```

These functions move the node `id`, or in other words, dynamically adjust the left and right fields, based on the value set in `number`. If `number` is set true, `moveUp()` will set the node to the topmost, or first, position; `moveDown()` will set the node to the last position.

getParentNode and getPath

To fetch the parent of a given child node, use `getParentNode()`. Simply provide an ID for a given node, and this function will find its parent and return the contents. To retrieve the path to a given node, supply the ID of the record, and `getPath()` will return an array of the topmost node down to the current one. This function is handy for displaying breadcrumb links.

recover, removeFromTree, setParent, setup, and verify

Recovering a corrupted tree, meaning that the left and right fields are realigned by the Tree behavior, is done with the `recover()` function. No passed value is necessary when calling `recover()`; just make sure that the database table in question is set up properly in the `$actsAs` property.

To remove a node from the tree, use `removeFromTree()`. Simply provide the node ID, and this function will remove the node from the tree and re-parent all the remaining children up one level.

Normally, as already demonstrated in this chapter, the Tree behavior automatically assigns the parent so long as `parent_id` is properly set up in the view and passed to the model through `$this->data`. However, the `setParent()` function is available as a backward-compatible method for assigning a parent manually. When used, `setParent()` takes the ID value provided as its first parameter and assigns the matching record as the parent of whatever record is currently being saved. This function should be used when the model is undergoing a save.

To manually adjust the settings used in `$actsAs` in an action or model function, use the `setup()` function. The first parameter must be an array with the same structure as the `$actsAs` property; in other words, set an array just as you would format the `$actsAs` property and pass it to `setup()`. Then the new settings will be applied to the model when invoking behaviors.

To test whether a model has a valid tree, use the `verify()` function. No parameters here are necessary. Simply call out this function in the model or controller, and it will return a `true` value if the model has a valid tree.

Using the ACL and Translate Behaviors

So far, I've explained the Tree behavior at length to demonstrate how to use a behavior in your Cake application. Without adding any more than one line of code (specifically, setting the `$actsAs` property), you were able to extend the model to behave differently. On the fly, the Tree behavior adjusts the tags to include associations between them, and you don't have to write any more functions in the model to maintain the data tree (unless, of course, you want to beef up the tree to include more methods and structures). But, in relatively little time, you can add basic tree structures to your database.

Other behaviors work in a similar fashion, meaning that they perform similar tasks for the model that make it easier to move data around. Unfortunately, the other two built-in behaviors, namely, ACL and Translate, are much more complicated than the Tree behavior. (The Containable behavior is easy to use, but I'll get into more detail on this behavior in a moment.) The very nature of managing access control lists (which is what ACL stands for) is one of the most complex tasks of establishing user control in an application. Delving into this behavior would certainly be useful for many developers, but it would also go beyond the scope of this book. I'll simply bring it to your attention and encourage you to take a look at this built-in behavior if your application calls for a detailed hierarchy of various user groups and individual users.

The Translate behavior also involves more complicated methods for working it into your application. A tutorial for this behavior would go beyond the general purpose of this book because it would require knowledge of another language (as well as English). So, keep in mind that if your project requires complicated data mapping for changing language settings, the Translate behavior is your best bet for working with those methods in a dynamic fashion. In short, Translate can map field names, routes, and more on the fly.

Using the Containable Behavior

By supplying the model with specific find conditions, you can effectively search through the database and filter out exactly what you don't want in the result set. Not only can you avoid writing and looping through complex queries by sticking with Cake's model functions, but you can work with a normalized database and expand your application to accommodate more elaborate schemas. But with all of these possibilities, you may notice that constructing find conditions that work with the database to give you precisely what you need can become difficult in its own right. Or, worse yet, you may find yourself writing complex loops or helper functions to filter through the data in the view, especially when you end up with elaborate many-to-many associations.

It's best to let the model provide the controller and view with the exact pieces of data, but when complex associations are used, extra find methods must be employed. This is where the Containable behavior comes in—it applies filtering methods to associated models and records that allow you to be more specific when retrieving associated data.

As with all other behaviors, Containable must be included in the $actsAs property. To illustrate how Containable works, consider how some of our blog application's tables are arranged: posts have many comments, tags have and belong to many posts, and users have many posts. Now, consider this scenario: suppose you wanted to fetch a post based on a specific comment author from the Post model. Containable makes this operation simple. In the controller, you could enter the following:

```
$this->Post->find('all', array('contain'=>'Comment.name = "Superman"'));
```

This string would return all posts that contain a comment whose name value is set to Superman.

Containable can also "contain" associated models, meaning you can restrict the result set to a specific model without using unbindModel() or changing the recursive parameter. For example, if you wanted to retrieve all the posts in the database but only the associated comments (not associated tags), Containable could simplify that operation with the following:

```
$this->Post->find('all',array('contain'=>'Comment'));
```

Without Containable, you'd need to use unbindModel() to produce the same result, like so:

```
$this->Post->undbindModel(array('hasAndBelongsToMany'=>'Tag'));
$this->Post->find('all');
```

Containable can also return specific fields in associated result sets. For instance, you may want only the name of the post's author and not the additional fields in the users table (like password and role). Using the following:

```
$this->Post->find('all',array('contain'=>'User.username'));
```

will still provide you with the associated user for each post but include only the username and id fields. An example array for one returned post using Containable in this way would look like this:

```
Array
    (
        [Post] => Array
            (
                [id] => 1
                [name] => A Sample Post Title
```

```
                [date] => 2008-12-01 00:00:00
                [content] => Sample content.
            )
        [User] => Array
            (
                [id] => 1
                [username] => sampleuser
            )
    )
```

Notice that only the ID and username have been returned in the User array. With Containable, you can apply more specific rules to the find operations the model performs and significantly reduce the amount of data that gets passed around your application, not to mention the amount of work done in the controller or view to process the result sets.

Attaching and Detaching Behaviors

Whenever dealing with data, any application can get inundated with information. Not just in web development but in programming in general, managing memory and CPU load is essential for keeping the program running at optimum performance. In the case of web development, anything you can do to decrease the load on the server will improve the user experience, especially since speed is a factor when considering how a user interacts with the site. The model trims the amount of data that gets pulled from across the datasource by making use of detailed find conditions, recursive settings, and its bindModel() and unbindModel() functions. In a similar way the model can curb its load on the server by efficiently attaching or detaching behaviors. Other reasons for attaching and detaching behaviors exist that generally center on streamlining the application, whether to decrease server load or to clean up code. A few functions are built into the model to manage how much it uses behaviors and which behaviors get used.

Detaching and Disabling Behaviors

There are two ways to trim down a model's use of a behavior: make the model "turn off" all a behavior's callbacks or make the model stop completely from adopting the specified behavior. The disable() and detach() functions, respectively, perform these tasks. Simply provide an array containing the name of each behavior to be either disabled or detached from the current model. The only catch is that these functions are called through the Behaviors class:

```
$this->Tag->Behaviors->detach(array('Tree'));
```

So, to completely remove a behavior from working in the current model, use the detach() function; to limit the callback responses the behavior will send to the model, use the disable() function. When disable() has been used, model functions may still use the behavior's functions. Just remember that automatic callback processes, such as when a record is saved to the database, will not run; these processes will have to be called manually in the model.

Attaching and Enabling Behaviors

Just as with detach() and disable(), you can tell the model manually when and where to use certain behaviors. With enable(), you tell the model to allow the behavior to begin working during callbacks. This means that the model will automatically consult the behavior as it performs callback methods such as saving to the database or deleting a file from the database. The attach() function is used to start the behavior. Settings here are passed along just as in the $actsAs array. Simply format an array as you would the $actsAs property, and place it as the first parameter in this function.

To test whether a specific behavior has been enabled or disabled (not necessarily attached or detached), use the enabled() function. This contains the name of a behavior and checks whether it is enabled in the model. The enabled() function will return either a true value or a false value indicating whether the specified behavior is enabled.

Writing Custom Behaviors

Conventionally, behaviors are used for extending the model, so they should not contain any logic that would normally appear in a controller or component. Here's a simple checklist for determining whether the particular task or set of tasks ought to be performed by a behavior:

- Does the task involve handling data for the model?

- Does the task do more than perform data validation?

- Does the task perform more than one query when fetching data?

- Does the task work with present data (in other words, it doesn't need to perform connection methods that ought to be managed by the DataSource)?

- Does the task involve more than a basic save, read, update, or delete method (in other words, are multiple updates required when dealing with one record of data, and so on)?

If you answer "yes" to all of these questions and you can't find a built-in or third-party behavior that matches the task, then you ought to write a custom behavior. Unlike DataSources, behaviors don't require a specific skeleton to work. They only need to be named conventionally, stored in the right directory, and called appropriately in the model. The model can use behavior functions in much the same way as the controller uses component functions. However, by writing certain callback functions in the behavior, you can run specific processes whenever the parent model does any of its own saves, updates, or deletions.

Setting Up the Behavior File

Like other resources in Cake (which you are probably used to creating by now), behaviors follow a specific convention. First, the file name follows the same naming convention as models: it has a lowercase name, with multiple words separated by underscores, and the .php extension. Second, the file must be stored in the app/models/behaviors directory. Lastly, the behavior must have the correct class name written; see Listing 14-17 for an example of a basic behavior.

Listing 14-17. *An Example of a Basic Behavior File*

```
<?
class UpdateBehavior extends ModelBehavior {
    function setup(&$model, $config=array()) {

    }
}
?>
```

Notice that the behavior class extends ModelBehavior and includes the setup() function. This function is called as a startup function when the behavior is instantiated. The parent model as an object is accessible in this function through the use of the &$model parameter, meaning that throughout setup(), everything in the parent model including its properties and functions can be called with $model. For example, $model->data in the setup() function would contain the current model's $this->data array. Performing data methods such as saving to the database or running a query can be done in the behavior by using the standard model functions, like so:

```
$rows = $model->find('all',array('conditions'=>array('id'=>$config['id'])));
```

Using DataSources in Behaviors with ConnectionManager

If your custom behavior must use a DataSource other than one available in the $model class object, then you must use the ConnectionManager utility to create an object of the DataSource. Listing 14-18 demonstrates the easiest way to do this.

Listing 14-18. *Using the ConnectionManager Utility to Instantiate a DataSource in a Behavior*

```
$db =& ConnectionManager::getDataSource($model->useDbConfig);
```

Notice that Listing 14-18 used the parent model object; this can be done only if the behavior function using ConnectionManager has the &$model setting as its first parameter.

With Listing 14-18, $db becomes the DataSource object to be used in the behavior. Just as the model uses a DataSource, the behavior can now work directly with the DataSource. For example, the behavior can invoke the XML DataSource you built earlier in the chapter with the following:

```
$xml =& ConnectionManager::getDataSource($model->useDbConfig['xml']);
```

and then run a find-all operation with the $xml->findAll() function.

Performing Callbacks in the Behavior

The Tree behavior, as you probably noticed, performed some functions when the model saved tags. By simply providing the model with a parent_id value when saving a tag, the Tree behavior automatically assigned the record a parent value and ordered the tree. These kinds of automatic methods are performed when using certain callback functions in the behavior. In other words, for all saves that the parent model will perform, the behavior will execute the `beforeSave()` callback function, so long as the behavior is attached to and enabled in the model. You can have the behavior automatically perform any logic for the model by using callback functions listed in Table 14-4. Remember that the parent model is available in the callback function as &$model.

Table 14-4. *Callback Functions in the Behavior*

Function Name	When Called
`afterDelete(&$model)`	After the model successfully deletes a record or set of records.
`afterFind(&$model, $results, $primary)`	After the model performs a find; can be used to modify results returned by `find()`. If the model is being queried through an associated model, then $primary will be set to `false`.
`afterSave(&$model, $created)`	After the model successfully saves a record or set of records; $created is set to `true` if a new entry was saved.
`beforeDelete(&$model, $cascade)`	Before the model deletes a record; if $cascade is set to `true`, records depending on the current one are also deleted.
`beforeFind(&$model, $query)`	Before the model performs a find; $query is an array containing the find conditions.
`beforeSave(&$model)`	Before the model saves a record or set of records.
`beforeValidate(&$model)`	Before the model validates data.

Things to Keep in Mind When Writing Behavior Functions

Behaviors are simple to build, though they can be as complex as any other Cake resource. Generally, they will contain only functions and some properties, or class variables, that simplify handling data for the model. These functions behave like helper functions in that they finish by returning either a set of values, an array, or a boolean value. Only when the ConnectionManager is used to connect to a DataSource or certain callback functions are written will the behavior interact directly with the datasource. The rest of the time, the behavior serves to house processes that would otherwise bog down the model.

Summary

Conventionally, the model deals with all the data while the controller handles all the logic of the application. To better extend the model, Cake includes two resources that separate out repetitive functions: DataSources and behaviors. Through DataSources, you can provide the model with all the connection and querying processes in a background layer of sorts and allow the same finding, updating, saving, and deleting methods to appear in the model without changing the code there.

In this chapter I explained how to build a simple XML DataSource that automatically opens an XML file, parses the XML, and displays each record there as a blog post. Through behaviors, you can provide the model with more complicated data-handling methods or methods that happen simultaneously without bogging down the model. By using the built-in Tree behavior to better organize tags, the blog application now has a more efficient hierarchy of categories. The user also benefits by you using the Tree behavior; when clicking a category, not only does the user see a list of posts directly associated with the tag but all posts associated with child tags as well. The Containable behavior, which is used to "contain" associated models—or, in other words, restrict the result set in specific ways to provide you with exactly the data values you want—also allows you to extend the functionality of the model. I showed some simple ways of using Containable in your application.

Writing custom behaviors allows you to house these types of model functions in a type of extension and thus streamline your application even more. Now that you've used all of Cake's resource files and have worked in the MVC structure, all that's left is to wrap up the blog application.

CHAPTER 15

■ ■ ■

Wrapping Up the Application

At this point, you've thoroughly explored the fundamentals of developing in Cake. With the blog application as your first advanced project, you built custom resources such as controllers, models, and views; and you extended those resources with others such as components, behaviors, DataSources, and helpers. But you are probably aware that the current blog application is not production-ready (you wouldn't make it available to any real users yet).

The blog does already have the main methods that allow you to add posts, tags, and users to the database and other methods that provide visitors with a way to comment on and read posts. Bringing the application into production just requires that you tie up a few loose ends.

In this chapter, I'll explain the final routines to consider when wrapping up a Cake application and making it ready to deploy. I won't go through the code line by line, but I will direct you to common tasks that put the finishing touches on your Cake projects. Consider the routines outlined here as exercises that will help you practice.

Designing the Home Page

Until now, I've pointed you to areas of the application by specifying a direct URL. For instance, when telling you to edit a certain action, I would write the path to that action with the full URL (like `http://localhost/blog/posts/view/1`). You will need to create a home page that contains all these URLs or at least a page that lists how to navigate to all the features you've built into the blog. Many novices begin with the home page before building the features of the application, which can lead to a cluttered starting point for their visitors. Design considerations aside, Cake, by its architecture and convention, promotes using dynamic methods as much as possible to generate site content. You can take advantage of what you've already built into the blog application to create the links that will direct the user to all other areas of the site.

The first step is to create a starting point. Then, you provide content and navigation that takes the user through the interface from that point to the next. You have two options for creating this starting point, or home page: you can use Cake's built-in Pages controller or choose an action to be the starting point, such as the Posts Index action.

Using the Pages Controller to Produce a Single View

Areas of the application that don't necessarily perform any logic or that assemble various methods from several controllers, like a home page, may need a view only. For your blog application, home needs to include only a couple of posts that link to their full-story view and the categories links you built in Chapter 14 with the Tree behavior. I would normally do this by adding onto the Posts Index action (which I'll describe in a moment) because I want some posts to appear on the home page. But what if I didn't want to display any posts on the home page or if the home page was a simple one with just a few links to the main areas of the site? In that case, it might be easier to write a simple view in static HTML.

The Pages controller is invoked out of the box; it is the method that renders the Cake welcome screen. Notice that in app/config/routes.php the default home page is listed as the top route:

```
Router::connect('/', array('controller' => 'pages', 'action' => 'display', 'home'));
```

You'll recognize from our discussion in Chapter 10 that this route connects the base path ('/') to the Pages controller's Display action. It also passes the parameter home to the action, thus rendering Cake's default home page, which is the welcome screen. Changing home to another value or creating a view file named home.ctp in the app/views/pages directory will point this base route to your own custom view. The Pages controller is already built into the core, so you do not need to create an app/controllers/pages_controller.php file by hand. Simply pass along the name of the view you want to render and create the corresponding view file (with the .ctp extension), and the Pages controller will automatically render the view for you.

Once you've created your own home.ctp file or created a custom one, you should be able to go to http://localhost/blog, and that view will be displayed. Simply add links in this view file that point to the Posts Index action and other areas of the site, and the user will be able to navigate through the blog just fine. Elsewhere in the site, you'll be able to point back to this home page by using the base path or by using more verbose links, like this:

```
$html->link('Sample Link',array('controller'=>'pages','action'=>'display','home'));
```

Making an Action the Starting Point

To make the Posts Index action the home page, simply change the base route in app/config/routes.php. One way you could do this would be with the following route:

```
Router::connect('/', array('controller' => 'posts', 'action' => 'index'));
```

Now, when the user comes to the home page, the Posts Index view will be rendered, rather than the Cake welcome screen. Then, in the app/views/posts/index.ctp file, you could provide all the navigation to access other areas of the site. The benefit of using an existing action as the starting point for your application is that the logic needed to pull together various methods is already in place. Creating dynamic content like categories links is possible because the controller and model are already at work fetching that data. I prefer this method for building my home pages, but I have used the other methods in the past for specific reasons relating to the project at hand. Most important, however, is that you provide a home page or starting point that easily provides the necessary navigation and displays from across the application dynamically. Most of the time you won't want to manually update the home page, so the more you can allow the application to do that for you, the better.

Generating Dynamic Navigation

More complex navigation will likely require creating some kind of menu system in the application. The blog is already equipped to handle categories and rendering posts. It's easy to make a menu that is rendered in every view. (Displaying a menu is a good time to use an element instead of a layout or a helper.)

You could create a menu element like I've done with Listing 15-1 and call it in the various views throughout the site. Notice that I've checked the Session component to see whether the user is logged in, changing what links are available to the user accordingly. Of course, the login process would need to be built, preferably with the Auth component, but the element does work well for adjusting the interface to supply the links based on the status of the user's session.

Listing 15-1. *The* `app/views/elements/menu.ctp` *Element*

```
<div class="menu">
    <ul>
        <?=$html->link('<li>Home</li>','/',null,null,false);?>
        <?=$html->link('<li>Posts</li>',array('controller'=>'posts','action'=>➡
'index'),null,null,false);?>
        <?=$html->link('<li>Tags</li>',array('controller'=>'tags','action'=>➡
'index'),null,null,false);?>
        <? if (!$session->check('User')): ?>
            <?=$html->link('<li>Log In</li>',array('controller'=>'users',➡
'action'=>'login'),null,null,false);?>
        <? else: ?>
            <?=$html->link('<li>Add Post</li>',array('controller'=>'posts',➡
'action'=>'admin_add'),null,null,false);?>
            <?=$html->link('<li>Edit Posts</li>',array('controller'=>'posts',➡
'action'=>'admin_index'),null,null,false);?>
            <?=$html->link('<li>Log Out</li>',array('controller'=>'users',➡
'action'=>'logout'),null,null,false);?>
        <? endif;?>
    </ul>
</div>
```

Remember to call out your menu element in the view with the `$this->element()` view function:

```
$this->element('menu');
```

Customizing the Overall Design

When preparing the application for production and when improving existing methods in the process, you will likely need to change the design of the views, usually on an individual basis. One important routine when wrapping up the application is to go through each view and interact with the site. Then, adjust the design as needed.

In this book, I stuck with Cake's built-in style sheet and HTML markup as much as possible. You will undoubtedly want to change the design to fit your needs. Most of the time, you'll work with CSS and HTML to tweak the design as you build the application. In the case of your blog application, now is a good time to go in and apply your own CSS and graphics to the design. Maybe you'll want to hire a graphic designer to do this part.

In any Cake project, reviewing the design and improving it where possible is an important routine when wrapping up the application. Sometimes you'll create new layouts, views, elements, and helpers at this stage to better separate the display elements and maintain a consistent structure for the code. Remember, where possible, to make sure that repeatable design elements are saved in a single place in the code. This is the programming principle called DRY—Don't Repeat Yourself. In this way, you're thinking ahead for any possible adjustments you may need to make in the future that will save you time.

Debugging the Application

Let's hope your Cake applications are built without too many errors creeping in. Nevertheless, an important routine when finishing the application is to double-check for any bugs. Testing deeper resources such as models, components, DataSources, and behaviors can be tricky when calling actions in the browser through the controller. Cake comes with a helpful test suite that allows you to run tests on models and components with sample data. You will need to have your `app/config/database.php` file correctly set to link with a test database and then run unit tests through what Cake calls *fixtures*. But performing unit tests with sample data can ultimately cut down on the amount of time you spend making your application's models error-free, especially if you build a lot of custom model functions. As you explore ways to work better with Cake, consult the online Cake community for details on running the test suite. Many features are still in development with some promising methods set for later release. (Mariano Iglesias has written an excellent tutorial on model testing with the built-in test suite at `http://bakery.cakephp.org/articles/view/testing-models-with-cakephp-1-2-test-suite`, which will help you get started working with fixtures; you can check out other test suite articles at `http://bakery.cakephp.org/tags/view/test`.)

Running the Application on a Remote Host

Once your application is ready for use on the Web, your final routine will be to move the project from your localhost environment to a remote host. If the remote host has the same settings as your localhost, you should be able to upload the parent application folder "as is" to a remote directory, and it should run just fine. You will need to run a MySQL dump file of some kind to mirror the remote and localhost databases.

To secure your application, you should place the Cake libraries and app folder outside the document root on your remote server. This requires that you make a couple of adjustments to the folder structure of the application and that you change a couple of global variables.

The three main folders you can move around on the server are cake, app, and webroot. The main catch when you do change the folder structure of the application is that the webroot folder must be available in a public directory or document root. Let's assume that my remote host is set up with a home folder (outside the document root) and www as the document root, while the domain points to user/home/www. To better secure the application, I place the Cake libraries and the app folder in user/home, and I take webroot out of the app folder and place it in user/home/www. Cake can handle this structure, but I must change some variables in user/home/www/webroot/index.php before it will compile correctly.

I open the webroot/index.php file and scroll to where I see three global constants: ROOT, APP_DIR, and CAKE_CORE_INCLUDE_PATH. Table 15-1 shows the path on the remote host that each constant should be assigned, given my current folder structure.

Table 15-1. *Paths for My Remote Setup*

Constant	Server Path
ROOT	/user/home
APP_DIR	www
CAKE_CORE_INCLUDE_PATH	user/home

Cake uses DS as the directory separator. So, I reassign these constants to their new paths following Table 15-1 and end up with what is shown in Listing 15-2. (Normally, there are a few comment lines in this file; I've omitted them from the listing.)

Listing 15-2. *Changing the* webroot/index.php *File to Work on My Remote Host*

```
if (!defined('ROOT')) {
    define('ROOT', DS.'user'.DS.'home');
}
if (!defined('APP_DIR')) {
    define('APP_DIR', 'www');
}
if (!defined('CAKE_CORE_INCLUDE_PATH')) {
    define('CAKE_CORE_INCLUDE_PATH', DS.'user'.DS.'home');
}
```

Summary

This chapter explained some important routines to consider when completing your Cake projects. Remember to provide a starting point in app/config/routes.php and to create navigational methods throughout the application to improve the user experience with the blog and any of your other Cake applications. Also, don't forget to check thoroughly for bugs in the code and to alter the design of the views to fit your methods. When deploying the application to a remote host, be sure to place the Cake libraries outside the document root and to adjust the webroot/index.php file accordingly.

PART 4

Appendixes

APPENDIX A

■ ■ ■

Installation Issues

The best way to set up your development environment is to configure a localhost server on your computer. Let me explain what that means. When you access a web site, you're sending and requesting information from another computer through an Internet connection. That server can communicate and process the information in a plethora of possible configurations. For example, when you buy a computer, you have the option of getting a Mac or Windows-based machine. Or, if you want, you could run Linux, Unix, or even DOS. All these possibilities mean that for you, the user, the experience will depend on which operating system you choose. But let's say you want to print a document. Well, regardless of the operating system or how that operating system prints something, once the document is printed, it doesn't really matter what configuration the computer had; it's all the same to the reader of the document.

The Internet is a lot like this example. The computer/server at the other end that will be processing the requests and creating output could run just about anything. But the final output will be a web page of some sort or some kind of web output. For you, the developer, the configuration will matter a great deal. In fact, it will affect everything you do to create and serve a web site.

Developing in a Localhost Environment

When you set up a localhost, you're actually setting up a server on your own computer. You'll fire up a web browser like Firefox or Safari and type in something like http:// localhost to access the server like the user would if the web site were live. In effect, you're tricking the computer into thinking that it's talking to a web server when really it's talking to itself.

Using the Localhost First, Remote Last

As long as your configurations on your localhost are the same as the configurations of the remote web server where the site will be hosted, you can develop on your own computer. Once the site is running well, you'll move the entire contents of your root directory or application to the server, and you're done. If you've done it right, the site should run all the same on the remote server.

Why Doing It All Remotely Is Bad

Should you circumvent the localhost setup, you'll be forced into developing everything remotely. That's fine, I suppose, if the following things don't bother you:

- Running a continuous FTP session

- Uploading every time you want to test the slightest alteration to your code

- Timeouts because of your Internet connection occurring during program executions

- Users accidentally stumbling on your half-baked programs

- Buying up test domains to keep users from accidentally stumbling on your half-baked programs

- Eating into your own bandwidth (which for some hosting plans may be tight as it is)

Setting Up a Localhost

Whatever operating system you're running on your computer, installing a localhost environment is easy. If running on a Mac, I recommend installing Living-e's MAMP. If on a Windows-based PC, install XAMPP.

Normally, creating a localhost setup will require installing various server programs via a command-line interface that takes a good understanding of PHP, MySQL, Apache, ProFTPd, and other server technologies. What MAMP and XAMPP do is simplify these complex server setups so that essentially you run an installer program and the setup is complete.

Setting Up on a Mac

Mac OS X already comes with a localhost setup built in. But if you want to run MySQL and upgrade PHP to version 5.0 or higher, you'll need to install each element manually, which can be a little tedious. Running MAMP will likely save you a lot of time. The following sections outline how to do it.

Step 1: Download the Software

Go to http://www.mamp.info, and locate on the home page the MAMP download link. It will ask you whether you want MAMP Pro, and if you do, go ahead and pay the $49 to download it. Otherwise, download the latest free version of MAMP.

Step 2: Open the Disk Image and Install the MAMP Folder

This step is simple enough. It will ask you to drop a folder into the Applications folder. This is necessary for the localhost setup to work properly. Make sure you do not use any subfolders or rename the MAMP folder to anything else. If you dislike having to do this, you may want to consider more elaborate localhost setup methods.

Step 3: Run the MAMP Application Program

At any time you can manage your localhost setup by running the application /Applications/ MAMP/MAMP. The main screen looks like Figure A-1.

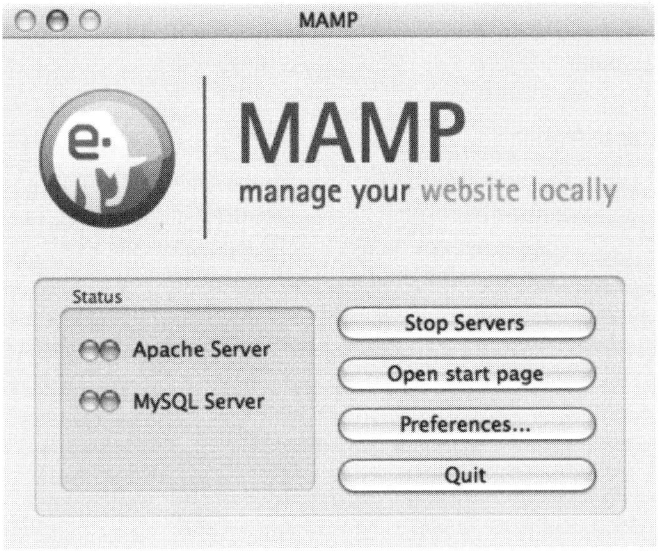

Figure A-1. *The MAMP main application screen*

This program, when you click Start Servers, will maintain the localhost environment. You now can begin executing PHP code, but you have to know where to access the localhost on your hard drive.

Step 4: Configure the Localhost Root Folder

By default, any file contained in the /Applications/MAMP/htdocs folder can be accessed in the localhost environment. This isn't too bad, altogether, but I personally prefer having my web sites outside my Applications folder. Changing this setting is as simple as going into the Preferences area of the MAMP application.

Click Preferences to open the Preferences area. Click the Apache tab, and you'll find a field called Document Root. It should read /applications/mamp/htdocs or something simi- lar. Click Select to change the document root to something else. In this case, I'll select the ~/Sites/ folder (if my Mac OS X username is dave, then the path will look like /Users/dave/ Sites). Now, from here on out, any folder or file places in the Sites folder will be executed by the MAMP localhost setup and not Mac OS X's default web sharing.

Step 5: Change the Localhost Ports

Now click the Ports tab, still in the Preferences area. It lists the Apache port and the MySQL port. The values in these fields are set to 8888 and 8889, respectively, by default. To better mimic a typical remote web server, these should be changed. In the Apache port field, type **80**, and in the MySQL port field, type **3306**. (You can also click the Set to Default Apache and MySQL Ports button.)

Because these ports are configured this way, you can now open Safari and type `http://localhost` instead of `http://localhost:8888` whenever you want to execute scripts and files. Also, when configuring programs to work with MySQL, you can simply enter **localhost** in the server setting instead of **localhost:8888**.

Step 6: Make the Localhost Easier to Manage

It can't get much easier than this to get a localhost environment running on a Mac. But one flaw with the MAMP application is that it must be running for the localhost environment to be running. So if you quit MAMP, you will no longer be able to run PHP code via the localhost. Fortunately, Living-e provides a Dashboard widget that does exactly what the MAMP application does to keep the localhost active. Simply launch the `Mamp Control.wdgt` file, and click Start Servers to make the localhost active. It will now run in the background through Dashboard.

Setting Up on Windows

Windows XP Pro has Microsoft's web server built into it, known as Internet Information Server (IIS). Installing IIS is pretty easy to do. However, most PHP and MySQL scenarios are more easily handled in a bundled localhost installer available from Apache Friends called XAMPP. The following sections outline the steps to take when installing and configuring XAMPP on your PC.

Step 1: Download the Software

You can download XAMPP from the Apache Friends web site. As of the printing of this book, a direct link is right here:

`http://www.apachefriends.org/en/xampp-windows.html`

You can download an installer application, a ZIP file, or a self-extracting 7-ZIP archive. The easiest option is to just run the installer application. So, scroll down to the download area of the page, and click Installer. The download should immediately commence.

Step 2: Run the Installer Program

The program will walk you through installing XAMPP. It will ask for a destination folder for XAMPP, and the default location is at `c:\xampp`. I recommend sticking to this configuration since you will likely want XAMPP to be able to access any area of your C drive. Click Next, and on the following screen leave the Service Section check boxes blank. To wrap it all up, click the Install button at the end. It will extract all the necessary files and leave you with a convenient localhost environment in the `c:\xampp` folder.

Step 3: Open the XAMPP Control Panel

After installation is complete, you'll be taken to the XAMPP Control Panel. This panel is accessible in the future by clicking the shortcut icon on the desktop or by going to `Start/Apache Friends/XAMPP/XAMPP Control Panel`. The screen looks something like Figure A-2.

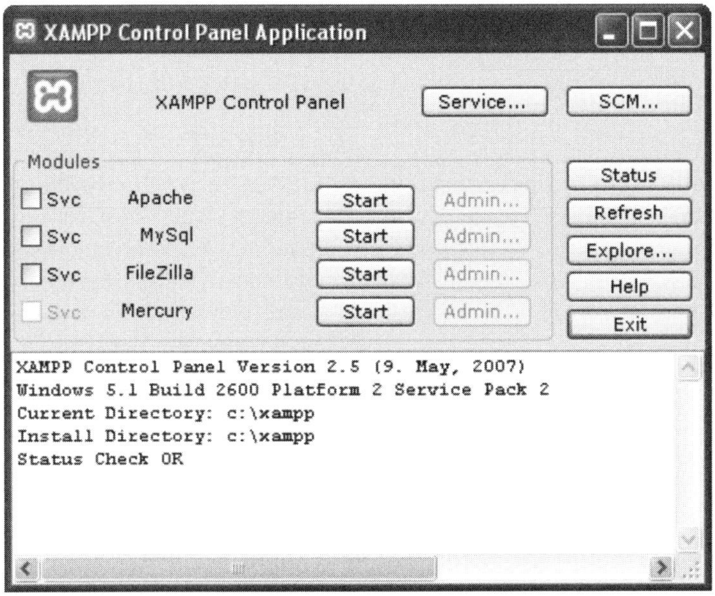

Figure A-2. *The XAMPP Control Panel screen*

Clicking the Start buttons starts those important web server services such as Apache, MySQL, and more. Start up Apache and MySQL using the Start buttons, and fire up your web browser. In the URL field, type `http://localhost`. You'll be taken to the XAMPP welcome screen.

Step 4: Secure the Localhost

Unfortunately, XAMPP doesn't come preinstalled with a more secure localhost environment. In some ways this may be a good thing, but for right now, the last thing you want is to compromise your network or your computer. If you think there is little to worry about other users accessing your localhost (which is really only the case in a work environment when other co-workers are using the same subnet or network), then you can bypass this step. If there is any chance of other users having access to your localhost in the least, then you may just want to take a moment to make XAMPP more secure. On the left side of the XAMPP startup web page is the Security link. Click it, bringing up the security information page. Most items, if not all, will be marked "unsecure." Let's make those all light up green.

A link below the main table called `http://localhost/security/xampsecurity.php` takes you to some fields that will allow you to secure the localhost. Change the MySQL root password, and click Password Changing. Below the MySQL root password fields is another set of fields to protect the XAMPP directory (`.htaccess`). Put in a username and password there. For both, make sure you do not save the passwords in a plain-text file.

From here on out, you will be asked to log in to access the XAMPP control pages. Restart Apache and MySQL to propagate the settings you've created.

Running MySQL

The most powerful web-based tool for setting up and running MySQL is called PHPMyAdmin, another open source application that comes installed with MAMP and XAMPP. The startup screens for both localhost environments contain a link to PHPMyAdmin. This is the quickest way to begin working in MySQL, since we've already installed a localhost that has the program preconfigured and ready to go. Many developers prefer PHPMyAdmin over other desktop-based MySQL applications because it's web-based and free and, quite honestly, a great application. I prefer desktop-based applications because of their speed, and I can avoid screen refreshing, which PHPMyAdmin is locked into because it's a web application.

Where to Find Other MySQL Tools

If you'd like to use a desktop application to manage your databases, you can find some listed in the following sections. They will likely require an extra level of configuration to get them working with your localhost environment. I'll list them and then explain some of the necessary settings to get them working right.

CocoaMySQL

On the Mac, probably the simplest freeware application for running MySQL is CocoaMySQL. It's available by going to `http://cocoamysql.sourceforge.net`.

MySQL Query Browser

On both Mac and PC, MySQL Query Browser is a reliable and easy freeware application that lets you navigate MySQL through a graphical interface (see `http://dev.mysql.com/downloads/gui-tools`).

HeidiSQL

This is much like CocoaMySQL on the Mac, except built for Windows. The layout is, in some ways, much easier to navigate than MySQL Query Browser and will require less MySQL prowess to get started. It, too, is open source, so giving it a try can't hurt (visit `www.heidisql.com`).

Typical Settings When Running MySQL

No matter what application you decide to use, each one will need some parameters before it can connect to MySQL. The following sections highlight the common ones that get you connected.

Host

This will almost always be just localhost, even when you're setting up a script to run on your remote server. If you are trying to access a remote database, it might be the domain name of the site, but you'll need to have the details provided from the web-hosting provider. With the configurations outlined earlier, simply enter **localhost**. Should this not work, just identify the IP address of your computer, which is usually defaulted to 127.0.0.1.

User and Password

MySQL supports multiple users and groups for administering and maintaining databases. These can be added or changed once you've logged into your application and accessed the necessary areas to add or change an account. In this example, this will be both root for the username and password, unless you entered something different instead. Sometimes web hosts will set up shared hosting accounts for you; in these cases, you may need to add a prefix to the username, like cake_.

Socket

When MySQL is running, the connecting point for the application and PHP is called the *socket*. The default path for this is /var/mysql/mysql.sock, but with these quick and easy localhost setup configurations, this will be a dead end. If you know that the MySQL socket is stored in its default location (like on most hosting setups), then you can leave this setting blank. On the localhost, you'll have to specify the path. On the PC, the defaults connect correctly if you followed the tutorial. On a Mac, Table A-1 contains the path strings, if necessary.

Table A-1. *Path Strings for Connecting Your Application to the MySQL Socket*

Web Server Software	Path
Mac OS X Server	/
MAMP	/applications/mamp/tmp/mysql/mysql.sock
XAMPP	/applications/xampp/xamppfiles/var/mysql/mysql.sock

Port

The default port for MySQL is 3306. Enter this only if the application asks you or if you somehow altered the port number to something else.

APPENDIX B

How CakePHP Compares with Other Frameworks

To give you a sense of what to expect from Cake, this appendix compares it to some other popular web frameworks.

PHP Frameworks

Currently, the most popular PHP frameworks include the following:

- CakePHP (www.cakephp.org)

- CodeIgniter (www.codeigniter.com)

- Symfony (www.symfony-project.org)

- Zend Framework (http://framework.zend.com)

Each of these frameworks is built in the PHP language, but they differ in their methods and libraries. Other frameworks could be listed here as well (PHP has a large and growing number of frameworks compared to other languages), but I'll stick with these four. No doubt others will emerge, but I expect these to continue to be the most dominant players in the PHP frameworks market. For a comparison of some of these frameworks' basic information, see Table B-1.

Table B-1. *Basic Information*

Framework	Official Support Group	Latest Version[1]
CakePHP	Cake Software Foundation	1.2 rc1
CodeIgniter	EllisLab	1.6.2
Symfony	Sensio Labs	1.1 rc2
Zend Framework	Zend Technologies	1.5.2

1. As of the writing of this book.

Using the Various Frameworks

Each of these frameworks has been released as open source projects, which means that a lot of the development work relies on community support. Tracking bugs, writing supporting documentation, and providing general support are tasks that involve developers like you. Many times, regardless of the framework you choose, you'll go to the online community for help. The size of the community and the available online resources may have an impact on how well you experience the framework.

In the following sections, I discuss some of the current features of each framework's online community and how they assist their users in developing software. I'll also describe some basic observations when using the various frameworks and compare each one to Cake. I recognize that much more could be said about each framework, but my aim is to give you an overview of the user experience relative to Cake, not to write an exhaustive comparison of all the frameworks. You'll get a general sense of what it's like to move from one of these frameworks to Cake and where to begin when considering making Cake your primary development framework.

CakePHP

Throughout the book, I've mentioned some main web sites where you can participate in the Cake community. Table B-2 lists these and other web sites to check out for more information on CakePHP.

Table B-2. *CakePHP Community Web Sites*

URL	Details
www.cakephp.org	Home page of CakePHP
http://bakery.cakephp.org	The Bakery; contains articles, code, and other announcements about CakePHP
http://groups.google.com/group/cake-php	Discussion group; contains thousands of discussions about the framework and is a great resource for getting questions answered
www.cakeforge.org	Repository for open source CakePHP projects; great resource for downloading third-party Cake applications and plugins
http://trac.cakephp.org	Cake's support web site and tracking system; here, you can view and submit tickets related to releases of Cake
http://live.cakephp.org	The Show; a live Internet radio podcast for all things CakePHP
irc://irc.freenode.net/cakephp	Main IRC chat room for discussing CakePHP

The amount of activity on the web sites and chat room listed in Table B-2 is high; to date, Cake has been downloaded more than 680,000 times and remains one of most often searched web frameworks.[2] The discussion group has almost 9,000 active members and has an archive of more than 54,000 moderated threads. At any given moment, the IRC chat room usually has between 100–200 visitors.

Duplication throughout the community is kept to a minimum, so expect to be directed to a thread or blog post that someone has already used to address the same topic when asking a question or requesting support. You will also probably sense a feeling of perfectionism in the community. What I mean by that is this—the Cake Software Foundation, which manages Cake's development, could have easily taken shortcuts when developing the framework. Compared to other frameworks, Cake would already be considered a version 3.0 or 4.0, but it's currently at 1.2. This is due more to really tightening up the framework rather than cooking up something fast that could perform a large plethora of methods. The result of this strategy is that Cake really is more robust, mature, and well written than it otherwise would be, and you can count on it maintaining its robustness as it takes on more fancy methods. I, by no means, am diminishing the large quantity of built-in methods that rival any other framework's functions; I'm merely pointing out that one of Cake's key advantages is its architecture, or, in other words, its methodology—which has been very carefully designed and tested.

Perhaps Cake's most competitive feature is its find methods for data handling. In this book, I've explained how to use the `find()` model function to easily fetch database records without writing SQL or other data source queries. By setting find conditions and other parameters effectively, you cut down on the amount of looping and matching thanks to how the model neatly returns result sets. CodeIgniter, unfortunately, comes with basic database helper functions that require you to still write most of the queries in SQL. Symfony uses rather complicated criteria syntax to set find conditions in the model layer that only marginally improve upon PHP's database functions. And Zend Framework relies almost entirely on your knowledge of SQL syntax to use its database adapter classes. Because Cake's find methods are designed independently of a data source, they don't have to follow a specific query language, which makes running finds through the model much easier.

CodeIgniter

CodeIgniter's community is relatively small when compared to CakePHP but does have a good support network online. Its user guide (`www.codeigniter.com/user_guide`) is well designed and has a nice layout for navigating through the table of contents. Many of the concepts used by Cake are also used by CodeIgniter, such as the MVC structure, helpers, routing, scaffolding, and caching. The support network is great, with a forum that boasts more than 66,000 topics and more than 400,000 posts. However, a lot of the topics there aren't directly related to code development issues like Cake's discussion group. In a sense, CodeIgniter's forums and wiki are more like combining Cake's discussion group, Bakery, and CakeForge. The number of web sites built on CodeIgniter is smaller than that for Cake, but CodeIgniter is off to a good start and will likely become a more popular framework in the future.

---

2. When compared to other frameworks using Google's Trend History tool (`www.google.com/trends`). Of the PHP frameworks, CakePHP is searched the most.

Starting a CodeIgniter application takes less time than setting up a Cake application; however, some configuration methods that come preinstalled with Cake are left out with CodeIgniter. For example, setting up routes to behave like they do in Cake will require that you manually write an `.htaccess` file to pass paths through a similar routing engine. By default, CodeIgniter is more lightweight than Cake, which is one of its chief selling points. However, as you expand your CodeIgniter application, expect to have to perform an extra step here or there to achieve the same functionality you get from Cake.

The MVC structure in CodeIgniter is similar to Cake's. Because of this, the general process of creating models, views, and controllers is nearly identical to what you learn when building Cake applications. Aside from minor differences in passing data around the application and naming conventions, running CodeIgniter is largely the same experience as in Cake. However, where Cake wins is with its powerful core classes, helpers, routes, and data-handling methods. The available resources and built-in functionality are more robust in Cake and, frankly, more cohesive. In other words, Cake developers will probably think they have taken a step backward when fully immersing themselves in CodeIgniter, though they will undoubtedly think they are in familiar territory. That's not to say that CodeIgniter isn't already a fabulous framework; it's just that it separates methods into its several resources less effectively than Cake. In a nutshell, the Cake paradigm is more about making the model fat and spreading out the various methods; CodeIgniter makes for very large controllers.

Symfony

Symfony entered the PHP frameworks arena early on and has remained popular. Its community is also large with developers groups, forums, a chat room, a wiki, and more. All of the main links to these various online groups and sites are available on Symfony's community web page (www.symfony-project.com/community).

Symfony actually is much different from CakePHP in its approach. In this book, I showed how to create a Cake project by renaming a folder and placing it on your server or localhost. In Symfony, you learn important commands that you run through a Symfony console script, much like using Bake. You can install Symfony manually by downloading a packaged file and configuring its files to work with your server, or you can use PEAR to have an installation script handle most of the work for you. I find that getting Symfony to work correctly generally requires more time than Cake, simply because so many steps are required for both the server and the console to work right with the whole framework. But once these configurations are in place, starting a new Symfony application is as simple as entering a one-line command.

After you have successfully begun a Symfony application, you will need to initialize your data source connections using the command line as well as perform other setup tasks. Generating the scaffolding is also done in the console, but the final result is similar to Cake's scaffolding. Building models is primarily done using YAML-based configurations together with the `symfony` console script. If you prefer YAML to JSON or XML for configuring your database schema, then Symfony will probably suit you well. Cake really doesn't compare in this regard because its methods for connecting to a data source don't involve the command line (even though you can use Bake to write your `database.php` configuration file and build models).

When extending the Symfony application to take on more methods, many of the same concepts that make Cake effective are used. The learning curve is steeper when going from Cake to Symfony, mainly because the benefits Symfony offers are usually found in its command-line interface. However, Symfony users shouldn't find learning Cake all that difficult. It may take some getting used to running fewer commands in the console, but on the whole, you shouldn't have to perform any more steps to build your Cake applications than you would expect for a Symfony application.

Zend Framework

Zend Framework was arguably the first framework to be built for PHP. Its corporate sponsor, Zend Technologies, has a long history with the PHP language itself; its founders include two of the original authors of PHP, Andi Gutmans and Zeev Suraski. Much of what has made PHP one of the most popular web programming languages started with Zend Technologies and its contributions to the language. That being said, no wonder Zend Framework has had early success and continues to be a major player in the PHP frameworks market.

In terms of community support, Zend Framework has probably the largest online following of any of the PHP frameworks. Its documentation is extensive and thorough, and unofficial blogs and forums make it possible to get online support for just about any question. Code submissions to the core are passed through rigorous testing methods, which makes Zend Framework an incredibly robust framework. However, Zend Framework is much more of a large set of libraries than a lightweight MVC framework. For instance, its main library folder is almost 16MB, more than three times the size of Cake's libraries. Getting Zend Framework off the ground requires much more customization and configuration, whereas Cake has adopted more of the "convention over configuration" paradigm. You could likely use Zend Framework with just about any PHP project, which I demonstrate in Chapter 12 when explaining how to use Zend libraries in Cake, but the trade-off is that you'll have to write or at least configure much of what Cake does automatically with its dispatcher methods.

Zend Framework has no single development paradigm like Cake, CodeIgniter, and Symfony, and that appeals to many developers. Patterns like MVC are therefore possible in Zend Framework, but these require you to manually write configuration methods, which are automatically built into Cake and other frameworks. Cake is certainly ahead of Zend Framework in how the framework cuts down the amount of code needed to extend it. Learning Zend Framework is generally more time-consuming than learning Cake, mostly because of the design of the framework. Getting an MVC variant of Zend Framework off the ground is usually more difficult for a beginner than Symfony, not to mention Cake.

True, Zend Framework is more well known than Cake in most PHP circles; it's the veteran on the team, if you will. But Cake is proving to be more like the rising star that moves faster and is strategically sounder. Given Cake's effective implementation of the MVC structure and its structural design, it will likely continue to attract former Zend Framework developers and remain the top player in the PHP frameworks arena.

.

Index

You Need the Companion eBook

Your purchase of this book entitles you to buy the companion PDF-version eBook for only $10. Take the weightless companion with you anywhere.

We believe this Apress title will prove so indispensable that you'll want to carry it with you everywhere, which is why we are offering the companion eBook (in PDF format) for $10 to customers who purchase this book now. Convenient and fully searchable, the PDF version of any content-rich, page-heavy Apress book makes a valuable addition to your programming library. You can easily find and copy code — or perform examples by quickly toggling between instructions and the application. Even simultaneously tackling a donut, diet soda, and complex code becomes simplified with hands-free eBooks!

Once you purchase your book, getting the $10 companion eBook is simple:

❶ Visit **www.apress.com/promo/tendollars/**.

❷ Complete a basic registration form to receive a randomly generated question about this title.

❸ Answer the question correctly in 60 seconds, and you will receive a promotional code to redeem for the $10.00 eBook.

THE EXPERT'S VOICE™

2855 TELEGRAPH AVENUE | SUITE 600 | BERKELEY, CA 94705

Offer valid through 01/09.